JOHN

Goodbye to a River

John Graves was born in Texas, was raised there
(in Fort Worth), was educated there (at Rice),
wandered from there (to the Marine Corps,
Columbia University, and many far places)—and
after returning there in the late 1950s wrote *Goodbye to a River* (1960). Over the years Graves has
contributed stories and articles to *The Atlantic,
Holiday, American Heritage, Esquire, Texas
Monthly,* and other magazines. He has written on
conservation for the Department of the Interior
and for the Sierra Club—in *The Water Hustlers*
(1971)—and has taught college English. He lives
with his wife and two daughters on some 400 acres
of rough Texan hill country that he described in
Hard Scrabble (1974).

ALSO BY JOHN GRAVES

The Water Hustlers (with T.H. Watkins and Robert Boyle)

Hard Scrabble

The Last Running

From a Limestone Ledge

Blue and Some Other Dogs

Self-Portrait, with Birds

A John Graves Reader

John Graves and the Making of Goodbye to a River

Goodbye *to a River*

The
Upper-Middle BRAZOS

⊗ *Approximate locations of proposed new dams.*

Weatherford

JACK CO.

PARKER

Black Springs
(Oran)

LAKE MINERAL WELLS

Mineral Wells

Millsap

GRINDSTONE CR.

PATRICK'S CR.

BIG KEECHI

TURKEY CR.

ROCK CR.

Denn

Graford

Old Painted Campground

Littlefield Bd.

U.S.80 BR.

Lazy Bd.

Welty

Post Oak Bd.

LITTLE KEECHI

B.C. Harris Bd.

Hart Bd.

Moffit Bd.

U.S. 180 BR

Pollard Bd.

Oakes Crossing

Edmondson Bd.

Cyclone Bd.

INSPIRATION POINT

RED BLUFF

Soda Springs

Mary Meeks Bd.

TEXAS 4 BR.

DARK VALLEY CR.

ELM CR.

Dog Bd.

Bath Bd.

Hittson Bd.

John Hittson Bd.

Dobbs Valley Bd.

Dalton Bd.

KYLE MT.

Village Bd.

Poke Stalk Bd.

U.S. 281 BR.

Brazos

POSSUM KINGDOM LAKE

LOW-WATER BR.

SHUT-IN

Flint Bd.

Chick Bd.

Chestnut Bd.

Garland Bd.

EAGLE CR.

Palo Pinto

WARD MT.

DAM

Fortune Bd.

CRAWFORD MT.

IONI CR.

PALO PINTO CR.

PALO PINTO CO.

ERATH

Scale of miles
0 1 2 3 4 5
palacios

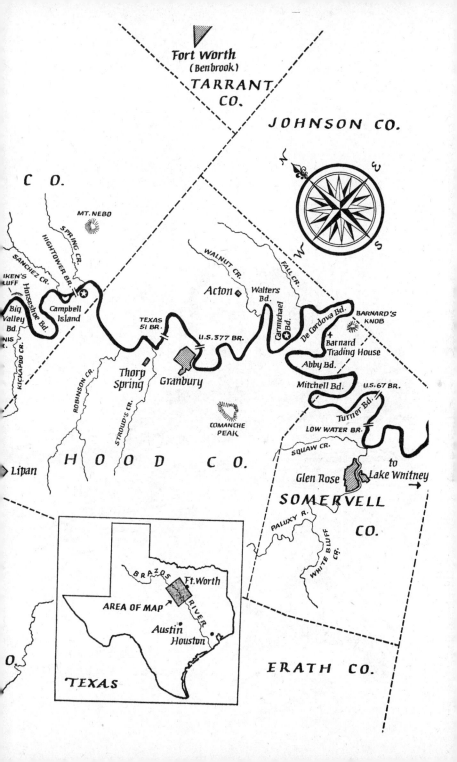

Illustrations by
RUSSELL WATERHOUSE

A NARRATIVE BY
JOHN GRAVES

Goodbye *to a* River

VINTAGE DEPARTURES · VINTAGE BOOKS
A DIVISION OF RANDOM HOUSE, INC. · NEW YORK

FIRST VINTAGE DEPARTURES EDITION, JULY 2002

Copyright © 1959 by The Curtis Publishing Company
Copyright © 1960, copyright renewed 1988 by John Graves

All rights reserved under International and Pan-American Copyright
Conventions. Published in the United States by Vintage Books,
a division of Random House, Inc., New York, and simultaneously
in Canada by Random House of Canada Limited, Toronto.
Originally published in hardcover in the United States by
Alfred A. Knopf, a division of Random House, Inc.,
New York, in 1960.

Certain passages in this book first appeared in *Holiday*
in somewhat different form.

Vintage is a registered trademark and Vintage Departures
and colophon are trademarks of Random House, Inc.

The Library of Congress has cataloged the Knopf edition as follows:
Graves, John, 1920–
Goodbye to a river, a narrative / John Graves. — [1st ed.]
p. cm.
Includes bibliography.
ISBN 0-394-42690-8
1. Brazos River (Tex.) 2. Brazos River Valley (Tex.) I. Title.
F392.B842 G7
917.641 60-10954

Vintage ISBN: 0-375-72778-7

www.vintagebooks.com

Printed in the United States of America

20

for H.,

who came along at about the same time.
I hope the world she will know
will still have a few rivers and
other quiet things in it.

A NOTE

THOUGH this is not a book of fiction, it has some fictionalizing in it. Its facts are factual and the things it says happened did happen. But I have not scrupled to dramatize historical matter and thereby to shape its emphases as I see them, or occasionally to change living names and transpose existing places and garble contemporary incidents. Some of the characters, including at times the one I call myself, are composite. People are people, and if you put some of them down the way they are, they likely wouldn't be happy. I don't blame them. Nevertheless, even those parts are true in a fictional sense. As true as I could make them.

PART ONE

By heaven! cried my father, springing out of his chair, as he swore,—I have not one appointment belonging to me, which I set so much store by, as I do by these jack-boots, —they were our great-grandfather's, brother Toby,—they were hereditary.

CHAPTER ONE

USUALLY, fall is the good time to go to the Brazos, and when you can choose, October is the best month—if, for that matter, you choose to go there at all, and most people don't. Snakes and mosquitoes and ticks are torpid then, maybe gone if frosts have come early, nights are cool and days blue and yellow and soft of air, and in the spread abundance of even a Texas autumn the shooting and the fishing overlap and are both likely to be good. Scores of kinds of birds, huntable or pleasant to see, pause there in their migrations before the later, bitterer northers push many of them farther south. Men and women are scarce.

Most autumns, the water is low from the long dry summer, and you have to get out from time to time and wade, leading or dragging your boat through trickling shallows from one pool to the long channel-twisted pool below, hanging up occasionally on shuddering bars of quicksand, making six or eight miles in a day's lazy work, but if you go to the river at all, you tend not to mind. You are not in a hurry there; you learned long since not to be.

October is the good month. . . .

I don't mean the whole Brazos, but a piece of it that has had meaning for me during a good part of my life in the way that pieces of rivers can have meaning. You can comprehend a piece of river. A whole river that is really a river is much to comprehend unless it is the Mississippi or the Danube or the Yangtze-Kiang and you spend a lifetime in its navigation; and even then what you comprehend, probably, are channels and topography and perhaps the honkytonks in the river's towns. A whole river is mountain country and hill country and flat country and swamp and delta country, is rock bottom and sand bottom and weed bottom and mud bottom, is blue, green, red, clear, brown, wide, narrow, fast, slow, clean, and filthy water, is all the kinds of trees and grasses and all the breeds of animals and birds and men that pertain and have ever pertained to its changing shores, is a thousand differing and not compatible things in-between that point where enough of the highland drainlets have trickled together to form it, and that wide, flat, probably desolate place where it discharges itself into the salt of the sea.

It is also an entity, one of the real wholes, but to feel the whole is hard because to know it is harder still. Feelings without knowledge—love, and hatred, too—seem to flow easily in any time, but they never worked well for me. . . .

The Brazos does not come from haunts of coot and hern, or even from mountains. It comes from West Texas, and in part from an equally stark stretch of New Mexico, and it runs for something over 800 miles down to the Gulf. On the high plains it is a gypsum-salty intermittent creek; down toward the coast it is a rolling Southern river, with levees and cotton fields and ancient hardwood bottoms. It slices across

Texas history as it does across the map of the state; the Republic's first capitol stood by it, near the coast, and settlement flowed northwestward up its long trough as the water flowed down.

I have shot blue quail out by the salty trickles, and a long time ago hunted alligators at night with a jacklight on the sloughs the river makes in the swamplands near the Gulf, but I do not know those places. I don't have them in me. I like them as I have liked all kinds of country from Oahu to Castilla la Vieja, but they are a part of that whole which isn't, in the way I mean, comprehensible.

A piece, then . . . A hundred and fifty or 200 miles of the river toward its center on the fringe of West Texas, where it loops and coils snakishly from the Possum Kingdom dam down between the rough low mountains of the Palo Pinto country, into sandy peanut and post-oak land, and through the cedar-dark limestone hills above a new lake called Whitney. Not many highways cross that stretch. For scores of years no boom has brought people to its banks; booms elsewhere have sucked them thence. Old respect for the river's occasional violence makes farmers and ranchers build on high ground away from the stream itself, which runs primitive and neglected. When you paddle and pole along it, the things you see are much the same things the Comanches and the Kiowas used to see, riding lean ponies down it a hundred years ago to raid the new settlements in its valley.

Few people nowadays give much of a damn about what the Comanches and the Kiowas saw. Those who don't, have good reason. It is harsh country for the most part, and like most of West Texas accords ill with the Saxon nostalgia for cool, green, dew-wet landscapes. Even to get into it is work. If you pick your time, the hunting and the fishing are all right, but they too are work, and the Brazos is treacherous for the sort of puttering around on water that most people like. It snubs play. Its shoals shear the propeller pins of the big new outboard motors, and quicksands and whirlpools occasionally swallow folks down, so that generally visitors go to the predictable impounded lakes, leaving the river to the hard-bitten yeomanry who live along it, and to their kinsmen who gravitate back to it on weekends away from the aircraft factories and automobile assembly plants of Dallas and Fort Worth, and to those others of us for whom, in one way or another, it has meaning which makes it worth the trouble.

PERSONAL MEANING, maybe, that includes trips when you were a kid and, with the others like you, could devil the men away from their fishing by trying to swim against orders where the deep swirls boiled, and catfish on the trotlines in the mornings, sliced up then and there for breakfast . . . And later trips when they let you go out with a friend named Hale and a huge colored man named Bill Briggs who could lift entire tree trunks to lay across the fire where you camped under pecans by a creek mouth, above the wide sand flats of the river, and who could fry eggs, rounded and brown on the outside and soft within, in a way you have never seen since . . . Later still, entrusted with your own safety, you went out with homemade canvas canoes that were almost coracles in their shapelessness, and wouldn't hold straight, and ripped on the rocks of the rapids. Squirrel shooting on cold Sunday mornings, and ducks, and skunk-squirted dogs, and deer watering while you watched at dawn, and the slim river bass, and bird song of a hundred kinds, and always the fly-fishing for fat bream and the feel of the water on bare skin and its salty taste, and the changing shore. The river's

GOODBYE *to a* RIVER [1]

people, as distinct from one another as any other people anywhere, but all with a West Texas set to their frames and their faces which on occasion you have been able to recognize when you saw it in foreign countries . . . Even first bottles of beer, bitter, drunk with two bawdy ranchers' daughters you and Hale ran across once, fishing . . .

Enough meaning, enough comprehension . . . Not the kind that might have ruined it for you, though. It had always the specialness of known good places where you had never actually lived, that you had never taken for granted, so that it was still special when in later years you would come back to it from six or eight years away to find it still running as it had run, changed a little but not much. After the dam was finished at Possum Kingdom near the beginning of the war, it began to filter out the West Texas drainings, and that piece of the Brazos ran clear for more of the year than it had before, and the old head rises no longer roared down, and the spring floods were gentler and the quicksands less quick. But it was there still, touchable in a way that other things of childhood were not.

The history was in it, too. When we were young we would beg tales from surviving old ones, obscure and petty and always violent tales, hearsay usually and as often as not untrue, and later we confirmed and partly straightened them in our minds by reading in the little county histories and the illiterate memoirs, and they were a part of the river. All the murdered, scalped, raped, tortured people, red and white, all the proud names that belonged with hills and valleys and bends and crossings or maybe just hovered over the whole— Bigfoot Wallace, Oliver Loving, Charles Goodnight, Cynthia Ann Parker and her Indian son Quanah, Peta Nocona, Satank, Satanta, Iron Shirt . . . Few people outside of West

Texas ever heard of most of them, and long ago I learned that the history of the upper-middle Brazos was not the pop of a cap gun in the big pageant, but that knowledge never stopped the old names from ringing like a bell in my head.

Meaning, yes.

~~~~~~~~~~

To NOTE THAT our present world is a strange one is tepid, and it is becoming a little untrue, for strangeness and change are so familiar to us now that they are getting to be normal. Most of us in one way or another count on them as strongly as other ages counted on the green shoots rising in the spring. We're dedicated to them; we have a hunger to believe that other sorts of beings are eyeing us from the portholes of Unidentified Flying Objects, that automobiles will glitter with yet more chromed facets next year than this, and that we shall shortly be privileged to carry our inadequacies with us to the stars. And furthermore that while all the rivers may continue to flow to the sea, those who represent us in such matters will at least slow down the process by transforming them from rivers into bead strings of placid reservoirs behind concrete dams . . .

Bitterness? No, ma'am . . . In a region like the Southwest, scorched to begin with, alternating between floods and drouths, its absorbent cities quadrupling their censuses every few years, electrical power and flood control and moisture conservation and water skiing are praiseworthy projects. More than that, they are essential. We river-minded ones can't say much against them—nor, probably, should we want to. Nor, mostly, do we. . . .

But if you are built like me, neither the certainty of change, nor the need for it, nor any wry philosophy will keep you from feeling a certain enraged awe when you hear that a river that you've known always, and that all men of that place have known always back into the red dawn of men, will shortly not exist. A piece of river, anyhow, my piece . . . They had not yet done more than survey the sites for the new dams, five between those two that had already risen during my life. But the squabbling had begun between their proponents and those otherwise-minded types—bottomland farmers and ranchers whose holdings would be inundated, competitive utility companies shrilling "Socialism!" and big irrigationists downstream—who would make a noise before they lost, but who would lose. When someone official dreams up a dam, it generally goes in. Dams are ipso facto good all by themselves, like mothers and flags. Maybe you save a Dinosaur Monument from time to time, but in-between such salvations you lose ten Brazoses. . . .

It was not my fight. That was not even my part of the country any more; I had been living out of the state for years. I knew, though, that it might be years again before I got back with time enough on my hands to make the trip, and what I wanted to do was to wrap it up, the river, before what I and Hale and Satanta the White Bear and Mr. Charlie Goodnight had known ended up down yonder under all the Criss-Crafts and the tinkle of portable radios.

Or was that, maybe, an excuse for a childishness? What I wanted was to float my piece of the river again. All of it.

CHAPTER TWO

⊶§ *When Michaelmas moon was come*
with warning of winter, then thought Gawain
full oft of his perilous journey.

OCTOBER is the good month, in a normal year at least. But normality in Southwestern weather is at best a stacking together of extremes, and that was the year the drouth broke that had been the norm for seven burning years—from the tree rings, they said, the worst since early Spanish times. Oil money from the cities, looking for a place to invest itself, had kept land from selling quite so cheaply as fat Jack Falstaff's stinking mackerel, but otherwise it would have. No one was certain that the region was not about to become another Middle East, its tenuous fertility transmuted by misuse into desert. Some fundamentalist ministers expressed gratification and said sin had brought it on, and maybe that was so, if in another sense than theirs. . . . But in the spring it broke with tropical flooding rains, and summer was lush with weeds and flowers, and even scrub stocker steers brought show-cattle prices on the hoof, and in October there was rain again, all month long.

With luck, though, November can be all right. . . .

A merchant of Weatherford, an old friend somewhat

monomaniacal in matters of regional lore, hated to let me go when we stopped by to see him on our way out to the river. He piled papers and maps on me, and instructions to see things he knew of and to look for things whose existence he suspected—Indian sites, beavers, an eaten-away silt cliff where longhorns' skulls and the remains of bison still came occasionally to view. Though he was older now and couldn't explore much, the countrymen brought him reports at his store. They were fond of him but maybe ironic among themselves afterward, in a café on the square, over his pleasure in rusty adze heads and branding irons and the hieroglyphics on old chimney stones. Most of his interest was focused tightly on his own county (once, when I'd told him of a good log house I'd located in the Littlefield Bend, he said with impatience: "Yes. I think that's over the line in Palo Pinto. . . ."), but within its boundaries he knew most of what could be known in a latter day of the turbulent local past.

He said: "There's a spring near old Brannon's Crossing. Two years ago they were blasting for a pipeline there and it disappeared and then came up three hundred yards away, stronger than ever. Someone told me."

"I'll look for it," I said.

"Do," he said. "They all used to get water there, the river so salty."

In the yard around his baroque Victorian house he has shrubs transplanted from the Hermitage, and a pecan grown from a nut picked up at Governor Hogg's grave, and roses from cuttings at the site of the cabin his grandfather built east of the town in the 1850's. Not many people like him will still be among us in another few years. In this country they are mostly of the South and New England, retrospective cultures, and the time has lurched up onto the horizon, as it must inevitably for retrospective cultures, when the South and New England will not exist.

So much the better, someone forward-looking answers.

All right. But he is an entire man and a bright one, and if we're establishing viewpoints this early I can tell you that I like knowing someone who can read to me from a school composition book, with enthusiasm, the epitaphs of Indian-victims buried in the graveyard at the defunct farming community of Soda Springs in western Parker County, Texas. Or who can show me with exactness, if I drive him out there, where Mr. Couts the banker stood when he had his mighty gunfight. A point of taste, certainly . . .

From there Hale and I—he was taking me out—drove across the stripped and eroded farming section to the north-west which had once been a solid forest of oaks, and into the jagged Palo Pinto country, strewn with big sandstone boulders, less totally raped in a century's exploitation be-cause less had been there in the first place worth the raping. Where the narrow dam blocks what used to be the canyon at Possum Kingdom, we turned up a hill and came out on a flat above the lake, beside the concrete control tower. The afternoon was leaden. When we got out, a raw north breeze picked at our clothes and grayed the surface of the big lake, and Hale said again, with a kind of satisfaction, that it was a hell of a time to be starting a canoe trip. I said again that I knew it, and rattled the gate of the chain-link enclosure around the tower and a grim humming network of wires above squat finned transformers classified deadly by red-painted signs.

A short, thin man in a Stetson, seam-faced, came out and looked at us and at the canoe on the car, opened the gate, and

showed curiosity and a willingness to talk. November is a
quiet month for sociable people at lakes. . . .

"All by yourself?" he said. "Without no motor?"

I said yes.

He looked disgusted and, walling his eyes across the lake,
said as though to a fourth, disinterested person that he'd
never had no use for canoes, not even in summer. But he was
friendly, and said they'd likely be letting water out just as
they were now, full and strong through two gates, for another twenty days at least without much variation, unless
more big rains came upstream. In that case they'd be letting
out more—probably too much, he said ironically.

"You watch them big rocks in Post Oak Bend," he said.
And then, in much the same tone as Hale's: "Hit's a hell of a
lookin' kind of weather."

Below the dam the river cuts next to high cliffs of stone,
yellow-gray and red and stratified like laid brick, with the
dark cedar all along the top, though on an afternoon like that
one you had to take the yellow and red for granted, remembering them from times of sunshine. Standing there at the
low bridge after we'd loaded the canoe, I doubted the dark
sky, and the bite of the wind and its ruffle on the water; and
under that grayness even the rapids below, rolling now with
the two gates open above, looked sullen and dangerous.

But rivers tend to look that way when you start a trip, and
so does the ocean when you clear the breakwaters and hit
the gray swells, headed out on a cruise. . . . They say our
protoplasm, the salt of its juices the same still as sea water's,
yearns back toward that liquid that brewed it, and I guess
that may be so, but the air-breathing, land-walking structure
the protoplasm molded itself into sometimes argues otherwise. Familiarity helps, as the skin divers know, and living

beside the sea you lose the caution and can swim out daily a half-mile or more to float bobbing for hours with the slow rise and fall of the big, smooth-crested waves. I've done that, and then have left the sea for a few months, and, returning, have found the fear there again, to be fought down again. It's the same with a rolling, roaring river. I didn't want a Bold Journey; I wanted the quiet October Brazos, and it wasn't there. . . .

Hale had been going partway down the river with me till business and his wife's opinion got in the way. He glared at the equipment stowed and tied into the canoe.

"I wish. . ." he said, and didn't finish. He said: "You call from One Eighty. Maybe I'll drive out and float with you a couple of days."

I said: "I'll call. You won't come."

"There won't be any ducks," he said. "You saw those on the hatchery ponds. They don't like the river when it's high."

"All right," I said. Getting in, I collared the pup to keep him from scrambling ashore, and pushed away. Hale yelled something as I swept into the bubble-hiss of the rapids. It was fast but smooth, and spewed me into a long flowing pool below. With only enough paddling for steerageway, the current carried me swiftly the mile and a half down to the sharp turn of the Flint Bend and around it, under the cliffs. In the clear water I could see the tip of the paddle with the blade and half the loom submerged. Sandpipers flushed, and a kingfisher and a great blue heron. Hidden in the brush, chickadees cursed one kind or another of bad luck in that buzzing code they use, and a redhorse sucker shot four feet clear of the surface and fell back onto it in a smacking belly-buster totally unconsonant with the clean grace of his leap. . . .

By the time I pulled onto a sand bar below a narrow flat that lay between the river and a mountain, the wind on my neck carried flecks of cold rain. I set up the little tent under a twisted mesquite, threw my bed roll into it, chopped dead limbs into firewood, and finally carried up the other things from the boat—the map case and the shotgun and the rods and the food box, heavily full, and the cook box and the rucksack, all of them battered familiarly from other trips long before. With a juvenile shame from those days when we had tried to model ourselves on the old ones, going out only with a blanket, tarp, skillet, ax, twenty-two, jar of grease, and sack of cornmeal, I knew that I'd brought too much gear for one man. But it was November, and our stomachs had been tougher then, and anyhow the point was no longer to show one's hardihood. The point was to be there.

From inside the tent the pup watched me with houndish melancholy, never having seen a tent before but knowing it to be better than the wind and the rain. As the evening light failed, the wind dropped; the rain kept on, a steady, soft, autumn drizzle. I got a fire started between two sandstone blocks, piled logs on until it roared, dropped in a foil-wrapped potato, and settled back with a cigarette in the tent beside the pup, the rain's tapping on the canvas full of remembrance of other rains, on other tents, in other places, back through a war and into childhood. I hoped it would let up a little when the time came to cook bacon and eggs, or whatever, though I wasn't yet hungry.

The aloneness of it was good. I didn't know how long it would remain good, but at the moment it was. I would have liked to have Hale along, but not many other people I knew.

"All by yourself?" the little man at the dam had said.

It is a nasty question to answer, the way he put it. It is the question of gregarious, colonial man, and it contains outrage, and it means: What the hell's the matter with you? Few people are willing to believe that a piece of country, hunted and fished and roamed over, felt and remembered, can be company enough.

I don't always believe it myself.

But what you answer them is simply yes. And they say they've got no use for canoes, for which you can be maybe a little grateful, since if they did have, they'd pullulate all up and down the river. . . .

From nearby on the mountain above, a goat bell tinkled, and then a barred owl put *his* old peremptory ungregarious question: *Who cooks for you? Who cooks for YOU ALL?*

The pup edged against me. He was a six-month-old dachshund and weighed about twelve pounds, and even after he was grown he wouldn't be a very practical dog, but he was company, too—more concrete, perhaps, than memories and feelings.

"Passenger, you watch," I told him. "It's going to be a good trip."

In the firelight he registered disbelief, and I was afraid I shared some of it. Rain already, and the damned river high . . .

CHAPTER THREE

LIKELY there were few Spaniards who came this far up the Brazos, and those who came didn't stick. Ad majorem Dei gloriam, they wandered through in their dented armor, sweating or freezing according to the seasons, hard and enduring as bleak Castilla and sad Estremadura that had bred them. They named the river, though which of them did so and why he called it the Arms of God are lost lore. Over the past century local chroniclers have built legends around that name: that some strayed Iberians out on the drouthy plains shrank their swollen tongues in the river's salty pools; that a divinely-original head rise hissed down just in time to save a party's rear from whooping savages . . . But those accounts smell of romantic wishfulness, and nobody seems really to know. They were here, the durable Moor-Visigoths, and left place names and casks and chests of gold at each night's stopping place—"Ef a man only had him a good witchin' stick"—but for the most part who they were and how many and when is unknowable, unregistered in that scattered, paper-and-parchment, half-reliable racial remembrance that we call history.

They were a swarming and persistent folk, the Spaniards of the old breed, and that even their missionaries did not manage to knot their toes into the grasses of northern and western Texas is testimony to the greater persistence of another, tougher breed. This was the Comanchería, this and eastern New Mexico and western Oklahoma and big swatches of Colorado and Kansas, or the lands we call those names now. And by the time the Spanish were set to extend themselves into those lands, the Comanches had the horse.

"Had" is inexact. The Comanches were squat pedestrians, incapable on the wide grass, until probably the early 1600's, when they began to learn to use the strayed Spanish stock for something other than barbecues. Then, within a century, they made themselves into one of history's great races of riders—and made riders too of the other plains tribes northward and westward to whom they traded ponies. During all human time, it seems, the Comanches, like their cousins the Tatars and the Cossacks and the Huns, had been awaiting that barbaric wholeness the horse was to give them. "Had"? If it was having, it was having in the sense that a man has a thigh, or a hand, or a heart. In the eighteenth and nineteenth centuries on the South Plains the separate abstract ideas of Comanche and Horse were not in fact separable. . . .

Within a simply attuned natural-religious framework, they existed for pleasure, but their pleasures were war and hunting and ravishment and kindred proud patriarchal violences. No other breed within their reach could or did like them except, finally, the closely similar Kiowas, but that fact sweated them very lightly. Those who did not like them could not whip them, either. They were The People, only a few thousand strong in their most numerous times, but total possessors of an empire of grass and timber and wild meat, and constant raiders, for pleasure, far outside the limits of that empire.

The Spaniards had horses, too, and guns, and a stark shoving religion, and a pride and greed that had carried them through conquests that nobody still would believe if the results weren't there to see. But the horse to them was a caparisoned pride, a tool rather than an appendage, and more of them now were comfortable mestizos and criollos than tough Spain-spawned seekers, and maybe a good bit of the shovingness had bled out along the flinty rich road from Vera Cruz. . . . What is certain is that by the middle of the eighteenth century the Comanches had them content to remain in their settlements in New Mexico and South Texas, and fearful enough to pay annual tribute in addition to the stolen horses and mules and women that flowed steadily outward to the plains. Braves with greasy ribboned braids lounged sardonically about the streets of San Antonio. Raids stabbed Old Mexico as far south as Durango. It was a kind of tangential retribution for Moctezuma and the burned libraries of the Mayas—not that the Comanches thought of working retribution for anyone's wrongs but their own, if they had any at that point. They were The People.

And that's what one forgets, looking back, feeling sorry, knowing the shame of what his own people did to the Comanches when his own people came and won. Forgets that for two arrogant horseback centuries they *were* The People, steady winners, powerful beyond any reverie of power their foot-bound Shoshonean ancestors could ever have shaped in the smoke of northern campfires. Dominant in the world they had selected, rich in the goods they prized, dexterous, cruel, wild, joyful, unbearable, lousy, bowlegged, and magnificent . . . So that the pathos one is prone to see in their destruction—apart, different from the destructions of the other red peoples to the east—is not pathos at all, because they had ejaculated the germs of that destruction into the womb of fate, and it was right. They had accepted the magnificence with its risks, and in accepting they chose. Not pathos, no . . .

But that is Big History, and beforehand, too, for that matter. What has relevance here is that the upper-middle Brazos was a part of what they owned. Other Indians lived along there also (the Comanches lived nowhere, but moved with whim and the north wind and the buffalo), docile farmers for the most part, scraps of Caddoan and other tribes who had fled as the Anglo-Saxons advanced unsharingly from the east and the south, and who in their common, constant disaster lived near each other without much friction now. In the flat bends and up the creeks they built villages and raised pumpkins and corn and squash, and the Comanches, granting them no respect and no claim to any corner of land, half tolerated them perhaps because it was pleasant to have them there to raid occasionally.

That the upper-middle Brazos ran through the Comanchería had a good bit of relevance a century ago. Because, though the Comanches were still calmly certain of their ownership, a new brand of un-Spanish whites had been moving in with the odd notion that *they* owned it, if they could grab it. Anglo-American tejanos and Comanches had been feeling each other out in the south of the state since the 1820's, and each breed had found the other rough, acquisitive, and treacherous. Neither was to change its mind in the Brazos country. . . .

~~~~~~~~

CHAPTER FOUR

⋖§ Have not all races had their first unity from a mythology, that marries them to rock and hill?

Yeats, The Trembling of the Veil

~~~~~~~~

RAIN . . . Even in gray heaped cities it has a privacy and a sadness. Tented, cocooned in warmed quilted feathers (the pup lumped snug between your calves; you had sworn you wouldn't, but in the night he wheezed and shuddered on the chewed blanket brought for him), you come awake to its soft-drumming spatter and the curl of the river against a snag somewhere, and move your shoulder maybe against the warmth of the bag, and the shoulder prickles in separate knowledge of its wellbeing, and the still cold is against your face, and that tiny blunt wedge of sheltered space is all that exists in a sensed universe of softly streaming, gently drumming gray sadness beyond the storm flaps. And the sadness is right, is what should be. Knowing you do not have to get up at all, for an hour or for two hours or for a year, you lie there warmly sad and then you go back to sleep without dreaming.

And after the hour or the two hours or the year (though, without logic or the need for it, it is only now grayish dawn at the crack between the flaps), a fox or a coon or just the constantly rehearsed utile fear that grips wild things spurs a blue heron into action and he flies downriver screaming with precise panic: *Help! Help! Help! Help!* except that with distance it becomes the same old querulous *Frawnk, frawnk!* of all your life. The pup, though, it being the pristine first heron's *Frawnk, frawnk!* of his life, tenses and gruffs in the bottom of the bag. The rain has stopped; there is only a staggered drip from the leaves of the mesquite. A cardinal chits, and what lies outside the canvas wedge is no longer a void but a tentative stir of leaves and light, wings and water, and the ragged beginnings of breeze.

Day . . . Time now . . .

In the pocket notebook I carried is scribbled, early among the entries for that morning: "The hard thing is to *get slowed down.*"

What that means in relation to my activities just then is a bit mysterious to me. Probably it means I was impatient with my own dawdling slowness, prodigious and no trouble at all to attain, and that I then grew irked with my impatience. Impatience is a city kind of emotion, harmonious with "drive" and acid-chewed jumping stomachs, and I presume we need it if we are to hold our own on the jousting ground this contemporary world most often is. But it goes poorly on a river. One's repetitious clumsiness, byblow of irregular years away from the rock-bottom facts of ax and wood and fire and frying pans, and wet feet inside boots one forgot to grease, and the hauling of buckets of water up from the beach, and the endless packing and unpacking of sacks and boxes and the stowing and unstowing in the boat, is as solid a consideration as bird song and mesquite smoke and the lilt of a canoe in a rapids. To let it erode one's calm, for the time that it must last, is to deny the worth of being there, and is furthermore generative of still more slow clumsiness. Did one, in rage that all the good wood was soaked, chop logs carelessly against the rocky ground? If so, one had good cause for thirty minutes' more rage later, while honing out the nicks. . . .

"One" gave up on the fire, finally. The morning was not all that cold, though cold enough, with a lowering sky and a cutting breeze. I put on an extra wool shirt under my windbreaker and made coffee on a little German alcohol stove, eating store bread with it and a can of apricots. The pup lay in the tent atop the tumbled sleeping bag, shivering, gasping pneumonically, showing his eye-whites. I felt guilt for having brought him so young, and decided not to strike the tent until I saw whether or not it was going to start raining again, as the sky swore it would. Resigned or impatient or however, you can stay reasonably dry in rain if you're set up when it comes; to have to scramble muddily ashore and make a new camp under a downpour is a pure and lasting misery.

Redbirds called weakly, and then a canyon wren, and a Carolina, and chickadees, titmice, killdeers, kingfishers, gulls. I saw none of them. As the wind picked up, it hushed them as wind does, and drove them to cover. Three or four thousand robins in a strung-out, undulating flock flew from around the mountain, barking, and disappeared into wet autumn-bright woods across the river. For me those great aggregations connote the bleak time, the bare months, and I supposed the weather was what I deserved for having started so late in the year.

My watch had run down during the night; I set it again by guess, and with a second big cup of coffee smoked the last of my ready-rolls, throwing the crumpled pack on the night's fire's paste-pounded ashes.

Finally three or four patches of blue showed improbably in the west, and disappeared. The rest of the sky looked as bad as ever, but taking the brief blue for my omen I knocked the tent down, rolled stakes and poles inside it, and tied it into the canoe with the other gear. I lashed a tarp over the whole cargo and of its rear edge made a protective awning for the pup. When I picked up his blanket, he came to life. His existence theretofore had been a series of known rituals, one of them tug of war with that moth-perforated sheet of wool. He squealed and growled and shook his head, pulling backward as he held onto it. I dragged him that way down to the canoe, wadded the blanket between the awning and the white-cedar ribs, and put him there on top of it. From beneath the canvas then he gazed out at me with sadness, or what looked like it. . . .

The wind was stout and wetly cold, and seemed southerly. But you can seldom tell exactly on the river; the snaking trough of its valley twists wind and turns it back against itself and usually, it seems, against a canoe. I had loaded badly; the heavy boxes were amidships rather than forward, and the wind catching the light bow shoved it perversely upstream as I pushed away, and I was drifting backward through a fast riffle. I fought it around in time to see and miss a rock, and kept it straight by hard paddling, and knew I would have to stop again before long and rebestow the load. It didn't matter much; I had no idea of making distance and wanted only to be ready to quit when the rain started again.

Gray sky, gray pale green of the willows not yet turned by frost, and gray black-green of the cedar on the hills, gray-red and gray-yellow of the tall oaks and cottonwoods and pecans, ingrained gray of great sandstone boulders tumbled along the shore. Gray blow of the gray wind, counterthrust of the gray current . . .

At Shut-in Crossing I tired of the needless fighting and stopped on a sand bar with a half-inch of mud spread evenly over its surface. Skating about the canoe on clogged boot soles, I made the laborious rearrangements and tied things down again and tarped them again and then, unwilling to start out again in the day's unpromising monotony—it seemed somehow a waste of good river—walked followed by the pup into the valley above the crossing. Backed by steep hills, it lies on the other shore from where most of the old ones settled along that bit of the river, which I guess is why they called it Shut-in. A man named Davis homesteaded there in 1857, a year or so before the Comanches (restricted by then legally, if not in fact, to a reservation up the Clear Fork) reached a startled awareness of the newcomers' solidity and began the really bloody fighting.

They were diverse, the first Saxons who came here, the old ones, and it is hard to talk knowingly about them from a century's distance. There was very little Hollywood about them, and not much Fenimore Cooper. Rough, certainly . . . Mainly Southern, but not altogether, and even the Southerners heterogeneous in origin and type—rednecks and slaveholding younger sons from the cotton states, Texas-Revolutionary veterans from the older cattle counties far down the Brazos and the Colorado, hillmen from Tennessee and Carolina. Judging from the dialect they passed down, and the religion, and the narrow, straight-line living broken occasionally by sprees and murder, the hill people may have predominated, but a lot of them came later, when other people had moved on after exhausting a farm or so.

Sharp around the edges, not tender . . . They couldn't

have been, bringing wagonloads of women and kids and chattels where they brought them. Like the Comanches, they were unlovable to neighbors of other breeds, but like the Comanches too they did not care. They had a notion, handed tangled down from the dank European forests, that *they* were The People. There wasn't room enough in the Comanchería for two tribes with that illusion.

What part John Davis played in the consequent uproar is not recorded, but someone relayed a sad, sentimental story about his floorboards. He drove a wagon south to Waco to get them, and brought them back to lay them in his cabin for his bride; it was the first floor in the Palo Pinto country which was neither flat dirt nor puncheon. They say she was proud of it, and a few months later she died in childbirth and John Davis tore up the floorboards and made them into a coffin. . . .

Maybe then he stayed in the valley, morose, and proceeded with mule and plow and straight uncontoured furrow, with cotton and corn year after leaching year, to wear it out. Someone did. It lies fallow now, its old small fields choked with briars and the low second-growth oak brush they call shinnery. I didn't know where the old Davis cabin had stood, or whether any signs of it remained, but near the river I found what was left of some log corrals, and beyond that a bulldozer had been at work and a bright goat-wire fence stood taut, evidence probably of new city ownership. Up through the thirties and the war and even till the drouth of the fifties, individual families still subsisted on some of those little farms in the valleys and on the flatlands inside the river bends. It was a hard-scrabble life. Most of them have moved away now, leaving the farms to lie brushy and neglected, convalescing from a century of abuse. Businessmen buy up blocks of them as ranching investments, dozing away the scrub and the cedar that has moved down from the hills, and replanting in grass. If the land is to be used at all, that practice probably does it less harm than the other did, though a kind of people, backwash of the old ones, are disappearing with the change.

Towhees and cardinals hopped about in the brush, untouched by the wind that hissed in the treetops, ignoring me and the pup in the assurance that thick undergrowth gives them. Bewildered by so much untailored shrubbery, the passenger stuck by my heels. Mud . . . An old corncrib, collapsed at one corner, and the rat-chewed gray cobs spilling out between the logs like a travesty of a cornucopia . . . Frostbitten sumac the color of arterial blood speckled the high hillsides. Deer tracks pitted the old corral. Silence. Ruin . . .

Trespassing, I climbed over the new fence. The old kind of owners didn't worry much over that kind of property rights, roaming the country as if it were still open, letting others roam, too. The new ones are testier, when they are there, but they're usually not there and even then they're fretful only if you're hunting. I'd left the gun in the canoe. Having climbed over, and crossed the sterile slash of the bulldozer's path, I found nothing on the other side different from what I'd already seen, and climbed back over again. . . . At the canoe, I got out my fly rod and was setting it up when a yellow Cub came flying up the river low along the wind, with two men in it. They waved. I jerked my head in answer.

Irked perhaps by my calm—people who fly around near the ground seem to require delight and awe from earthbound watchers—they banked into a tight circle and came back to buzz me, too low now, and with the plane's wheels slapped the top branches of a cottonwood.

It scared them. They pulled up steeply and flew off in the direction they had come from, and the roar of their dive became a drone. . . . The pup yapped after them.

The silent air of ruin is fragile.

Though the day was bleak and low still, moseying up the valley had cleansed my feeling about it, a little. Below the crossing's fast water, bream were surface-feeding on midge nymphs or something else too small to be seen. Anchoring with a rock, I cast a little Rio Grande King to where the rippled water turned slick, but it wasn't little enough. They ignored it for a dozen or so casts, and when one finally took he was the size of a silver dollar with tail and fins, a goggle-eye. To me, bream on a fly rod are as pretty fishing as a man can want, but there are times when they aren't worth working for. I put the little one back in the water, reeled in, and shoved on.

Just around the bend there, the canoe balanced now and shooting smoothly along, I saw another cleanness. A bald eagle came flapping easily down the wind, passed within short shotgun range of me, and lit in a dead tree upstream. I put the glass on him and he sat there, spruce black and white, fierce-eyed enough for anyone's Great Seal. . . .

They practically do not exist any more in our part of the country. Those who study such matters believe that the whole nation, not counting Alaska, contains only a couple of thousand or so of them now. They don't adapt. They need big space and big time and big solitude for their living and their breeding, and not finding them, perish. . . .

Most people who feel at all about birds and animals seem to have a specialized affection for those species that adjust tidily to the proximity of man and man's mess. I lack it, mostly. A robin's nest in a pruned elm in one's garden is pleasant to watch, and English sparrows' squabbles and loves are worth laughing at if you haven't got anything better to laugh at, and gulls do circle with white grace about our coastal garbage dumps. But for me they lack the microcosmic poetry that some see in them. They lack the absoluteness of the spacious, disappearing breeds—of geese riding the autumn's southward thrust, of eagles, of grizzlies, of bison I never saw except in compounds . . . Of wolves . . . Of wild horses that have been hunted down in twenty years or so and have been converted into little heaps of dog dung on the nation's mowed lawns. And antelope, and elk grazing among the high aspens, an old bull always on guard . . .

I'm aware that the bald eagle eats carrion and has other unaesthetic habits, noted by good Benjamin Franklin. It doesn't affect the other feeling. Sheepmen shoot the goldens now with buckshot from airplanes, in the western country. We don't deserve eagles; they will go.

What hurt was knowing that when I was younger I would have shot this one. The gun lay by my foot, and an ancient itch had stirred my hand toward it as he passed. . . . For nothing, for pride of destruction that has marked us as a breed . . .

"Hell," the old-timers used to brag in front of the feed stores in Weatherford and Granbury, "I've done wore out three farms in my time. . . ."

Anyhow, he sat there on a barkless worm-runed branch, twisting his neck to set the full yellow glare of his eye upon me, and when my own neck was twisted around too totally for comfort, I waved him goodbye and took up the paddle again.

A long gravel island . . . Along one side of it lay a calm pool that would end, I knew, in a safe riffle where I might be able to float or might have to get out and ease the canoe through, wading. Down the other side the main force of the river ran in a hard fast roaring chute with willows lying out horizontally and a big rock or so sticking up. Earlier, in quenched mood, I would have chanced wet feet on the safe side; now I steered into the chute without even considering a walk down the island to see what the water did below, this high. Startled by the sudden bumpy speed, the pup came out of his hole and stood up with paws on the gunwale to watch, just in time to get a harsh willow branch across his muzzle. It caught me, too, and for a moment about my ears and neck there was the itch of the little insects that manage for a time to survive frosts among the thick leaves. . . . Then a rock to slew past, twisting the bow aside and jumping the stern over with a levered side stroke, and finally a long rough clear run with the gravel to the right and the root-woven overhanging shore to the left . . . Straight and coasting fast, I glanced across the flat island and saw, parked in its center, the little yellow airplane that had buzzed us upstream. No one was near it. While I watched it, puzzling, we bore down on another rock, and I didn't move fast enough to avoid a long scrape that made the ribs crackle. Though the canoe had a new fiberglass covering and the gear was lashed down, I craved no holes or overflips or other emergencies. I think as kids we used to; certainly we had enough of them. . . . Cursing, I settled to business, and in a minute or so the chute vomited out into a great calm pool below the island.

On a boulder two old countrymen were still-fishing with casting rods. They looked at me. An eddy caught the boat and drifted me close, and I got out my pipe to fill it.

"Come down in at air airplane?" asked one, a cadaver in overalls.

I said no.

"Tole you not," the other said to him.

"Catch anything?" I said, because one has to. . . .

With monosyllabic unwillingness, the cadaver confessed that they hadn't. I lit my pipe, and from the corners of narrow farmers' eyes they flicked glances at my boat and possessions. The second one, short and wiry, reeled in an empty hook above a huge sinker and began to rebait it from a jar.

"Hod-damn stuff stinks," he said.

"What makes it good," the cadaver averred.

For a few moments I sat, smoking and resting, in the aura of their strained indifference, then shoved on down, having given them fuel for an hour's taciturn, conjectural conversation. There was a fine long piece of river below, deep but with a pull, and running somehow—a miracle—sidewise to the wind, so that the water next to one bank was sheltered and smooth. I steered there and drifted quietly. On either shore the castellated sandstone mountains rose. The day held sadness still, but I had the feel of the river now, and the boat, and the country, and all of it was long-ago familiar.

There is no way to equate canoeing with the ways of the old ones in that country. We used to try, reading books of northern Indian lore, but it was an alien injection and I guess we knew it, imitation Chippewas in the Comanche country. The whole tradition there, Indian and white, was horseback; they didn't need to travel the alternately dry and flooded streams. But their kind of penetration into the country is no longer a possibility; barbed wire and the universal privacy of property obstruct passage, and the highways are mere gashes across the land, having little to do with what the land is. . . . I can't give you three unanswerably good reasons why one should care a damn about what the land is, but if one does, one does, and rivers thread through it and are still public domain—a reasonably rare phenomenon in proud Texas, which retained title to its public lands when it came into the Union, and then gave them all away.

Canoes, too, are unobtrusive; they don't storm the natural world or ride over it, but drift in upon it as a part of its own silence. As you either care about what the land is or not, so do you like or dislike quiet things—sailboats, or rainy green mornings in foreign places, or a grazing herd, or the ruins of old monasteries in mountains. . . . Chances for being quiet nowadays are limited. Those for being unquiet seem to abound—vulgarity, as Huxley has written, being like adultery largely a matter of opportunity. But I saw a coon waddling along the riverside path that afternoon, and an old boar squirrel tightwalked unsuspecting down a branch just ahead of the boat, and having skipped lunch I shot him for supper.

Hale had been right about the ducks. I saw none. Wet years in the Southwest are good for wildlife, but you see less of it than in the dry times, when cover is scarce and all creatures have to use the scant remaining patches of water. The river now was incidental to tanks, creeks, and even ruts as a water supply, and its heavy flow would make it unpleasant feeding for waterfowl.

Somewhere on Schoolhouse Mountain, in the Fortune Bend (Old Man Fortune brought his slaves there in '56 to work the land, but wisely left his family in Waco; I never read what happened to the slaves when things got rough in that country), a man was calling cattle in the old, long, melancholy way. They called back, wending probably toward his feed-laden pickup truck. . . . In another drifting mile or so it was four thirty by my guess time, and I pulled out at the mouth of Ioni Creek, above a tumbling rapids, and made camp in a bed of thick, tough, oily, dark green weeds, below willows. It was the sort of place that in summer would have been insect-ridden, but the footing was sandy turf instead of mud, and I wanted to get settled before evening brought whatever weather it might bring.

Jesse Veale fought the old, useless fight just up Ioni, one day in 1873. . . .

I skinned and quartered the old squirrel, thick-hided and with testicles as big as a dog's. Since the war, somehow, I don't much like to skin them. You cut them at the wrists and make a slash or two and peel away the tough pelt, and what you then have suddenly in your hands is a bug-eyed, naked, dead homunculus whose looks I do not care for. It isn't the same with other animals. . . . I remember, from somewhere, a story of Kentucky politicians arguing over the composition of burgoo, and whether or not the squirrels that went into it ought first to be decapitated. One point of view holds that the cheek meat is the best of all. . . . In the story, the proponent of headlessness wound up shouting: "By God, I don't care. When I look in a pot, be damn if I want it lookin' back at me!"

Which, in male company, could lead to the proctologist and the swallowed glass eye, and along many another colorful byway, but won't . . . I would have been a headless-burgoo man—in fact am, since that standard stew one boils up out of squirrel and potatoes and grease and flour and whatever else is at hand is essentially the same dish. It wasn't much good that night, but on the other hand I was hungry and willing to use my teeth.

I ate about dusk and sat staring at a little stick fire that needed constant fueling. The pup had dry dogfood with squirrel gravy, and sought the tent. Aloneness is most striking at evening, however it may happen to be striking you at the moment. Day's absorbent busy-ness is past, and the dishes are stacked dirty, and you are confronted with yourself and confronted too with whether or not you like being where you are, by yourself.

I didn't like it overmuch just then, with blackness attacking a low gray sky. It takes time for the habit of people to wear off of you, especially at evening. I sat and listened to the rapids, and thought for no good reason about Jesse Veale, who rode to Ioni with two of his brothers and a friend from Palo Pinto town a few miles away, to fish and to hunt turkeys and to camp and, probably, to stick cockleburs under one another's saddles and tie knots in one another's bed rolls and laugh the kind of laughter you laugh with friends out that way, young.

In '73 there was not much reason to expect Indians in that neighborhood—in fact, Jesse Veale was the last man killed in that county by them. The fighting had gone on hot and heavy all during the War and afterward, in the bitter Reconstruction years, when the Northern whites at the Oklahoma agencies had not only tolerated but sometimes abetted the raids down across the Red, with the full moon. But by '73 it was last-ditch and sporadic, and its center had moved out north and west of the Brazos country. . . .

Inheritors of the old sharp-edgedness, though, Jesse Veale

and his companions likely went around hoping for trouble, any kind. If so, they got it. One afternoon, setting fishlines near the Garland Bend, they ran across some Indian ponies staked out in the cedar, and some saddles, and took them. (The assumption with Indian ponies was always that they had been stolen, or if not that others had been.) The next morning Jesse Veale and Joe Corbin crossed Ioni a half-mile above its mouth, on their way back to camp from checking some hooks at the river. At the crossing, in a race to see who'd come second and get splashed, they hit the water hard at about the same time and sprayed each other mightily and raced on through, yelling. On the other side Joe Corbin pulled up and knuckled water out of an eye and unholstered his old cap-and-ball Colt.

"You scutter," he said. "You done wet my loads."

"You ain't gonna shoot nothin' nohow," Jesse Veale said.

Joe Corbin said: "Jesse."

"What?"

"Jesse," Joe Corbin said, "they's two Indians a-lookin' at us from on top of that bank. They's more than two. . . ."

Afoot, likely because it had been their ponies the boys had taken upriver, the Comanches began to shoot, and an arrow hit Jesse Veale in the knee, and his horse went to bucking off to one side. Joe Corbin yelled: "What the hell we gonna do?"

Jesse yelled something back. To Joe Corbin it sounded like: "Run it out!" He did, snapping his useless pistol at an Indian who tried to grab his reins and ducked aside from the misfire, lashing his pony on up the bank's rise. . . . When he last looked back (how many times did he see it again, the rest of his life, how many times did he wonder if what Jesse Veale had said was: "Fight it out"?), Jesse was on the ground shooting and clubbing with his pistol, and they were all over him. And when Joe Corbin came back with help from a ranch not far away, they found Jesse Veale sitting dead but unscalped against a double-elm tree, his pistol gone, Comanche blood on the ground around him. Though the Indians were gabbling over their wounded in a ravine near at hand, and someone's dog went there and bayed at them, the whites were only three and did not follow them, then. . . .

Some of the lines they had been checking must have been set where I was camped just then, a good fish hole still.

Sometimes you take country for itself, for what shows merely, and sometimes it forces its ghosts too upon you, the smell of people who have lived and died there. They do not have to be individual ghosts like Jesse Veale's; often they're only the feel that a time past has for you, the odor of an era. . . . And they don't have to smell good.

My canteen was empty of its sweet city water. I filled it at the river, propped it in the coals with dry sticks around it, and sat watching its contents boil to purity if not to palatability. They say Old Man John Chisum's cowboys, accustomed to water from the same mineral-laden redbed that taints the Brazos far to the west, used to carry shakers of salt when they trailed into strange country, that their drink might taste the same as usual. . . .

Sizzling rain began, unheralded by any gust of air. I dragged the boxes and sacks into a hasty pile and put the tarp over them, and tumbled into the tent. The pup was having one of his shivering, gasping seizures. Heavy, the rain drowned the fire's small flicker, and since the lantern in its box was with the flashlight under the tarp outside, I shed my boots and pants in the dark, trying not to rub the canvas with my shoulders, and slid into the bag.

Young, one *was* Jesse Veale, or Charles Goodnight, or sometimes an Indian, a brave one. . . . One saw them heroic in size and posture, and transmuted them into myth, and tried in reverie and play to live the myth; it is the process that in this day has shaped the whole Western legend into a raucous lie flooding out from bluely glowing television screens.

There was heroism, but there were people, too. Older, having seen a few heroics at first hand and having probed one's own possibilities, one knows more about Joe Corbin, feels what he likely felt, leans down with him along his running horse's hot neck and glances back with him past his biceps at a clot of screaming, hating, hacking savages, knows the panic, and the pointlessness of turning the pony back and dying there, too. . . .

Young, one moves in upon the country and thinks himself a tile in its tesselated ecology, and believes that he always would have been such a tile, and hoots with the owl, and scorns even tents.

Older, one knows himself an excrescence upon the landscape and no kinsman to any wild thing; one hears the bass drumbeat and the gabble of the rapids below and the roar of the rain and feels abrupt depression and wonders why he barged out alone into the wetness and the winter. And thinks that perhaps, in the old time, he would have been one of the cautious who stayed in the jammed East.

I lay awake for a long time with a kind of three-o'clock-in-the-morning apprehension on me. The pup shivered against my side. The river boomed and burbled against its rocks. At last, half-awake, or I thought so, I heard the booms and burbles change into drums and voices, and it was Comanches and Kiowas somewhere off across the creek. Multitudes of them, in angry fiesta, and there was in me a wonder whether or not they'd find me . . .

For a time I had a consciousness too that the sound was not really voices and drums but the Brazos. With full sleep, though, that consciousness went away, and the delusion went into a dream in which the celebrants were angrier and louder and knew I was there and were searching in a loud line, while I scrabbled away on hands and knees in the wet scrub. . . .

"*Kah-seh!*" one screeched from nearby, and another answered in syllables as clear.

In life, I have only known that feeling in war, at night, on bitter little islands in the Pacific. That tangled into the dream until the hating Comanches were not distinguishable from hating Japanese in the underbrush beneath palms. . . .

When the dream had ended its feel still rasped my sleep, so that later when a cramped shoulder woke me and I rolled over, the rain still roaring, the rapids still booming, I felt relief and chuckled. I was on a whimsical trip down a river, and the trip didn't amount to much. The little tent was warm. The flavor of wartime was still on my mind, but now what I remembered was the tents of an encampment we had far up on the side of Haleakala, on Maui, where in the days the yellow sunshine splashed off the red slopes around us and the Pacific far below and the crags of the volcano above, and where at night it used to rain so hard that there was nothing in the world but roaring rain and a tent and oneself, young and tight-bellied, on a dry warm cot. . . . The evening's foreboding was gone, and I decided rather cheerfully that if the weather didn't change, I'd pull out at the Dark Valley bridge and telephone home for a ride.

It was that simple. I went back to sleep.

~~~~~~

MORNING CAME damp and dark with a low fog and ducks calling as they flew half hidden in mist overhead. The rain had stopped, but the dark green weeds around the tent were dripping and quickly soaked the passenger and my boots, socks, and pants. The rapids' sound was muted; what water I could see lay like murky glass. My gathered wood was saturated; I gave up frontiersmanship and used a dollop of my scant lantern gasoline to start a big roarer for warmth and coffee and stewed fruit.

The fog had a fine privacy. In a jacket pocket I found a little rosined bird squeaker that someone had given me, and tried it, and called up a wintering house wren that sat in a scrub hackberry and scolded me much like a chickadee. Then I walked up a hillside behind camp, wooded with mesquites and elms and drouth-dead stubs. Birds were thick there, feeding and moving about with the want of fear that quiet foggy air, like brush, seems always to give them. I picked out two kinds of flickers, Mexican and red-bellied woodpeckers, lark sparrows, cardinals, and more wrens, and sat for a time trying to see specific distinguishing marks on a flock of streak-breasted finches that flitted about singing a clear little finch song. But I'm not a meticulous enough student to keep the less flamboyant Fringillidæ straight in my mind, and finally gave it up. . . .

Before leaving, I paddled up Ioni to the crossing where Jesse Veale died. It is still there, though dozed out wider for present ranch use; I looked for the old double elm's stump, not remembering whether I'd actually seen it when young or only had seen a photograph, but however that may have been, it was no longer there. Mesquites stand thick on the flat above the crossing now, though probably in the old days they didn't; like cedar, they move onto overused land. Except for a few birds, it was a silent place.

Across the creek the black bulk of Crawford Mountain grayed upward into the overcast; the Comanches went there after the fight at the crossing, and the next day a big mob of avengers swarmed out from Palo Pinto and trailed them up among the cedar and the rocks, and found a dead one wearing Jesse Veale's hat. . . . Live ones were waiting, too, slowed down probably by wounds, since they rarely stuck around to fight after a raid—not in '73, not that long after the old arrogant days when they stormed Durango and San Antone. They winged a couple of citizens before being run into a cave under a high cliff. The Palo Pintans besieged them there all night, using up a lot of ammunition on the cave's dark entrance, and in the morning, fired with rage and maybe other stimulants, Jesse Veale's brothers ran in with pistols in one hand and knives in the other. But the Indians had slipped free during the night; later someone found their signs up near Shut-in, where they had passed on their way out to Oklahoma. . . .

That had been a long time ago, but the place was eerie in the fog with a little of the held-over eeriness of my nightmare. Feeling it, the passenger got back into the canoe and sat on top of the tarp and barked, scattering ghosts with sharp sound.

If any were there to scatter . . .

CHAPTER FIVE

THAT afternoon I got only to Eagle Creek, still probing uncourageously against weather's ire. Rounded gray-stone cliffs stand beside the creek mouth; in the river itself massive, split-away, rhombic blocks twist and slow the green current of a long pool. Big oaks gone red, and yellowed ashes rose precariously from slanted alluvial soil beneath the cliffs, piles of drift against their boles in prophecy of their own fate; it is on the outside tip of a bend, and in those places the river lays down rich sediment for maybe centuries and then in a fit of angry spate cuts under it and carries it away, trees and all. . . . A canyon wren was singing there; one always is. They love high rocks above water, and the wild falling song itself is like a cascade.

For want of other level ground, I made camp on a high yellow sand bank under the oaks and the cliff, and built a big drift-hardwood fire against a boulder to drive back the chill damp and to dry my wet feet a little. Before dark I crossed the creek to look for the stones of a little circular Indian rock shelter I remembered there, but couldn't find them; in their place was a great hump of gelatinous silt piled up by the springtime floods.

I ate creamed chipped beef on the last of my store bread and drank coffee laced with whisky and honey and slept hard despite an old chariey horse's digging under my shoulder, the pup an established bedfellow now. What old man had it been, somewhere in books, who'd slept with a dog to cure his aches? I couldn't remember. The passenger cured none of mine.

In the morning it was raining again, with thunder. I waited it out in the tent, and when it had stopped I ate, washed, and loaded, cursing sore hands and slick riverside mud and the cumbersome boxes and bags, though still without knowing how I'd have managed with less gear at that time of year or how, having what I had, I could handle it more easily. In summer or a drouthy fall, when the river is low and you know it is going to stay that way, you can camp on low bars almost beside the boat and can reduce lifting and staggering and sliding to a minimum, but not with the big water running and two-foot rises and falls commonplace.

The big water scooted us on down—I know the "us" is an anthropomorphism, but in the absence of other company a dog makes a plural, and not a bad one either—and through a fine, pounding rapids above the Boy Scout Ranch at Kyle Mountain. I wanted to go there as a kid, but for some reason never made it. Maybe it was the smoking; most of us started that when we were thirteen or fourteen and felt morally obliged to give up Scouting with its insistence on physical rectitude.

After that a quick sweeping shower wetted us. Chilled, we passed under the east face of the Chick Bend mountain, where they once bushwhacked an old warrior at dawn while he stood guard for his companions, and to the right around the Dalton Bend, named for Marcus Dalton, who settled there. This region was thick with cattlemen in the old days; they had brought the craft with them from the south of the state, where their fathers had learned it from the Mexican vaqueros. Many of their families moved west and north with the frontier and the cattle trails, and their names are familiar all the way to Canada now—Reynolds, Goodnight, Loving, Slaughter, Waggoner. . . . Once after the War, not for the first time, Marcus Dalton took a herd to Kansas and sold it. When he was back in his own county again, headed home (home for him now was up the river a way) in a wagon with two friends, the Comanches killed them and scalped them and looted their baggage, but overlooked $11,000 in cash in the toe of a boot. Dalton's little dog that had gone all the way to Kansas and back with him (sleeping in his bed roll as they camped?) was still alive to yap at the whites who found the mess.

Just below the Dalton country old George Slaughter lived, a book in himself if you wanted to write it—a Mississippian who reached Texas in time to fight the Mexicans and, they say, deliver a message to Travis at the Alamo before it fell, and moved to the frontier when he was nearly fifty to preach Baptist hellfire and fight Indians and punch cattle and found a range dynasty. In Andy Adams's book, it was a Brazos-bred Slaughter who showed the stopped trail herds how to get across a flooded river. The Slaughters showed lots of people lots of things.

It showered yet again. I knew that around the next curve, a mile and a half below, I'd be able to see the Dark Valley bridge, and knew too that that was the place to quit. But the river was pretty where I was—wide and clean and even-flowing, with curious, arching, limestone overhangs along the right shore—and after the rain had stopped I dawdled, reluctant, only steering in the current, wondering if a house I remembered near the bridge would have a telephone, or if I'd have to hitch to Palo Pinto. On those country roads the first car along usually gives you a lift.

Except that just then, with the abrupt autumn changefulness that I'd just about quit believing in, a big wind blew up out of the southwest and cleaned the clouds from the sky in a scudding line, and all of a sudden everything was the way it was supposed to be. The pale green of the willows came alive; big frost-golden cottonwoods flared where I hadn't noticed them. . . . A cardinal flew dipping and rising across the river, red as a paint splash in the washed sunlit air, and five feet under the canoe I could see stone by stone the texture of the bottom as it slid past. The passenger came out of his hide-hole to climb up onto the tarp and growl at a Hereford cow and her calf, dubious-eyed, who watched us move by.

There was no guarantee the weather would stay good; I doubted that it intended to. . . . We rounded the curve. The new bridge was there beside the creek, skinny and tall on its concrete piers.

(It was up Dark Valley that settlers saw the last of 600 good stolen horses in one bunch, pointed north to the Territory ahead of the big band of Indians who had hit the Landmans and the Gages and the Browns and the Shermans, cruelly hard. But that story goes later, if it goes at all. You can't get them all in.)

I said: "Hell, bridge."

The bridge said nothing.

I said: "Passenger, are we going to quit?"

The passenger construed it as an invitation to play, and came scrambling back to gnaw on my pants cuff. There is a big rapids under the bridge, an ugly one. It has old rusty car bodies sticking up out of it, and crashes straight in against a rock bank before veering left into a long shallow chute. Smart boatmen don't run it when the river's high, but walk the gravel bar on its inner curve, letting the boat down gently by a line.

But I had the feeling that if I stopped there, I might be obliged to quit, and dawdled still until the sucking funnel at the head of the rapids caught me. Because my stupidity didn't deserve good luck, I had it. We flicked the jagged remains of a Ford and then I was pulling deep and hard on the right, the paddle spring-bending in my hands, to bring the bow left and clear of the stone bank at the turn, and did bring it left, and rammed the paddle head-on against the rock to keep the stern from hitting, and yelled aloud as we straightened into the long run.

Then I was ashamed in the way that you're ashamed when someone else hears you talking to yourself. A man and a woman were fishing at the lower end of the chute; those are the places where the countrymen drop their lines, the places where the big catfish feed. They watched me slide down toward them, and as I passed the man tossed his head in resentful greeting. They were alone and liked being alone, and hadn't liked my crazy shout. I resented their being there, too, and so respected his right. . . .

Hungry, I stopped on a gravel bar and made bouillon on the little alcohol stove, and with it ate crackers and cheese and slices of onion. The sun bit warm into the knotted muscles of my back as I ate, and relaxed them. The sky and the water and the multicolored chert gravel of the bar shone with a brightness that I'd forgotten, and made me a little sleepy. It was payment for three bad days and I took it so, and lay down for a while, and threw pebbles up into the air and heard them fall in the current, and drank coffee and smoked.

Across the river a gap showed in the cottonwoods where Elm Creek comes to the Brazos from (inevitably) still another historic spot, a vale they used to call the Indian Hole. People are less "married" now, in Yeats's sense, to surrounding rocks and hollows and prairies, and think less of them, so that the old names get lost. I don't know whether they still call that the Indian Hole or not, or even if anyone knows just where it is. A friend of mine and I walked a couple of miles up the creek once, trespassing, and thought we'd found it but were never sure. . . . There, in 1858, an old fellow named Choctaw Tom, together with a band of his relatives and friends, learned what an ineluctably sweet privilege it was to be a red man on the white man's fringe of settlement. The lesson didn't do most of them much good because they didn't survive it, but they learned it anyhow.

They had all been jammed together on a reservation up the river by then, scraps of ten or a dozen tribes—all but the Comanches and Kiowas, a few of whom were resisting agricultural education on their own reserve up the Clear Fork while the rest ran as freely as ever in West Texas and Oklahoma, raiding down into the settlements occasionally for horses, or for cattle to trade to the New Mexican comancheros at plains rendezvous, but not usually for scalps. Not yet . . . It had been a number of years since any major bloodshed, and that had been farther to the south.

Major Robert Neighbors, cataloguing Indians in '47, and General Cooper three or four years later, had liked the peaceful Ionies and Wichitas and Kichais and Caddoes and the others in their villages along the Brazos, and had dreamed of little Utopias for them. The first settlers, tough but knowledgeable Texans for the most part, had tolerated them well enough, swapping horses and food with them and letting them hang around the log barns to beg milk. An Anadarko chief named José María used to take white children for wild rides on his pony, and his squaws made moccasins for them, and other pleasant tales have come down from those brief friendly years. Nobody liked the Comanches and Kiowas, but nobody ever had, and they were little in evidence except when they came, on the full moon, to steal and hoot in the nights. . . .

Less knowledgeable whites came cramming in soon, though, and wanted the Indian farmland in the bends and the valleys, and got it. Major Neighbors, trapped by his sympathies into taking charge, herded the farming tribes up to their reservation (God knows they must have been pessimists by then, some of them having been driven from as far away as the Mississippi in one generation) and taught them by his own example that good white men existed, which was about the least useful thing he could have taught them at that point in history. It seems now much like those ladies who train titmice and chickadees to eat from their hands, that the next brat who comes wandering down the alley may have a sitting target for his air rifle. . . . They loved Neighbors, and the stories that have filtered down of how they labored to make the Brazos Reserve a model of agronomic efficiency have a pathos, in the light of what was to follow, that twists in you like a knife.

Neighbors had sorrier luck with the Penateka Comanches on the Clear Fork, but one wonders if he expected much of them. Maybe so. It would have taken more than his pure kind of humanitarianism, though, to make plowmen out of The People. They ate up the seed corn and the brood stock that were furnished them, converted their tools to arrowheads and battle axes, and on horseback drifted in and out of their reservation pretty much at will. The great Comanche Trail, ancestral route of thievery and rapine, lay near. In the fifties buffalo, the big southern herd, still teemed on the plains to the west. Two centuries of sweet wild tradition urged the Comanche to follow them, to ride and hunt and fight. Hand mirrors and hoes and occasional begged whisky and strings of colored beads and the stink of a mule's behind were not a fair trade for that. . . .

The newer frontiersmen didn't distinguish much among the different kinds of Indians. Likely they didn't want to. They were the cutting edge of a people whetted sharp to go places, to wear things out and move on, to take over and to use and to discard. It is doubtful that any of the people in history whetted in that way, from Alexander to a Russian lieutenant-colonel of tanks in Budapest, have wanted to dwell much in their minds on the humanity of the people in their path, on abstract justice. If they had, they wouldn't have been able to go where they went. You do not, for instance, conquer an Aztec empire with 400 men and a set of developed humanistic impulses.

Drunken, shiftless Choctaw Tom was no Aztec, but he shared with them a fate. His Hernán Cortez was a man named Peter Garland—Captain Garland, they called him; the frontier seems to have bred titular soldiers like maggots. He lived forty or fifty miles south of the Reserve, but he had been losing stock to Indians, and one day in 1858 he gathered up a crowd of bravos with similar grievances, or maybe just

with a wish for friction, and headed for the Palo Pinto country with blood in his eye.

Choctaw Tom's motley little party had left the Reserve to
graze their stock, with army permission. He had no reason
to think of trouble; he was known and liked and joked at
by the white men of that neighborhood.

"Hey, Tom!" maybe a young one would shout at him
along the road. "Gotty purty gal? Wanty whisky?"

"Whisky, yes, God damn," he'd yell back, the old black
eyes with their yellow whites sparkling. "No gal. Pony?"

A clot of his own people followed him around usually; he
had status among them. With some other old men and some
women and children he was encamped at the Indian Hole,
unluckily accessible, when Garland reached the area. Maybe
what Garland did shows a sense of abstract justice after all.
Of abstraction, anyhow. Certainly it had no concrete connection with Choctaw Tom's outfit. Garland and his volun-
teers hit them at dawn while they slept, loping through the
lane between the lodges and shooting right and left, turning and loping back through. . . . When they rode out, pre-
sumably well satisfied ("Indians" had stolen stock; "Indians" had been dealt with), seven men and women and
children were dead and the rest pretty thoroughly shot up.

Afterward, in Palo Pinto town, the captain with pride told
someone: "We have opened the ball, and others can dance
to the music."

Others did, though Garland was probably overestimating
his own role in history. It is unlikely that his little ugliness
lighted the fuse to the main powder keg, because the main
powder keg was labeled "Comanche," and he hadn't ven-
tured to touch them. But he set a pattern for other settlers
like him, and it seems that more were like him than were

like, say, Robert Neighbors. Many more . . . In Jacksboro
some blood howlers started a newspaper, *The Whiteman*,
dedicated to those propositions implied by its name. And
The People themselves were getting restive, resentful of the
white encroachment on so much good land and grass and
water, covetous of the big, fast, American riding stock. That
was the year they massacred the Cambren and Mason families in Jack County just to the north, the first real bloodiness
of its kind in the area. Companies of white Rangers, official
and otherwise, were organized and began vengefully to track
war parties and stolen stock across the wild prairies.

Things were shaping up. Old Sam Houston the Raven,
ally of all Indians by tepee marriage and temperament,
hurled objections from the southern seat of government
but got nowhere. "I agreed," Austrian George Erath wrote
in his memoirs—he knew the Brazos country—

> I agreed, but I said that no man would dare tell them so unless
> he wanted to be hanged, and that if he, Houston, went up there
> preaching peace they would hang him.

Houston was the one who sadly, somewhere along the
line, said there was no solution. He said that if he could
build a wall across Texas which would keep all the Indians
securely to the west, the God-damned Texans would crawl
over it from their side. . . . He was right. The Brazos whites
finally organized a full-scale attack on the Lower Reserve,
the peaceful Indians. Because of the firmness of the army
commander there, and the unexpected backbone of the Indians themselves, it came to nothing; but in 1859 Robert
Neighbors had to lead an official removal of all Indians
from Texas, farmers and fighters alike, up across the Red and

into the Territory. After he had them there, he sent Washington a bitter message:

I have this day crossed all Indians out of the heathen land of Texas and am now out of the land of the Philistines. If you want to have a full description of our exodus, see the Bible where the children of Israel crossed the Red Sea. We have had the same show only our enemies did not follow us to Red River.

When he returned south, one of the truly decent men of his time and place, he was immediately shotgunned down by a drunken Indian-baiting Irishman, whom he had never before seen, in the street at Fort Belknap up the Brazos. It had something to do with his having spoken out against the murder of some Reserve Indians, or, some say, with his having accused the Irishman's brother-in-law of stealing horses and letting the Indians take the blame. There was a lot of that, then and later. . . .

The heterogeneous little collection of farming tribes stayed in the Territory, those who survived their new proximity to The People—and many did not survive it. Their racial will to endure seems to have ebbed; disease ate at them, and their women munched abortifacient weeds to avoid letting the long-continued nonsense go any further.

The Comanches and the Kiowas, on the other hand, simply had a new base from which to continue that fighting their ethos impelled them to. From that time onward, it was illegal for them even to hunt buffalo in Texas. But the old gap between law and enforcement was wider than usual in the wild western country. They ran as they had always run, and had a good clear focus for hatred now—the frontier's tejanos—and for another fifteen years or so, helped by the confusion of the War and Reconstruction, they raked that frontier and, indeed, practically froze it on one line for a good while.

~~~~~~~

ALL SUCH ANTIQUE VIOLENCE, though, seemed to have less than it might to do with a drifting, sparkling, sunlit afternoon between the mountains, and the solid feeling that we deserved it, the passenger and I. . . . Little Keechi, the Harris Bend, and down the slick fast water into Post Oak where redbirds sang from both shores and big rocks glided past beneath the keel, the ones the little man at Possum Kingdom had warned me of . . .

The Brazos belonged to me that afternoon, all of it. It really did. The autumn-blue sky (fair skies in Texas at other times of year tend to be white, bleached), the yellow-white air, the cedars and oaks green and gold and red, the rocks the size of buildings, the sun on my back, the steady, comfortable stroke of the paddling, mohair goats kowf!-ing at me from the shore when they caught my scent . . . Belonged to me and the whistling birds and the unseen animals (deer and coon tracks overlaid each other in the shore's silt) and to the big suckers that leaped and splashed . . . People's sounds and a consciousness of them touched me from time to time—an ax's chock up in the cedar, a cow call, a tractor sputtering in the flatland of a bend, a jet's scar across the high blue and its blowtorch blare and the crack of its sudden liberation from its own sound—but it was fall, and they weren't on the river. It was mine.

Savoring its possession, I ran too late in the bright evening and had to camp hastily among sandburs on a Bermudagrass flat. They stuck to so many parts of the passenger that he went into the tent and sulked, picking them off onto our bedding.

Bacon for supper, and lumpy biscuit bread baked by the fire . . . It occurred to me that I'd been making a less than maximum effort toward hunting and fishing, toward living off the land. It was somehow, at that point, a rather guilty realization. Though I had kept a rod rigged and the shotgun by my hand, I had hardly used them. Little had shown up to use them on, but when we were young, we had poked and probed and poached and had ended up always with the meat we needed, albeit often of strange textures—robins, snapping turtles, frogs, armadillos. . . .

Sport was not a main purpose of this trip, but if, during most of your life, your given reason for going out of doors has been to hunt and to fish, then even after you know that the real reason is different, a faint compulsion toward those things remains like a consciousness of sin. I thought of the sour old Midwestern-Scowegian outsider, Veblen, and what he said about it. Despite his hydrochloric wit, to me he is abstract and not very quotable, and all I could remember was a phrase: "the risk of disrepute and consequent lesion to one's self-respect." It was what he said happened to the member of the leisure class who sallied afield for purposes other than slaughter.

But one gets many lesions as he goes along, anyhow, whether or not he is classified leisurely. The hard thing in the long run consists not in loss of self-respect but in decid-ing how much of yourself is sportsman and how much not, and how much you want to exercise the one or the other part at any given time. Saint Henry David Thoreau, incisive moral anthropomorphist that he was, implied that blood sports were for juveniles, not men, and was conceivably right. Prince Ernest Hemingway implies the opposite. . . . One's nature, if he owns more than a single mood, implies both views at one time or another and sometimes in cramping conjunction. It knifes through you, for instance, after waiting through a long golden evening for doves beside a stock tank in someone's pasture, watching your first bird coming in high and swift on the north wind, laying down knowing before you fire that you are on him, watching him contract raggedly and fall in a long parabola to baked hard earth and then going to pick him up—it knifes to feel suddenly in his warmth against your palm, in the silk touch of the feathers at his throat, all the pity of that perished gentle wildness. . . . No fiercely nature-loving female could ever have felt it stronger than I have, at times, and those people I care about hunting with feel it too. It goes away if you keep shooting and is replaced by a stone-hard exultation that is just as real, just as far down inside you, and before long you're twisting off the heads of the broken-winged ones without even full awareness of what your hands do, your eyes searching up for another bird, another shot.

It was there, nonetheless.

But even Saint Henry had impulses to gobble woodchucks raw. Eating does get into it. Leave sports and ethics out of consideration and you still like meat in your belly. . . .

There was time. There was river below, lots of it. After that bright afternoon, I knew they were going to let me have at least a little autumn.

CHAPTER SIX

I SAW my first deer of the trip there in the morning, a medium-sized buck in the cedars above camp where I went to get wood. He coughed at me before I saw him, and I ducked down to glimpse him beneath low-hanging branches as he ran off, flag high. The season would open in three days, but not for a lone man with one average stomach. . . . Despite drouths and people and domestic stock, there is still a good bit of game in the Palo Pinto country. Little, probably, compared to what the old days knew when all the country's productivity went cyclically into the nourishment of only wild creatures . . . But the brush and harsh hills still hide deer and turkey, and the goats and cattle have not yet reached an exact balance point against the supply of grass and hardwood browse. The last lion was shot in that country in the twenties. Occasionally someone claims to have seen bears, and a friend of a friend of mine, truthful, I'm told, was hunting there a few years ago and heard a funny snuffling on the other slope of a knoll, and when he walked up onto it a full-grown buffalo was grazing just beyond it. It looked at him without fear until some swirl of the air carried his scent to it; then it lumbered off into the brush. He couldn't account for its being there, nor could the landowner, nor could I unless it had escaped from one of the big ranches a good bit farther west, where well-to-do descendants of the old ones have a few small keepsake herds under heavy wire. Even after ten or twenty generations of captivity, there is something in buffalo which doesn't accept wire, and sometimes it isn't heavy enough.

Fog, but bluing above into the promise of a clear day . . . And a little after sunup a stout south wind came to scour the air clean again. Stewed apricots and coffee . . . Neat mud-printed coon tracks lay along the gunwales of the canoe when I went to load it. Around the turn there, two drinking does stood still thirty yards ahead of me as I drifted, and let me take their picture before easing, not much alarmed, back into the brush, and a big flight of ducks passed over the river high. Then the wind slapped in behind us. I cut a little willow and jammed it upright in the bow and we sailed up out of Post Oak into Hart at a good five knots with no paddling, even though the river was down a foot or so from the day before. Sand bars were close to the surface now, and I had to watch for their telltale pallid diagonals and zigzag with the channel, though in most places the canoe could slip over. With normal low water in the river it can't slip over; navigation turns into a hard game of second-guessing the sand bars and tricking the breeze. Wind and channel, channel and wind . . .

Speeding along with no effort was pleasant for a change, though the wind was cold and I disliked the thought of fighting it later when the river twisted back south. Canoeing, most of the time, you prefer no wind at all; it destroys quietness and whips your scent about and makes animals lie low and even squelches the birds. And if it turns against you, it makes a trip pure labor. But preference hasn't got much to do with it; days without wind in West Texas are few.

Goats, wild as deer . . . The herds of them in the Brazos country mushroomed with the grassless drouth and the Japanese market for mohair. Cattle went gaunt and were sold off, even cherished private herd-strains built up through forty years, but the Angoras stayed healthy on the tough bitter leaves of the oak brush. They are little trouble to own. If the screw worms eat one up, you are only out five dollars, and if he lives his hair pays that much every year. Some say they ruin land; some say not; I don't know. They have yellow, wise, evil eyes, but also a self-sufficiency that I like and that our present blocky kinds of beef cattle have lost. *Kowf!* one says, reading your presence on the wind, and the whole bright hair-haloed herd goes twinkling off into the brush on sure legs.

Whatever their effect, I tend to think they symbolize a further degeneration of the country; there is about them a smell of the burnt Near East where their breed began; they seem a portent. This region raised antelope and buffalo with rich fat on their ribs once, and later its longhorns were the sturdiest that went up the trails. Now the cedar has spread its sterile shade in the flats where grass no longer grows, and though some of the upland ranches with sentient owners still show thick carpets of curly mesquite and grama and buffalo and blue-stem grasses, and some even of the damaged parts can be brought back, most of the earth's surface there will never again be what it was. Goats and other such Mediterranean fauna—burros, and magpies, and tawny water-thrifty rodents that live among the rocks—somehow symbolize for me those lands that will never again be what they were.

One waxes pessimistic? Not so much . . . There is a pessimism about land which, after it has been with you a long time, becomes merely factual. Men increase; country suffers. Though I sign up with organizations that oppose the process, I sign without great hope. . . . Islands of wildlife and native flora may be saved, as they should be, but the big, sloppy, rich, teeming spraddle will go. It always has.

Nevertheless, the Brazos was there, and I was on it. Two tall sand-hill cranes, forerunners of the big flights, flapped up from a bar at the old Welty crossing as I bore down on it. I had business there, a minor expedition that, like many others, I'd never gotten around to making before.

Good hard-bottomed fords were prized in the days before bridges. With normal water, horses and cattle and high-wheeled wagons could traverse the river at them without fear of holes or quicksand. They were all known and were named, usually for the man who settled nearest them. Henry Welty settled there quite early, west of Big Keechi, and by 1863, when a good many of the country's males were away with the Confederacy and the Comanches were lashing the frontier like a whip, he and his wife had five children scrambling and yelling about their cabin, and a good herd of stock.

One evening Henry Welty saddled up and went to bring in his milk calves, to keep them off their mothers' teats. He gathered them up, and was driving them toward the corrals when, in the bend of a draw, about ten of The People fired at him from brush. Wounded, he loped away, but they followed, yelling, and when he fell from his horse they finished the job and scalped him and stripped him and took the horse. All that night, hour after dragging hour, they wailed and hooted about the house where Mrs. Welty and her children huddled fireless and lightless. . . .

It wasn't an unusual story, nor did I think to ferret out any new aspects of it. I just wanted to see if I could find the place. The gullied trough where the wagons had come down to the crossing since more than a century before was still sharp; I climbed up through it into a wide pasture dotted with mesquites and post oaks from which the wind was whipping yellow leaves, and followed the ruts of the old road to a second rise maybe a half-mile inland. There, where they should have been (the old ones seldom built next to the river), I found a roughly rectangular jumble of squared sandstone blocks, what was left of a foundation and chimney. Even a rotten log or two would have been too much to expect; most of the cabins went long ago for fence posts or cordwood, or burned down.

The real settlers, the old ones, were gone by the time I'd grown up enough to ask many questions. But some of their children were living, and those who remembered back into Indian times remembered, more often than not, nights like that one Mrs. Welty spent in the house that had rested on those sandstone blocks. No light, no fire, no sleep, no explanation, maybe, except a sweat-cold hand over your mouth if you started to whine from the discomfort and the felt fear; the woman herself wondering (yet not wondering either, because knowing) if the flesh that had cloven her flesh to produce these children lay now out there somewhere cold and hacked . . . And the feel of the murderous wild men in the moonlit dark all around the house, and not knowing if a screech owl's quaver was a screech owl or a wolf's yell was a wolf. Always moonlight, that was when they came. . . . It must have been hard to forget, the feel of those nights. Those were the years when some settlers moved together and forted up; more got back away from the frontier entirely.

I stared at the blocks for a time and kicked a couple of them and looked about a little for pieces of iron or china. Then, finding none and having proved nothing, I went back to the canoe well satisfied. Either you care or you don't. . . .

Big Keechi . . . I rounded down at its wide rock-strewn eddying mouth, and two army helicopters rounded down at me. Poised against the wind just over me, their pilots waved and shouted; they were young, and came probably from Camp Wolters twelve or fifteen miles to the south. I waved back. They gestured toward the creek, but I couldn't make out their meaning and shook my head. Together, as if maneuvered by one set of controls, they veered back over the land and flew down the creek and, from waters I couldn't see, flushed fifty or more bluebills toward me. Meat or no meat, beaters in helicopters weren't a part of my personal leisure-class ritual, and I had no notion of killing any ducks that way. But if you were once young and harebrained in a uniform yourself, you keep some tolerance for the breed. I picked up the shotgun to humor them. The bluebills flared away before they came in range, so that there was no need to play out the show. One of the pilots hovered over me again for a moment and held his nose between his thumb and forefinger; then, as I laughed, he flew off over the jumbled cliffs of the shore.

During a second I envied him, dominant as a hawk over the country and the river, minutes away from places it would take me a week to reach by water. But the envy was a spasm and without point; I was on the river in the way

I'd chosen to be there. And I'd had enough of the young, uniformed, harebrained business to last me three lifetimes.

Big Keechi (if you're of those who don't care, I guess you probably won't have come this far with me) is about as historic as places get in the upper-middle Brazos country. It is a biggish and dependable creek for that part of the world, and it runs far up into Jack County in a wide valley that caught the eye of cattle-minded men when the whole country was free for the choosing. Like the other north-south tributaries, it was a road in and out of the Brazos valley for The People, and consequently it heard the bowstrings' thrum and the rifles' pop, time and time and time again.

Old Man Charlie Goodnight lived up there when he was young, at Black Springs. It was where he settled when he first struck out on his own with a little herd and a big set of guts and considerably more direction and determination than most of his neighbors. Mr. Charlie's life spanned about three eras, and he was vigorously central in all three. Born in Illinois, he came to Milam County, Texas, as a child at just about the time when Texas entered the Union, and grew up in the hunting-farming-stock-raising aura of that time and place. Young, he earned cattle of his own by tending a herd on shares, set himself up on the Keechi range, and by the time the war and the bad years came along knew about as much as anyone in the region about Indians, Cross-Timbers cattle raising, and how to stay alive. He served out the war as a scout and ranger on the plains, fighting Comanches instead of Yankees (Texas had its asterisk on the Stars and Bars, but on these fringes there were many men who had no stake in slaveholding nor any particular excitement about the whole fracas), and he could, they say, practically tell you how many miles you were from usable water by fingering the foliage on a chittamwood tree. . . . Indians and neighbors stole him blind while he was away, but he built up another herd and joined with another Keechi cattleman, Oliver Loving, to open the harsh trail to New Mexico and Colorado. Old, he had the JA in the Paloduro Canyon where the Cap Rock breaks away to rolling prairies, and was, more than any other man on the South Plains, a symbol of the cattle baron. He was a tough and bright and honorable man in tough not usually honorable times, and had respect and a kind of love for the Indians even when he fought them. They called him Buenas Noches.

Old people around that country will tell you also, with some bitterness, that Buenas Noches had a big mouth and took credit for much that Loving did. It is so. But the Comanches got Oliver Loving on the Pecos (there's a hair prickler, but it's a long way from the Brazos), and Mr. Charlie lived to tell both their stories. He lived a long long time, and when he was ninety-one and a widower he took a second wife, twenty-odd years old.

A tale exists. I heard it once about Goodnight and once about another of the old ones who stayed alive long enough to get rich, and it may not be true about either of them. But it could be true—ought to be. . . . When Goodnight was old, he lived on what was called the Quitaque ranch, having been eased out of the JA operation by the New York socialite widow of his Irish milord partner. Once a scraggly band of reservation Comanches, long since whipped and contained, rode gaunt ponies all the way out there from Oklahoma to see him.

No buffalo had run the plains for decades; it was their disappearance, as much as smallpox and syphilis and Mac-

kenzie's apocalyptic soldiers, that had finally chopped apart
The People's way of life. Jealously, Mr. Charlie had built up
and kept a little herd of them.

He knew one or two of the older Indians; he had fought
them, and later had gone to see them and reminisce with
them in Oklahoma. They asked him for a buffalo bull.

He said: "Hell, no."

They said: "They used to be ours."

"They used to be anybody's that could kill one," the old
man said. "These are mine. They wouldn't even be alive if
it wasn't for me. You go to hell."

"Please, Buenas Noches," maybe one of them said. Maybe
not—The People seldom begged.

He said no again and stomped in the house and stayed
there for a couple of days while they camped patiently in his
yard and on his porch, the curious cowhands gathering to
watch them. In the end he made a great deal of angry noise
and gave them the bull they wanted, maybe deriving a sour
satisfaction from thinking about the trouble they'd have
getting it back to Oklahoma.

They didn't want to take it back to Oklahoma. They ran it
before them and killed it with arrows and lances in the old
way, the way of the arrogant centuries. They sat on their
horses and looked down at it for a while, sadly and in silence,
and then left it there dead and rode away, and Old Man
Goodnight watched them go, sadly too.

I parked the canoe in eddying water between big rocks,
thankful for the casualness that fiberglass permitted, and
climbed up to a nose above Keechi mouth, a picnic spot. A
good place, with the hills rolling up behind and the green
stream junction swirling below among its boulders . . . In
an overhanging tangle of roots a mass of daddy longlegs

clung each to all the others and vibrated with the rhythmic ecstasy that seizes them in the fall; the pup charged into them and they scattered. Under a cedar stood a table made from an old barbed-wire reel set on its side. Strewn thick about it were layers of that heterogeneous litter whose concoction is one of our glittering talents as a people: paper napkins and brown sacks rain-molded to grass and shrubbery; bullet-pierced beer cans brightly plated and painted against the rust that alone might have made them bearable; bottle caps and bottle shards; a yellowed latex memento of love's futility; tarnished twenty-two shell cases by the hundreds.

Yes, ma'am, I've drunk beer and with others like me have hurled hillbilly songs against the woods' stillness, and have made country afternoons hideous with the pointless explosion of cartridges. Having done it doesn't make it look any better to me, though.

Above there the old Painted Campground lies, twenty or so acres of worked-flint chips, potsherds, burn-marked hearthstones. . . . There are dozens of places like that along the Brazos, traditional stopping places that, judging from the thickness of the midden in some of them, must have been in use for unknowable centuries before white men came, by tribes in migration or seasonally encamped. If you poke around any of them long enough, you can usually pick up a couple of arrowheads to rattle against each other in your pocket until a nephew or a friend's son begs them away from you—though, by the very principle of middens, most of what you find is fragmentary or faulty.

The main part of that one is now a pleasant pasture dotted with mesquites and turfed with side-oats grama. Like most of the other sites, it lies high above the Brazos; Indian and white alike gave the river respect. You don't have to be an old-timer in that country to remember when it was common, there being no dams above to take the shock, for a three- or four-foot curl of angry red water to roar around a bend upon a party swimming in quiet pools under a blue sky. A cloudburst far out on the plains could cause that.

I've never heard why they called it the Painted Campground. In '72, settlers trailed a raiding band to it, waited till dawn, and were easing in on their bellies when one of them lost the steel control that tactics require and let out a berserker yell. Fast wakers, the Indians hit the brush, leaving behind them a few artefacts, some stolen horses, and the distinctively long-haired scalp of Chesley Dobbs from down the river, whom no one till then had known to be dead.

No end, no end to the stories . . .

The river angles back south there, and the wind turned ferociously against me. For a time I fought it, the high old-fashioned bow of the canoe slewing back whenever I stopped paddling hard, and then camped early on the shallow-shelving west bank at about the place where they're going to put one of the dams, a couple of miles above Turkey Creek. The river was rising again, and the spate silt was still slimy from rain for six vertical feet or more above water level, so that I had to carry my gear a long way up into a little elm motte. As he was wont to do at stops, the pup ran about barking proprietarily; across the river there the land rises to a steep escarpment, which gave him a clear echo, and he had a fine time with his own reflected voice until I made him stop. Then he went in the tent and with industrious molars gnawed our covering, despite punishment, steadily till bedtime.

The night was black but starry. The wind kept on in the darkness, unnaturally; I woke once or twice as it popped the tent flaps. Big wind depresses when it continues without the normal wanings of evening and night and dawn, whether it's called sirocco or khamsin or whatever. I lay feeling soft muscles ache and wondered if they would tauten to the work or whether I'd finally arrived at that point where the body won't snap back into tone with a few days' misuse, and wondered too what weather the wind might portend, and what idiocy had brought me out there to lie on the graveled ground, in November. . . .

~~~~~~~~~~~~~~~~~~~~~~~

CHAPTER SEVEN

In solitude one finds only what he carries there with him.

Juan Ramón Jiménez, Maxims

~~~~~~~~~~~~~~~~~~~~~~~

A DOE . . . Deer go with mornings. Sleepy and unfocused, I went into the woods for breakfast fuel and stood out of the still big wind in a sheltered place by a heap of fallen post oak, unwilling to rive the silence with my ax. She came picking her way along a fence line at right angles to me. Half catching my scent, she flicked up her tail and went away soundlessly and without desperate speed; then another came the same route, snuffed the whirlpooling scent full, coughed, and tore off across a field with a big fawn behind her.

A shave and clean khakis, since I'd get to the One Eighty bridge that day and would have to locate a telephone to reassure relatives of my continued, undrowned, unfrozen, unstarved existence . . .

A disgust . . . Skating fifty yards down and back in greasy mud, and down and back, and down and back again, following my own slithering spoor as I bore boxes and sacks to the canoe, I wondered what Thoreau would have thought. Or, for that matter, Mr. Charlie Goodnight . . . They were both ascetics, the one in order to think and feel, the other in order to act. A kind of asceticism, undefined, was root and sap of the idea of my being there, on the river. Therefore I'd come out with 200 pounds or more of assorted unnecessaries. A blanket and a bag of meal were all you should need. Even making the blanket a sleeping bag, maybe, with a tarp to throw over it . . .

But then what of an ax and a knife and a gun and a rod and a lantern and a change of clothes and a cunning Teutonic burner for when the wood was wet? Not to mention compasses, maps, sides of bacon, apples, field glasses, books, pots, ditty bags . . . Goods swamp the shallow ship of yoga, Saint Henry; your spare cry of "Simplify, simplify!" rings more alien generation by generation.

A relief . . . Loading done, the feel of a well-trimmed boat on live water between yellow-and-russet autumn shores, the waxen slim strength of a paddle's shaft. The sky was milky and the big wind still blew, but neither mattered much with movement and the fresh beginning of a day.

A frame house, at another high Indian ground . . . Since I'd climbed far out of public domain there and was carrying a gun, I came at it from brush, uncertain until I could see whether it was in use. Besides the poacher's unpainful sense of guilt, there is a shyness that gets into one after a few days, out alone. But nobody was there—nor, I could tell as I came closer, was anybody going to be. Ailanthus and chinaberry and a crumpled stone fence framed a bare yard space. The windows held only inpointed fragments of their lights, and the gray upright planks of the siding had never felt a paintbrush's wet kiss. In back stood a cedar-log corral and a crib and a shed, repaired with baling wire and littered with rusty junk, and on the front porch lay three beer bottles, an old white icebox on its side, a set of bedsprings, and a swollen, still aromatic dead goat. Under an eave a canyon wren sang, then flicked away.

It was of that ungothic shape—roof peaked high along a ridge pole in the middle over three rooms in a row, and flattening fore and aft over the gallery and a rank of lean-to rooms—which the double log cabin's form had suggested to a log-cabin people abruptly presented with lumber. The East Texas mills began shipping boards into that country on the new railroads in the seventies, and after that few log houses were built; the old arts of the froe and the maul and the adze and the broadax died. By then the good post oaks had just about been cut down, anyhow. Existing cabins were often planked over and their dog runs enclosed, but this wasn't one of them; its windows were not deep-set enough.

A low windmill, tailless and bullet-holed, groaned futilely without revolving above the well in the rear. A diseased pear tree stood by it, drooping with fruit. I went into the house. Whoever had last lived there had taken away little gear with him when he left; worthless chattels lay everywhere, upended and thrown about by other woods-runners who'd rooted among them before me. In the room I first entered, the floor was of dirty four-inch pine planks held down but loosely by nails whose flat heads were still shiny from the polishings of boot soles. A square of flower-patterned, worn linoleum lay beneath a fat wood stove marked in cast letters:

RIDGEWOOD
SEARS, ROEBUCK AND CO.
WORLD'S LARGEST STORE.

Browned wallpaper printed with rose leaves peeled away from browned wallpaper printed with Greek temples, which in turn peeled away from browned wallpaper printed with philosophical Chinese under weeping willows, and the damp-rotting smell of all three layers tinged the air. The cheese-cloth ceiling sagged down between its rusty tacks as if inflated from above, only scraps of paper still hanging to it; in its center, strangely, was tacked a panel from a corrugated sanitary-napkin box. Four calendars, one for 1947, two for 1950, and one for 1951, all by courtesy of John Haley's Gro. and Ser. Sta., had glazed, bright pictures bas-reliefed by some stamping process and showing happy matters: an un-tracked, snow-covered road beneath pines; a fat small boy fishing in very blue water while a brown-and-white mongrel watched; a smaller, fatter boy about to arrow an apple off his apprehensive browner-and-whiter pup's head; Jesus Christ with a gold halo blessing a crowd of children under their elders' grateful gaze. . . .

Two wire coat hangers on a nail, a straight-backed wooden chair with a woven-rawhide bottom totally sat through, an apple crate, half of a quirt, a paint can, feed sacks, a rocker with a bald, torn, plush seat and back piece and visible lumpy springs, a lone brown-and-blue-striped sock against a baseboard, crayoned fat geese and hoglike cows and cowlike hogs friezed in parade about the wall at the height a four-year-old might reach. . . . Besides the wallpaper's smell, there was an odor of the kind that individual houses get from their families, not unpleasant. When I was little, I used to think you could characterize families from the smells of their houses, but an early addiction to tobacco kept me from developing the theory.

The other rooms, accessible through doors that opened to latchstrings, were much like that one. In the lean-to kitchen, where mouse-gnawed stains of grease outlined the stove's square absence, a dome-topped rotten trunk had been dumped on its side, and letters flowed from it onto the floor. I looked at one. It was dated April 17, 1899, and was from someone named Elnora in Hood's Cove, Kentucky, to someone named Addie. It said that crops were what you might expect, but that Alfred had never given up his hanker to move southwest, what did Addie think? It said that Bella's baby had died of colic at six months of age, which only left her two, and that the new preacher had "gotten Alfred's *Irish* up" with what he said about Negroes, and it ended:

. . . I do not know where Time *goes* and when he said the other Day that it was *Twenny Five Years* since You All went out to Texas and I begann to cry, Dear Sister, because I do not *beleive* that we are Like to see Each Other any more. . . .

I knew that if I read any of the others I'd probably stay there all day, so I dropped it into the pile and went out back to prop a rusted Model-T fender against the pear tree's trunk and pick some fruit. The pears were good, bird-pecked and with maybe a worm or so in their cores, but sweet and not grainy like most Texas pears, which are fit only for preserving. Standing there, I ate three while a hungry mocker rasped at me from the shed's roof.

Axles and planter wheels and the old iron-bound oak hubs of wagons and a hundred unidentifiable rusty rods and bolts and straps of steel . . . Pieces of the same kind of junk were woven and wired into the logs of the corral in such quantity that you had to believe the intent had been partly ornamental. A Prince Albert can, its red gone yellow, letters scratched from the legend on its back (I wonder if any Texas boy ever failed to learn that dirtiness) to leave a mild obscenity . . . A huge old sandstone grinding wheel, without its frame . . . An automobile tire still showing patches of red, white, and blue paint, flush-filled inside with dirt for flowers. A rosebush against the house with one frost-speckled bloom . . .

On a mountain not far behind that place, there was a fight where the Comanches each wore one long white-lace lady's stocking, loot of a raid. It was said they made fine targets against the dark cedars. . . . That would have been only a couple of years before Addie came there, if the Brazos was where she and her man first came when they reached Texas.

Had it been their children who stayed on? If so, what had they been like? What music had they made in that stark shelter? What salt-rimed spot had there been in that bare yard where a man, heavy-eyed in the clean predawn, had emptied his bladder morning after morning, year after year, yawning gratefully at the goodness of Creation and the certainty of coffee, biscuits, and bacon? What daytime worries had wakened burr-prickling in his mind as he stood there? Where had he and his gone—to aircraft factories? to farms less tired? or, more probably, considering their leavings, each to take his thanatoptic chamber in the graveyard? Anyhow, they were gone, and neither they nor their kind would come back. We were not Like to see Each Other any more. . . .

Below the house, the field where the Indian midden lay was fuzzed silkily with needle grass, symbol of exhaustion. Figure-eighting about it, I kicked up a round mano and the forepart of a spearhead among charred hearthstones, and started back toward the river through descending brush. On the second narrow flat above the Brazos was a fine grove of big elms and pecans; squirrels there charked at me, and when

I stopped and let the pup run ahead, ignorant of his function, one came edging flattened around a tree trunk onto my side, watching the dog. I raised the gun, but then considered that there would be beef for sale somewhere near the bridge, and did not shoot, picking up a stick instead and throwing it against the tree. The squirrel arch-leaped to earth and ran to another pecan, and the pup, startled, danced after him screaming with tentative bravery. Nuts crackled underfoot; I gathered some and ate them as I walked—small, hard-shelled natives, but richer than the grafted commercial species. The wind soughed in the treetops, shut out of the woods' layered silence.

A rusted trap in a patch of shinnery oak, twisted baling wire attached to the end of its chain . . . Dragged there by what unknown brute in what unknown pain, when? . . .

Some days load themselves with questions whose answers have died, and maybe never mattered hugely.

BELOW TURKEY CREEK, I thought to put in and reconnoiter the area where George Eubanks played jumping jack with the Indians from behind an oak tree. But that stretch was a rapids, and trying to turn inshore I let the canoe sweep side-wise against a rock; when it tilted, I leaned compensatorily upstream and managed to ship half a boatload of ice water. . . . I jumped out into a current above my knees and led it ashore. Luckily there was sun, and neither the food nor my bed had gotten wet. I changed the morning's clean trousers, soaked and mud-marked now, for my old filthy but dry ones, put on moccasins in place of the squishy boots, and laid everything out to dry. It would put me at the bridge late. I dislike schedules, and on the river the idea that I'd let myself come to count on getting to any one spot at any particular time enraged me more than the accident my ineptitude had caused.

Not far above the bridge a dude ranch stood, tile-roofed and Spanish-stuccoed with dark oak trim, near where the Newberrys and some others fought half-white Quanah Parker's raiders, a long running horseback fight. The Comanches got Elbert Doss, characterized in the chronicles as a "promising young man," but Quanah, who wore a blue Yankee soldier's coat on that foray, told someone in the later peaceful time that he'd lost nine out of sixteen warriors before he made it back to Oklahoma.

Among the pursuers was a type usually described as "Bose Ikard (colored)." He would be a story, a long one. Most of the not numerous Negroes along this frontier—"buffalo soldiers," the Comanches called them—were pretty much background characters, leaving uproar to the whites whose supremacy forced heroics upon them. But a few like Bose Ikard and another one named Britt seem to have felt differently. In Weatherford cemetery Bose's stone says:

"Served with me four years on Goodnight-Loving Trail, never shirked a duty or disobeyed an order, rode with me in many stampedes, participated in three engagements with Comanches. Splendid behavior"—C. Goodnight

It was an Old Testamental God for whose perusal that commendation was issued, the stern Monarch in whose campaigns the stern generals like Mr. Charlie galloped. It seems clear, too, that Mr. Charlie considered that his opinion of Bose Ikard (colored) would carry weight with that Monarch.

Why shouldn't he so have considered? Nowadays the jostling millions around us, and an economy in which the "planned obsolescence" of both man and machine is basic, and such weighty concerns as whether or not Oscar will rise to vice-presidential rank and be able to live in Westport, Connecticut, convince us that Fate does things to us and that for sanity we'd better laugh about the things it does. People like Mr. Charlie had what was maybe an illusion, but a solid one; they believed they did things to Fate. They were engaged in the foreordained rape of a virgin land and they considered their task meaningful. It was. Most of them had pretty fair senses of humor, but they didn't feel obliged to laugh at themselves.

Once I'd gone to that stuccoed dude ranch as a respectable Sunday visitor in company with well-dressed friends who knew the owners. Now, it was a logical place from which to telephone. But I was feeling raunchy in aspect and shy in soul, and drifted by it uncertainly on swirling waters, and picking up my paddle flushed a great horned owl from a cottonwood tree.

The sound of gravel machinery announced the bridge below. The pit operation itself, northwest of the bridge, seemed at the moment too raucous a reintroduction to the world of men; I parked the canoe on the other side of the river and clambered, carrying the pup, through stickerburs to a house there. A pregnant, sallow woman in gingham, whose cheeks sagged where fat had used away from beneath them, checked her screen door's latch to make sure I couldn't get in by force, and said she had no telephone.

"Has the pit over there got one?"

"Naw," she said without embellishment, studying my stained pants and old wool shirt. I didn't blame her.

Less confident even than before, I tried hitching, holding the passenger under my arm and pointing a thumb in the direction of Mineral Wells as the pickup trucks and station-wagons and shiny sedans sh-h-h-OFFed by. It is one of the main east-west roads, and there were a good many of them, and the big transcontinental trucks that shake you as they pass. Some drivers looked at me with interest, or at the pup, but none slowed. Our world periodically respects Bold Looks and Successful Looks and Manly Looks and Ivy Looks and various other kinds of looks that advertisements tell it to respect, but since the proletarian thirties, the Unwashed Look has lacked admirers. . . . Rejected, I walked on across the bridge toward the clanking, squealing gravel pit. Inside its gate I set the pup down; he ran over and wet himself to the shoulders in the liquid red mud dripping from some sort of tall gravel-washing machine. In the little office shack an old man with a seamed scarlet face said no, they had no telephone.

I told him what I was up to.

"Hell," he said. "We close down here in five minutes. I'll run you somewheres, my way home."

I thanked him. . . . In the car, a well-tended and fairly new coupé, I put the pup on the floor between my legs, but after we'd started I forgot him, and he surged up and printed red mud over the seat covers and my benefactor's breeches and mine. I slammed him down and apologized.

The old man grunted. "Some dog," he said. "Where the hell you goin' to, down the river?"

"Around Glen Rose."

"Purtier up here," he said. "You know they was exactly three hunderd and sixty-five miles of the Brazos in Palo Pinto County? One for ever' day in a year."

He said it "Payla Pinta," as a lot of the old-timers do. "Colorayda," they say, too, and "Alabammy" and "Virginny." What he said wasn't true, though it was familiar. At Cholula southeast of Mexico City, where the Spanish built all those sterile little chapels on top of Aztec altar mounds to milk away their evil, people will tell you that the chapels tally *exactamente trescientas sesenta y cinco*, but they don't. I've heard the same thing about the depth in feet of some pot-hole lakes outside Roswell, and the number of steps in a tower stairway somewhere in Europe. . . . A slovenly roller-measure check of the Brazos map on my wall, just now, registers a little over a hundred river miles within that county. But people find a pleasure in such fabled correspondences; none of us is immune.

And the claim did have a little poetic verity—the river winds hugely. They used to tell about a fisherman who yanked out a catfish over his shoulder, and when he looked around he'd thrown it back into the Brazos ten miles upstream. And I wonder how many rivers *that* chestnut's been told about. . . .

Therefore, and because he was giving me a ride, I said appreciatively: "Is that right?"

He said it was, and let me out at a brightly lighted ser sta gro. It was getting dark. I hiked the filthy pup under my arm and again thanked the old man, who laughed and said: "Hell!" and drove on home.

I went into the ser sta gro. They're institutional in that part of the world; some for variation label themselves "gro mkt sta," or "gro sta," or whatnot. Practically every countryman below a certain level of prosperity seems to yearn bitterly to own and run one, maybe because from the times of drouth and depression and crop failure he remembers that storekeepers had canned goods on the shelves to eat and that everybody else in the county owed them money. Appearing and disappearing like May flies, enduring in proportion to their individual owners' popularity and skill at whipping off the wolves of bankruptcy, they vary in size from the one-pump station with a shelf or so of Days O' Work chewing tobacco and Van Camp's beans to a fairly elaborate approximation of a town grocery store, and serve as gathering places for the philosophical symposia of their neighborhoods.

Three or four philosophers in bib overalls with brown juice in the corners of their mouths regarded me as I dumped the pup on the floor. Countrymen are usually unfond of dogs indoors, but I was tired of carrying him and didn't trust him alone outside by the highway. Their gaze told me that I was dirty even by their standards, which by open evidence were not effete. A radio was shrieking out that synthesis of the old simple Anglo-Saxon music with Tin Pan Alley and electric amplification that is usually called hillbilly, but not around there. There it's just "music," and the neon-glaring tonks near the cities seem its most appropriate setting. If you're from that country, you usually have an unwilling affection for it, having listened to its evolution. Even twenty years ago it still retained a little of the old directness and innocence, but now the directness and the innocence have passed to not very direct and not very innocent people with guitars around places like Greenwich Village, and the country people take their music with heavier seasoning.

The proprietor was scratching beneath his belt and selling a lady green tomatoes. "Where to you want to call?" he said, not in direct answer to my question.

I told him and against the coolness in his pouched eyes added: "Collect."

"There," he said, pointing with the right rear surface of

his skull, still scratching. . . . Telephoning, I watched his ear monitoring me till it heard me repeat the magic word to the operator; then he sacked up the tomatoes and gave them to the lady and went to join the philosophers. One does not for long remain in command of a three-pump ser sta gro if he places confidence in grimy strangers; one is beset hard enough already by grimy acquaintances. When I'd finished a call to my people and was waiting for the operator to put one through to Hale, I saw the pup disappear behind the meat counter. I snapped my fingers. He ignored me. A dark young man behind the counter glanced toward the owner, and I snapped my fingers again.

"Don't matter none," the owner said, maybe because I had friends who would accept collect calls.

Hale said in a business voice, intimating weightiness, that he had to fly down to Houston the following day. I told him he'd be sorry, twenty years thence.

He said he already was.

I told him a yellow catfish that had looked to weigh forty pounds had nearly torn the paddle out of my hands that morning. It was true; I'd been shooting a clear heavy run with yellow leaves dancing down the water all around me in the sunlight, steering with just the edge of the blade, when suddenly something grabbed it with a bump and a twist, and as suddenly let go. Then he rolled in the current ahead of me, golden, sight-feeding as they sometimes do. . . . They run twice that big in the Brazos, some of them, though only a few are ever caught on hooks, and those by the patient catfish specialists. Some are wrestled ashore by the "grabblers," sturdy rural sportsmen who wade and tread water while they probe the recesses of the undercut banks with

· 79 ·

their hands, disregarding moccasins and game wardens and other dangers. Others are taken, just as illegally and less sportingly, by cynics with cranked magnetos, the so-called "telephoners."

Hale said: "Forty pounds is easy to say. I bet he wouldn't weigh what the one did that we sold that café that time."

"You go on to Houston and make some money," I said.

"No ducks?"

"High fliers. There'll be some, below Rock Creek."

"Not unless the water goes down," he said. "You ought to see geese before long, whenever there's another norther."

I said I guessed I would.

"Damn you," he said. . . . He wanted me to call him again, from farther down. I said I might, and hung up. He had always been a strong hunter and fisherman, and though he was a good friend I found that I'd fallen so much into the pattern of quietness and aloneness that it didn't bother me much that he couldn't come out. . . .

"Kind of motor you usin'?" the owner said, having listened. Four sets of hairy philosophical ears radared toward me.

"Canoe," I said.

And saw a quintuplicate reproduction of the expression on the face of the little man at Possum Kingdom dam.

"Tippy damn things," the owner said, and walking to the meat counter took out a little piece of liver and gave it to the pup, who gobbled it. The owner said: "Cute little sommidge. One of them dash hounds, ain't he?"

But the dark young man was sympathetic. He said he'd been fishing once on the river and a fellow had passed in a canoe and had talked to him.

"On his way to the Guff," he said. "Man, he was havin'

hisself a time. Didn't have no clothes on, nothin' but a pair of sharts. Brown as ara nigger. Talked Yankee."

One of the philosophers snorted the kind of snort that poets get in taciturn lands, defining for me the young man's rank among them, and obliquely my own. He waited on me while I picked out fruit and potatoes and biscuit mix and a little range-beef T bone, ruby red without marbling and by nature tough. Since they had no hamburger, he recommended neckbones for the pup, and I bought some. An outdoor-magazine reader, he said he'd saved up and bought a new .270 for the deer season that opened the next day, and asked me as a sylvan oracle what I thought about that caliber. Accepting the role, I said it was a sweet rifle, without adding that I had only three or four times in my life sought to kill any large mammals besides man, and then unwillingly and with a borrowed gun. . . .

The owner, partly because he liked the passenger and partly, Swissly, because I'd become a customer, had decided I was all right. He said so, which puzzled me till I saw that he and the philosophers had cans of beer sitting on a counter behind them; because of an army camp, a stretch around Mineral Wells is wet territory in that generally, justifiably prohibitionist land. He offered me fifteen dollars for the pup, and when I turned it down, he said he didn't blame me, and went out to commandeer a seat for me, regally, in a blue pickup truck that stopped to buy gas. The two men in it were brown lean small-townsmen headed out to a deer lease, and made room cheerfully for me and the pup. They were talking about how they'd packed the eggs and whether the milk would keep without ice and such matters, the talk of women-tended men magnifying the maleness of a three or four-day expedition away from their women. I'd talked that way myself, often, but listened now feeling different from them. They let me out at the bridge, and good wishes flew both ways through the air.

Thrashing . . . The armed night watchman at the pit, where the only level ground near the bridge lay, said it was all right if I camped there, but that I'd better make a noise if I came up around the machinery. The canoe, though, was on the other side of the river. Somehow I bulled it across in the dark, sloshed about in water and mud extracting an austere minimum of gear, and made camp by the light of the gasoline lantern tied to a willow branch. I was glad to be by myself again. There was no driftwood but only dry willow sticks, which make no coals; I scorched the little T bone a bit and ate it with store bread and tomatoes. The passenger found his neckbones too fresh and carried them off one by one, as I gave them to him, to bury each in a different spot for ripening; nor could I tell him that he was unlikely to be around at the time of their perfection to profit from his toil. . . .

He was an affable little brute, impractical but comic and good to have with me, philosophical under scolding and the occasional sleepy kicks he got when he wriggled too much in the bottom of the sleeping bag at night. In a few days he had developed more than in weeks in town, giving up his abject station at my heels to run about the woods on our shore excursions, learning to evade the cold by staying in the tent or by hugging the fire, sitting like a figurehead on the food box in the bow as we slid down the river in the long bright afternoons. At the ser sta gro he had been a help; elsewhere among countrymen he was as likely to be a drag, but I was glad I'd brought him.

Nekkebone, nekkebone, kept running obsessively through my head as I watched him dig. It was from Chaucer or somewhere; someone had smitten someone else and cleaved his head all the way vnto the nekkebone. . . .

Traffic roared with irregular steadiness across the bridge. Each car or truck that crossed rattled a loose bolt somewhere toward its center.

Near that bridge an old fellow used to live who was known generally, probably because somebody had read Mark Twain, as Indian Joe. He spent the latter end of his life scrambling up and down hills all through that country with a witching rod in his hands; he believed in buried Spanish gold. Unfortunately for Joe, the gold didn't believe in him; he died there as poor as ever, though I imagine he'd had a better time than many a more practical seeker has in country clubs.

The Brazos nurtures a few lonely ones like that, some of them pretty wild-eyed. They live on willow islands in driftwood shacks, and in holes among the high rocks, neighbors to the rattler. One of them near Palo Pinto used to sell reptiles to schools and laboratories. You hear about them more than you see them, though they probably see you as you pass. When landowners know they're there, they seem usually to tolerate them; some widowed or bachelor landowners get a bit that way themselves. In hard times there were more; now, with jobs easy to come by, the hermits who remain are the real ones.

We don't know much about solitude these days, nor do we want to. A crowded world thinks that aloneness is always loneliness, and that to seek it is perversion. Maybe so. Man is a colonial creature and owes most of his good fortune to his ability to stand his fellows' feet on his corns and the musk of their armpits in his nostrils. Company comforts him; those around him share his dreams and bear the slings and arrows with him. . . .

But there have always been some of the others, the willful loners. And out alone for a time yourself, you have some illusion of knowing why they are as they are. You hear the big inhuman pulse they listen for, by themselves, and you know their shy nausea around men and the relief of escape. Or you think you do. . . .

There was old Sam Sowell. He didn't live on the river, but not far from it either, in the limestone and cedar country near Glen Rose. His home was a dugout on a hill with a grove of live oaks, on the backest back end of 180 acres that belonged to him. In those depression days the land would have been expensive at seven dollars an acre, but it was his bank. He subsisted on flour and beans and fatback and squirrel and mustard greens and such luxuries, and he dipped snuff. When he needed to buy anything, he would chop two cedar posts out of the matted brake that covered most of his estate, and would shoulder them and walk straight across country the three and a half miles to a store on the Stephenville road. There he would trade the posts for two bits' worth of whatever merchandise it was that he wanted, and would walk back home.

The dugout held an iron cook stove and a bunk, and on sunny winter days Sam would come up through the slanting trap door and sit like a gopher on the forward slope of the turfed mound that covered his home, blinking out over the dark hills, skeeting amber snuff juice onto the limestone rubble. I've studied him like that from a half-mile off, through a field glass. He had no woman nor wanted any, could not read or write, kept no dog, and had reduced friend-

ship to a three-inch wave of his hand and a waggle of his
gray narrow head to briefly encountered persons who had
known him all his life. Anyone who hadn't known him all
his life got neither waggle nor wave. He bothered no one and,
it seemed to me, wanted more than anything on earth not to
be bothered.

One winter night with a raw spit out of the north, four
young men were drinking white whisky in a shack not far
from Sam Sowell's place. One of them was named Davis
Birdsong; he runs a kind of ranch for a friend of mine now,
but I didn't know him then. They had put out dogs after
bobcat, but the cats knew better than to run abroad on a
night like that, and after a while so did the hounds, who
were huddled now on the shack's little porch, having been
cursed and tethered. The young men were keeping warm
both by drinking white whisky and by burning what was
left of the shack's teetering furniture in a potbellied stove
with a big crack down one side, through which from time to
time live embers spilled out onto the wooden floor. This
disturbed none of them, since the shack wasn't theirs.

(It still stands, disastrous, with inch-wide gaps between
the grayed boards of its sides; I have slept there with the
cotton rats and the skunks, and at noon in summer sometimes the rattlesnakes' dry buzz sounds from beneath the
floor, where they lie impatient for cool night.)

Jim Lemmon said: "Listen at her whustle."

Davis Birdsong finished kicking a bureau drawer to pieces,
shoved them into the stove, and said: "Give me that jar."

Someone passed it and he drank. They hunched about the
stove, more conscious of their comfort than they would have
been with ducted heat and deep carpets, though none of
them, probably, had ever experienced either of those things.

They were of that place; a wet norther and a shack and a stove went together, and they had grown up in houses a little tighter and more rectangular than that one, but not much. The hills are not rich country, not since the old ones cottoned out the flat places and grazed out the slopes, and the topsoil went on down the Brazos, and the cedar moved in thick and sullen, letting nothing grow beneath it. That happened so long ago that a whole, spare, organic way of life has had time to grow up around the cedar itself, and even in the thirties only a few ancients recollected scraps of the brief richer time.

So that the shack represented more or less standard shelter, though outside the small circle of the stove's radiation its temperature was in the thirties and all of them were dressed in denim. They were cozy.

But coziness is not a lasting satisfaction to persons of that age and breed. . . .

"I wisht they was somethin' to God damn do," Jim Lemmon said.

"Could go maybe see old Rosie," said a third one hopefully, a thin sort named Ike Atterbury.

"*He*'s home."

"Oh."

"Could gang up and stomp old Bert," Dave Birdsong said.

Bert grinned broad-faced into the stove's glow, bull-necked, stump-bodied. "Could," he said.

"I reckon not," Dave said. They had recently tried it. . . .

They had a coal-oil lantern. He took it and rolled up its wick a little and went roaming with it through the corners of the shack. It had stood empty for three years now; the last family who had lived there, not owning it or paying rent, had taken off in a Chalmers touring car for California to go orange-picking and had not been heard of since. Their calendars moralized on the walls; their detritus cluttered the floor. Dave's foot rolled on a mustard jar; he slapped the wall to keep from falling, and cut his palm on a nail. . . .

"You come acrost any sixty-eight-carat gold thunder mug, you holler right loud," Jim Lemmon said.

Davis picked up a pair of overalls. Except for having no knees and only one strap, and having suffered the gnawings of mice, and being rotten, they were pretty good overalls.

He said: "Could make us a dummy."

Ike Atterbury said: "Tootie Anson got hisself shot, a-foolin' with dummies."

"Stood too closet," Davis said. "Looky here, they's a flarr sack."

"Nothin' to stuff the sommidge with," Jim Lemmon said.

"Straw," Dave told him, jerking his head toward a rear door. "Lean room's full of it. Seen it."

"Who you gonna dummy?" Ike Atterbury said, doubtful.

"We," Bert said. "Who *we* gonna dummy, you mean."

"What I said."

"Sam Sowell," Davis said. "Ain't walkin' no futher'n that, no night like this."

"That gold he's got hid," Jim Lemmon said, musing. "Five thousand dollars, somebody said."

" 'Pression's done growed it," Dave said. "Thousand, used to be."

It was a whingding dummy, he told me long years later. They finished the first Mason jar of whisky while they were making it, and started on another, and in the end they took Ike Atterbury's hat, knocking him down when he objected, and pinned it with baling wire to the dummy's head. Its flour-sack face glared white; they tied a dog rope to the overalls' one shoulder strap and jiggled it from a rafter. It looked fine. Single file then, sodden under the thin horizontal rain that should by rights, Dave said, have been sleet, cold as the air was, they threaded through the thick shinnery brush of the shack's valley and up a nose into the cedar. For secrecy they had left the lantern at the shack with the dogs, but none of them missed it. (You go hound-hunting with those people on a dark night and you're lucky to get home with two eyes; they feel out the slapping, scratching branches with another sense, like bats, and lift casual forearms to shield their faces, but you don't.)

A quarter-hour later they were standing before Sam Sowell's storm-cellar house. Smoke from its stovepipe bit warm into their noses; a thin line of yellow light showed at the edge of the trap door.

"Hod damn, I'm cold," Ike Atterbury said. "Whine we just go in, say hi?"

"Shut up," Jim Lemmon told him. "Drank some whusky."

"Thang looks like Bert," said Davis, who had been stringing the dummy to a live-oak branch, its feet just touching the ground, twenty feet from Sam Sowell's door. Bert snorted, and followed Davis and Jim Lemmon a few yards down the hill and to one side. Ike Atterbury remained standing by the live oak, thoughtful.

"Hello!" Davis yelled. "Hello, the house!"

"Naw!" said Ike Atterbury.

"You standin' about where he'd shoot," Davis said. "*Hello!*"

That was when Ike left them, at a run. They let him go, slapping one another's damp shoulders and doubling over with quiet, violent laughter as they heard him hit the heavy cedar below with crackles and swishes and a curse or two.

Then there was nothing more above the wind's big sighing.

"*Is* cold, a little," Davis said matter-of-factly.

"Sha," Jim Lemmon said. "Where's that old sommidge at? HELLO!"

The door's yellow line widened. Abruptly they all squatted beside a cedar, watching while it grew parallelogrammatically and old Sam Sowell's head projected dark from its center, swinging about, blinking against sudden blackness. In a minute, after his pupils had opened out and the night had erased lingering lamp light from his retinas, Sam's head stopped swinging and remained fixed toward the dummy a few feet before him.

"Who ooh?" he said.

("Didn't have no front teeth on top," Davis told me. "Worth your money, see him side-gnawin' a old tough piece of fried squirrel. Couldn't talk good.")

The dummy didn't answer.

Sam Sowell said: "Honnam ooh, who be ooh?"

Jim Lemmon had fallen over onto his side and was wheezing silently on the wet stones beneath the cedar. Bert was making a hl-hl sound around his gums which was as near as he ever came to laughter. . . . Davis watched: to this day he seldom even smiles, but only crinkles the corners of his eyes when great mirth seizes him.

Sam Sowell stared for a time at the dummy without speaking, then swiftly stuck out an old arm, picked up a rock, and hurled it. It missed; the dummy stirred a little under a gust of wind.

"Hunnamitch!" screamed Sam Sowell, and disappeared. Jim Lemmon whoo-whooed softly in the exhaustion of suppressed mirth, Davis watching still while the old head came out again behind a shotgun's barrel, laid itself down along the stock, and jerked as flame shot out in a loud five-foot-long streak at the dummy's midriff.

"Air, by Gog!" Sam Sowell cried, and came tearing up out of his hole like an infantryman riding the wake of a barrage. But the enemy no longer existed; he stopped where the upper half of the overalls still hung from the live-oak limb, and stared down at the blasted-away lower half on the ground. Bending over, he came up with a handful of straw, stood frozen for a second under the wind, and then began again to swing his old narrow head in search.

"Look out," Davis said, and laid a hand on Jim's shoulder.

But Jim had choked on a chuckle, and sputtered, and then the three of them were rolling, scrambling backward and downhill as the shotgun swiveled toward the sound. Davis said he started running while he was still on his knees and had just about worked himself erect, still moving fast, when he ran astraddle a small cedar. He clambered straight up and through it, treading branches, and had ridden it down on the other side when the second barrel of Sam Sowell's shotgun spoke. A pellet tugged at Davis's hat, and Jim Lemmon yelled. Then, like Ike Atterbury, they crashed into the heavy cedar of the lower hillside and tore on through it, their bat's radar awry. Davis lost his hat and could never afterward find it, to prove it had been hit. . . .

Finally they stopped, scratched and soaked and run out, in a little slit clearing near the bottom of the hill. ("Just spent a time a by God breathin'," Davis said to me. "Bein' a-scairt it uses up air. . . .") Sam Sowell, needing reloads, had not pursued. The wind blew. The rain spattered down.

"Three," Jim Lemmon said, having been groping at the calf of his left leg.

"Missed me," Bert said.

"Popped my hat," Davis said.

"Old bastard," Jim said.

"What we spected," Davis told him mildly. "What you'd do, too. Hit were a good dummyin'."

"Would of kilt us."

"Didn't."

"Could of," Jim Lemmon said. "Lost that whusky, too. I'll fix him."

"How?"

"Watch," Jim said, and headed back up the hill.

(" 'Bout half mean when he got mad," Davis said. "Worrit me.")

In the beginning Jim had Bert stand on the door, but then he brought some big flat rocks and laid them across it and Bert moved, so that by the time Sam Sowell got around to shooting up through it, he did no harm. . . . Jim got a leg from the dummy's overalls and wadded it into the top of the dugout's stovepipe. Dave stood discreetly aside and watched while the door's yellow crack and the hole that Sam had blown with his gun grew darker, smoke muffling the lamp light inside. Listened as the coughing began . . .

He said factually: "Gonna assaficate him."

"Sure," Jim Lemmon said, and did a jig step. "Hey!" he yelled at the dugout's door. "Hey, how's it smell, old ringtail?"

Sam Sowell coughed, and fired again. The shot lifted one of the boulders an inch or two, but it fell back into place. Jim Lemmon stepped back a yard.

"Thousand bucks, let you out!" he shouted. "By God, shoot old Jim, you'll see!"

"Tell him," Bert said with satisfaction.

("A-scairt of 'em," Davis told me without shame. "Old Bert he never said nothin' but he always run with Jim. Hopin' they'd quit by theyself, knowed it'd be a fight.")

It was. . . . He waited the four or five minutes that it took for the coughing to stop, then resignedly moved to the door and began to lift the big stones away from it. It was dark, and he had the last one off before Bert dived at him, the big belly hitting him in the shoulder, the oaken arms hugging. They rolled. . . . Davis got a rock in his hand and somehow found room under that hug to start pounding Bert on the back of the head with it. Bert abruptly relaxed. Davis came free, and scrambled back to open the door, and had a good grip on the armpits of unconscious Sam Sowell lying just below it when Jim jumped him, kicking and pulling.

"I helt on," he told me. "When Jim pult me away, old Sam he come out of there just like a rotten tooth out of your jaw."

"What happened then?"

"Old Jim he stomped me," Davis said. "Bert too when he waked up. Cracked me a rib. I had the old booger out, though, and they didn't stick him back in. Thought they might."

Sam Sowell caught pneumonia when he came to, and spent three weeks in bed at Davis's mother's house while she slept on a pallet on the floor. When he was well, he left one morning before anybody was up, without thanks or comment, and went back to his dugout. Not long after that, somebody took a shot at Jim Lemmon out of the cedar, and he quit hunting in that part of the county. He died later at Anzio; I never knew either him or Bert, who left for an automobile assembly plant or somewhere, the way people leave that country.

And didn't miss knowing them . . .

~~~~~~~~~

THERE WAS, too, a little fellow in the Northwestern cattle country whom a friend of mine told me about one time. The story could be researched, I guess, but I'll tell it the way I heard it. He was pathologically solitary like Sam Sowell and was considered to be a bit demented, though in the world of the Rocky Mountain slopes, where he lived in a one-room cabin, he could cope better than well. For cash sometimes he hired out to pack outfitters nursing dudes up into the game country he knew so well, a closed face with shifting eyes outside the circle of firelight where the big men from the cities joked and drank to build up in themselves an unconfident illusion that they were feeling that other pulse. . . . Probably he didn't even listen; most of their words would have been Urdu to him.

On his own, he hunted year in and out without regard for the game laws. Meat was wild meat; when you needed it you killed it and ate it, and, not needing it, you didn't kill it: that morality must have seemed higher to him than the one that applied to the licensed dudes. People knew about his hunting, but the West, maybe because for so long it was the big empty land where the loners went, has a tolerance most of the time for that kind of queerness, and he wasn't bothered.

Until one day the sheriff and the game warden of that county got to drinking together and decided it would be fun to go out and scare old John. It was not a very happy idea, any way you look at it. . . . They drove out over the rough trail, and went to his door, and when he opened it the sheriff said: "John, they tell me you got some elk meat up here."

Puzzled—they had joked at him from time to time in town, but he had never had trouble—John looked from one to the other of the plump, muscular townsmen, and finally said: "Why?"

"Why?" the sheriff mimicked, winking at his friend. "Why? We find any meat, you go to the jailhouse, John."

The countryman's eyes went back and forth faster, slitted down now, scared. "Don't want to go to no jail," he said.

"Ha!" said the warden. "Guess they's been others felt that-a-way, too."

As they grinned, he slammed the door suddenly in their faces and whipped the latchstring back through its hole. They started laughing, and after a moment he poked the muzzle of a Winchester out the window and shot the sheriff through the heart, and as the game warden turned to run, blew his head nearly off. . . . Then he hit for the hills with his rifle and a bag of cartridges, and for three weeks terrorized the region, not wanting to, just fighting back when they sought him. A battalion of the National Guard holed him up, they thought, on a rocky mountainside and sprayed it with eighty-millimeter mortar fire, but in the night, like an Indian, he slipped over a ridge nobody had thought anybody could slip over. He shot the hounds sent to trail him. Needing money for some unlikely scheme of escape his desperation had dreamed up, he hitchhiked into town once and held up the bank for precisely $500 (asking for that sum), killed a teller who made a jumpy gesture, and walked out through the streets to the mountains again. Having, like Sam Sowell, wanted only to be left alone, he had all the boosters in that country wearing nickel-plated pistols, and killed five or six men before they finally got him. . . .

~~~~~~~

THE MORAL? I think probably there is none. Leave loners be, maybe . . .

People had made me tireder than the river usually did. They had silhouetted my own temporary solitude and had shown me that I liked it well enough. The willow fire burned out and I went to bed, and lay listening to the periodic clank of the loose piece of metal in the bridge above.

Maybe that bit from Chaucer, if it was from Chaucer, wasn't about nekkebones at all. Maybe someone had cleaved someone's nekke vnto the brestebone. . . . It was the kind of thing likely to pester a part of your mind, alone.

Sam Sowell? He lived till well after the war, and changed in no respect. If cedar posts went up a little in price, so did snuff and fatback, and it all balanced out.

~~~~~~~~~~~~~~~~

CHAPTER EIGHT

⋖§ Out of whose womb came the ice? and the hoary frost of heaven, who hath gendered it?

~~~~~~~~~~~~~~~~

CRASHING BY six feet from where I lay, gravel trucks with hard brown faces laughing down at me from out of their cabs drove me breakfastless to the river that morning. I hurled in my gear and let it load the way it fell, and shoved off disgruntled, the passenger shrill in the bow. But it meant that I was moving early, and after I'd stopped on a bar a mile below to tuck things in and make coffee, I was glad of it. Some mornings I'd been puttering until ten or eleven o'clock, fire-staring, smoking another pipe of the tobacco that tasted so clean with another cup of coffee.

Shots, far back from the river . . . Deer season, and a Saturday, which would likely make for hell on the hills . . . I guessed that not even the normal quota of whisky-head sports would probably shoot a boat for a buck, but decided to wear a bandanna if I went rambling ashore. The river had risen eight or ten inches during the night. Three species of wrens were singing at the same time. It was a good morning, cool and with a dark line of clouds across the south, but the air had a muggy, head-aching edge to it somehow, the feel of weather that was going to change. By eight o'clock I was on the river again, the sun good on my back, the paddle good in my hands, the alternating pull and recovery of the stroke good against my toning muscles.

In a while I passed the mouth of a little branch where Hale and I, having put in at the One Eighty bridge late on a Friday afternoon, had once made an unfortunate kind of camp. It had looked like a good place, and, thinking maybe we'd stay a day or so to fish there, we had set things up solidly and even laid a sandstone fireplace to fit our grill. Just before dark the turkey buzzards started dropping into the trees all around us like flies onto fresh dung. It was a roost. When shouting at them did no good, Hale lost his temper and shot one, and it fell to the ground beside our tent and puked before it died, and stank; the rest flapped up five or six feet from their perches at the sound of the shot and then settled solemnly back down again. Others kept coming. . . . By dark we calculated that there must be 4,000 within a half-acre of woodland all around us; the fire didn't disturb them, nor did anything else. A hissing ran among them for a time like whispers, then stopped. We spent the night listening to the gentle rain-rustle of their droppings on dry leaves and breathing their vomital stink. A sky without two or three vultures wheeling and riding the thermals looks empty to me, but I saw less poetry in them after that night. In the morning they left, and so did we.

Fewer trees stood there than I remembered. But the floods the spring before had been big and had changed the look of the river's shore all along, scouring it, taking out healthy trees with the sick and dead ones that high water usually gets.

The shores flattened. In the Hittson and Village Bends the valley of the river's ancient scooping widens for a stretch before the sandstone mountains close in again tightly for a few miles of farewell. A squirrel barked from a tall Spanish oak. The sky was patchy, El Greco, its blue mottled with dark and bright wind-flattened clouds, pleasantly bleak. Sand bottom, sign of flatlands, bane of the low-water canoe-man, since it swallows up three quarters of the river's flow . . . Pecan trees and behind them fields with the growl of tractors . . . On the beaches, when we stopped to stretch from time to time, the pup dug great soggy pits, whining and barking at buried stones that balked his efforts to extract them, unaware that he wasn't after stones at all but ancestral badgers.

On the river the wind wasn't strong, but high up it was doing violence. The El Greco clouds suddenly, as though consciously, coalesced into a gray overcast that turned the day ominous. Two long skeins of big birds flapped across that grayness toward the south—sand-hill cranes, grating out their castle-gate croak—and I knew what the air's muggy edge meant. Geese confirmed it, the first I'd seen, four snows in a little disciplined V, winging solemnly and soundlessly south. The wind on the river died, and paddling I began to sweat. It was the kind of day that usually, in the Texas fall, is full of a kind of waiting; things are moving, the year is changing, a norther is coming. . . .

Winter there comes in waves, and keeps coming in waves till spring. For four or five months the wind rasps back and forth across West Texas like a great fiddlebow—north, then south, cold, then warm, so that even meteorologists don't know what overclothing to carry to work in the mornings. From Canada down across the Great Plains the cold, from the Gulf the wet warm or the cold blown back up at you wet, and always hard, and in the beginning it has the exultation of change in it, though after New Year more often than not it angers you, and you want again summer's quiet, burning stasis.

There is less talk of "northers" these days. People sit softly at ten fifteen in the evening and watch while a bacon vender points to highs and lows and fronts on a chart, and then they go to the wall to twirl their thermostats, and perhaps the windows rattle a little in the night, but that's about all. . . . In the country, though, a front is a fact still. There it's a blue line along the horizon, and a waiting, sweaty hush, and a hit like a moving wall, and all of life scurrying for the southern lee of things. There it's a battening down, an opening of hydrant valves, a checking of young and valuable stock, a walking across the swept lots with a flashlight, a leaning against the hard-shoving cold, a shuddering and creaking of old, tall, frame houses. There it's a norther, and there someone always, inevitably, rightly, cracks the old one about there being nothing between West Texas and the Pole except a bob-wire fence.

Therefore I had a little doubt about the exhilaration that lumped in my chest while I watched the cranes and the geese. I've always hoped geese would outlast me; my pessimism might not be stolid enough to hunch its shoulders over their destruction by insecticides, human encroachment, or whatever other agent it may be that will probably get them in the long run. They sum up the autumn and sum up the spring and sum up all the wide surge of the natural world, and your far ancestors and mine thought they were red-eared white hounds harrying damned souls across night skies. . . .

But a good norther in November can pare fifty or sixty degrees from the temperature in a matter of hours, and if it's a "blue" one, it can bring days of driving cold rain or sleet.

I had a visit to pay. A man who had been decent to me a couple of times, and whom I liked, farmed a stretch of the right bank in that neighborhood. I'd met him in a warm October that had turned suddenly cold, catching me under-equipped; I'd passed him where he was fishing from the rocks below his house, and after we'd talked a little he'd said: "Boy, you're gonna freeze. You pull out at my picnic ground down there and shoot you some squirrels and build you a far."

I did. The picnic ground—a good many of the river's farmers have them for extra money in the summer—was a sandy flat with big pecans and board tables and fireplace grills with stacked cordwood, and a doorless shack where I put my gear. Mooching through the woods in search of meat, I ran across ten new piglets whose mother made a run at me when I came too close. After shooting a couple of young squirrels, I fried and ate them and went to bed on the shack's floor, to wake a half-hour later to the slubber-slop of the old sow's champing as she ate up my bread and potatoes. Whacking her out with a board, I put the rest of the food on a table there, but she woke me again by damply sniffing my face, and I got up on the table, too. . . . In the morning the farmer, whose name was McKee, came down to get her. The piglets scattered to brush, but we caught one and tethered him by the leg to a stake and grabbed the others one by one as they came back to his squealing. It took all morn-ing; we spoke of churches and Indians and beer halls and a good many other things while we waited, and before I left he brought me a bag of fine cold biscuits to take the place of the bread. "You feed my hogs, I'll feed you," he said.

He wasn't at home this time. I climbed up through a cleft
in the rocks of the shore and approached the house past a
barn whose basic center was made of hewn, carefully fitted
logs that showed it to have once been a cabin. New red
machinery stood there, and six fat steers stared phlegmati-
cally between the boards of the corral. The house itself was
white frame, clean and orderly, with big elms overhanging
it in a fenced yard. Four pleasant mongrels met me and,
after barking dutifully, began to gambol, waving their tails,
to the pup's confusion and then delight.

His wife came out. I hadn't met her before. Standing at
the top of the back steps, she said she remembered his speaking of me. She was around fifty, in gingham, with black hair
pulled back on the sides of her head, and sun-narrowed
eyes—the big-framed, gaunt breed of woman that farmers
and ranchers so often pick to mother their sons after they've
finished with the pinch-faced pretties of the honkytonks.
Sometimes at town gatherings of people I have looked around
and wondered what happened to that physical type in the
process of urbanization, and then have seen them maybe
along the wall, standing round-backed, dressed to deprecate
their bulk among the slim-waisted twinkling blondes with
Empire hairdos. In the country they still stand straight, and
are prized.

Two married daughters, young and shorter than she, were
peeking past her shoulders. She lacked the frequent stolid
suspicion of farm women. She said: "Helped him cotch them
pigs, I know. . . . Think you'd git tard, chasin' up and
down in a old boat."

I said there wasn't much up to it, the way the river was
running.

"Ain't it nice?" she said. "Seven years I thought we was gonna end up with a dry creek there. You, Tookie, git away from that pup!"

One of the daughters asked if I'd seen any deer. I said I had.

"My husband kilt one this morning," she said. "He had nine points."

"Eight," her sister said.

"Nine, silly. That little old bump down by the head counted, he said it did. . . ."

She was pretty, dark-haired with blue eyes and as taut with life as her body was with young flesh, and I was glad she had a husband she was proud of. I liked all three of them; tone filters through families from strong fathers as it does in business from bosses, and McKee's women were a corroboration of what I remembered of him. Even his dogs were.

The women affirmed what the cranes and geese had told me; the television said that weather was on the way. They hadn't paid much mind to how bad it was to be, or when it was to hit. . . . *He* would know. How come I wasn't married? Didn't I get sick, eating junk I cooked on the river? . . . In the end, I had to argue out of an invitation to lunch two hours thence, when McKee would have returned; I said I had to get on down the river. It was true; if weather was to come, I wanted to be set for it. Mrs. McKee, in farewell, allowed that he would purely hate to have missed me, and that I was certain to get pneumonia. . . .

Near the Oakes crossing where the old road between Weatherford and Palo Pinto used to hit the river, the water's surface was much as I remembered the surface of the classic Test, in the south-English chalk country, from once when I stood there on a bridge watching the big, incredibly uniform trout at their feeding stations over the gravel. Smooth, with little swirls forming everywhere and drifting downstream to disappear, a dry-fly man's reverie . . . The Brazos runs wide there, with a large-gravel bottom about a foot and a half down like the Test's, and that was why they were alike. I wished it might also have held such trout, and in memory of not having been able to fish those rigidly owned foreign waters, I began to cast a little golden spoon with the spinning rod as I drifted.

Improbably, on the fourth cast I caught a one-pound white bass, and a few casts later another of about the same size. They pulled well in the current, and the second one jumped twice. They would make supper, if not an especially savory one. Most of the time I dislike them, to catch or to eat. An introduced species, they swarm in the big artificial impoundments and are good quarry for motorboat trollers and those who like to spot the feeding bunches of them on the surface in calm evening and race full-throttle at them to make a few casts. . . . They have coarse flesh and run in schools, and fishing for them lacks the studious, precisionist illusion that goes along with stalking trout, or black bass, or even bream.

It was pleasant, though, to have caught two fish of any kind in that pretty water. I strung them through the lips and drifted on down, past the old stone house at the crossing, wishing I could place in my mind what bird it was that was singing a thin, high, sad song off in the brush. . . . The sky seemed about to clear, then did not. The wind veered about from the east, and then back from the south, while the north side of me itched in expectation of that thrust which didn't come. Finally it did come, or seemed to, a cool push from the northeast behind me as I tooled down into the long ingoing stretch of the Village Bend on smooth-flowing water over shallow sand and gravel. Then it stopped, and the air was hot again. I gave up weather prognostication.

Many cranes were calling from a field somewhere off to the right and ahead; four wheeled in the air there. I was passing good Indian sites without heed; the Village Bend is rich in them. On the left, a goat lewdly surveyed me from a long, sloping, dead willow branch; he was perched at least twenty-five feet above the water, and had no business up a tree. The feel of farmhouses and people, though I saw none from the water . . . Smoky air, the sun hot through it, the wind in the east again now . . . I nearly went to sleep, and let the boat spin and drift backward as it willed in that obstructionless smooth glide, four or five miles of it. No fish, no ducks, no squirrels, no Indians, no pioneers . . .

Hills ahead against which the bend breaks itself to fold back in its long finger shape . . . Behind a low rise someone shot, and sixteen sandhills rose and came over me in gawky hasty flight, unformed, calling. Law enforcement in that back country is hard, and for that matter three-quarters even of the countrymen now think that cranes are geese, and the goose season was on. Further heavy flights of cranes passed over the river southward, behind me. . . . In the deep pool at the bend's tip, just under the rocks where Henry Belding gave an Indian chief the cramp colic, I intended to fish, having left myself time for it. But when I got there, two couples were car-camped on a flat beside the rocks, and the young men, sideburned and snickering, were firing a twenty-two pistol at chips and clots of foam in the water. I paddled on down a mile and, having time, picked a good campsite on a Bermuda flat ten or twelve feet above the water with a wide, clean, sand beach below it and brush sheltering it behind, on the north. Goats had cropped the grass like a lawn and had done the passenger the favor of eating up all the burrs, which they perversely like. Good solid driftwood was lodged among the brush from the spring floods. I pitched the tent tail-north, the stakes solid in good turf, dug a pit for the fire before it, and, liking the look of the whole business, decided I'd stay there until the norther had come and blown and shown the length of its teeth. I could hold out, there.

Except that it didn't come. Evening was dead still and rosy; from the farming flatlands north and east of me people-sounds rang faint—shots, shouts, the barking of dogs. . . . With the last sunlight at least 500 cranes came out of the north, spiraling and sailing down onto the river, grating their call. A dozen lit on the beach near my canoe, but took off again whistling and calling when the pup ran to the edge of the flat and barked down at them. Above and below, the other hundreds remained, stalking about the sand flats and bugle-croaking that stridulous sound as ungainly and wild and noble as the birds themselves. The pup went into frenzies until I quieted him.

For no good reason I went down to the canoe and took out the spinning rod and made one cast, reeling the lure in fast as it swept down the quick smooth water. As I was lifting it out, a good bass took it with a splash and a twist and tore fifty feet of thin line off the reel before it slowed him. Then he gave up and came to a quiet backwater where I beached him—a black of about three pounds, long and slim as the river fish are likely to be. Since the afternoon's two whites were still flapping-strong on the clip chain, I turned them loose and fileted the black for supper, and it was dark. The lantern's gas was exhausted, but its hissing would have been harsh against the calm starry night anyhow; I cooked and ate by the fire's flicker and used the flashlight to put out a throwline and to get myself to bed.

It was warm; the pup, finding me too efficient a heater, went off to sleep on my wadded pants.

I had given up prognostication.

~~~~~~~~

In the morning there I saw day come. Not in the way you usually see it if you're up, over a stretch of a half-hour or so. I saw it come. I was standing on the beach, with light fog eddying about my legs, and was looking down the river along the dark shoreline fading into mists. Everything was a dull blue-gray. Then the sand was yellow and the trees gold and red and green, and though clouds and fog still hid the sun I knew that I had seen the abrupt instant of its rising. . . . The throwline had one small channel cat, which I threw back, and two snarled stagings where larger ones had twisted free by that process they know. The cranes seemed to have concentrated below during the night; they talked among themselves for a time and then rose all together with an uproar of angry armies, and left.

Coffee, and a piece of cold fried bass . . . I felt no hurry to leave that place until I knew for certain that the big cold had hung up to the north of us somewhere, as it probably had. So I smoked, and drank more coffee, and made an expedition back into the brush after the high, sad, slow whistler's song:

———

— — —

———

Birds were there—a Harris's sparrow, a mocker singing a subdued winter song to fit the quiet morning, doves fat and

mature now that the season for their shooting was past (you
kill mostly pinfeathered infants in September, when it's legal), a spotted towhee, cardinals, the usual raucous mob of
robins, something black-throated with yellow cheeks. . . .
But it was none of them. The whistler stayed hidden, and
kept singing. The passenger impeded bird watching, bouncing about with sticks in his mouth and snarling at me for
refusing to play. He impeded bathroom matters, too. . . .

The thing was, I had once known what bird that whistle
belonged to. Knowledge of that kind takes so long to come
by, solidly at least, and there is so much of it to try to have
before you die, if you care anything about it, that to lose
any small part of what you do have seems unfair.

Cranes, battalioning about in high swarms, maybe having
decided too that the cold wasn't chasing them . . . Shooting, in the northwest where the rugged country lay, the
sound fuzzed by distance until you couldn't tell whether it
was rifles or shotguns . . . Deer? Ducks? Cans? Cranes?
Probably a little of all of them . . . I washed dishes, sloshed
out the canoe, and squirted Duco into a tear I found where
the rock at Turkey Creek had gouged the fiberglass. As I
was heating water for shaving, two girls in a pickup drove
down to the rocks above the opposite shore, and got out to
fish. Though they were maybe 250 yards away, I resented
them. So did the passenger, who stopped playing and sat
down to stare, not barking because they were women and he
was woman-reared, but growling low in his throat from time
to time. They stared back covertly; once while I was shaving
before the tent with a mirror in my hand, I heard them
giggling across the quiet air.

As the laughter of fools? What was it? . . .

Hale always claimed, and still does, that those other girls

that time were solid in their intentions toward us, and that I botched it. He seems still to feel strongly about it. . . . As I remember, we were walk-fishing in the limestone country below Granbury, ranging down the river afoot from camp at some farmer's pay picnic ground, wading the long shallow stretches in tennis shoes and climbing over the boulders beside the pools. The girls, older than we, were sitting under a cottonwood by their car with cold beer in an ice bucket; laughing, they offered us some, and Hale swilled two bottles in succession, declaring that he was an old beer drinker. I drank one, and since I was empty and hot it dizzied me, nor did I like its bitterness. The girls started a kind of banter that made me jumpy even without my understanding much of it. Hale answered with some truck-driver talk from a hamburger stand we frequented, and in a while one of the girls slapped him and started wrestling with him in the sand, laughing.

"Let's fish some more, Hale," I said.

His answer was muffled but negative.

The girl with him sat up, tugging her blouse straight. She said: "You ain't nothin' but kids!"

"Agnes, you old bat," her friend said. "Fred and them'll be waitin'."

Hale was in favor of wrestling some more, but got slapped in earnest, hard, and sat back. Then they were in the car with their bucket and driving away, their laughter trailing back at us out of the window. Hale said, with surprise, that he felt terrible, and proved it by being sick. . . .

Across the years that laughter trailed down to me when I heard the two girls' mirth on the other shore as they still-fished. It carried a weight of embarrassment, even now.

What had bothered me then, besides the hot pubescent confusion, was a feeling that the women and the beer hadn't gone with the river, with the way I felt about the river and being there. Years and beers and women later, they still didn't; I shaved resenting the girls' giggling long-range interest in me, and was glad when finally, having caught nothing, they got in their truck and drove away.

You get to be a kind of loner.

For as the crackling of thorns under a pot, so is the laughter of the fool! It wasn't only the girls who'd brought that bit up to boil around in the bottom of my consciousness; it was, too, the daily building and rebuilding of fires with twigs and debris that snapped as they burned.

From those same fires, I smelled like a smoked side of bacon. Which had been squirted by skunks . . . The sun had cut the thin fog and the wind wasn't yet strong, so I went down to the water and stripped and bathed, plunging in to wet myself in the current and jumping erect to soap and scrub, then plunging again to rinse. It made me feel fine, though I'd have been a silly enough sight, had there been anyone to see, standing naked in ice water up to my knees under an autumn sky and a rising breeze that was picking yellow leaves from the cottonwoods.

Geese were trumpeting somewhere in the sky. I couldn't focus and find them. Would they mean the real weather?

It seemed not. . . .

Worked-flint chips speckled the sand under the leaf mold in the brush behind camp when I scuffed it up with my foot. It was a site: for that matter, just about the whole of the Village Bend is. Its flat, flood-renewed alluvium must always have attracted the placid red men whose way of life was the hamlet and the planting stick and the harvests of pumpkins, beans, corn, and potatoes. In the forties of the last century, when roving loners were the only whites in that country, a big Ioni village of rush wigwams stood inside the bend, and the Anadarkoes had another across the river to the south. The Ionies seem to have been the Tejas for whom the state had been named when they lived far to the south. . . . Robert Neighbors visited them on the Brazos in '47, and General Cooper in '51, and both reported them peaceful, amicable, and a bit daunted by the always overhanging shadow of the drifting Comanche.

The Comanches (no, ma'am, I hadn't left them; when thou hast done thou hast not done, for I have more) slashed and stabbed and twanged their bows and banged their muskets as merrily around here as they did on the rest of the Brazos frontier. There were some good fights among the recorded ones and probably some better ones that never got written down. They killed Benjamin Franklin Baker, his horse slowed by a big load of fresh pork, just to the north of the bend. In the rough breaks at the tip a little group of Palo Pinto townsmen in '67, ired by the loss of horses from the village itself, caught up with the rusty thieves by using hounds, and when they found them they wished they hadn't; there were a lot of them. . . . The fight surged up and down the rough cedar-thick mountainside with little groups of cut-off citizens and Comanches meeting each other and fleeing and pursuing and dodging in a kind of Shakespearean comic confusion, nobody getting hurt much except a few horses. At the climax of things, when friends had found friends and lined up together on two sides, an old Comanche chief jumped up between the lines and began to strut and shout in Plains-Indian battle fashion. . . .

Henry Belding wrote forty-odd years later:

Directly I saw Buck Dillahunty shoot his six-shooter at the old Jabberer, but he never batted his eye, but came on like he was going to walk over us. Then I took deliberate aim with my shotgun at his side and at the crack of the gun, he went off, all doubled-up, as though he had the cramp colic pretty badly. . . .

About ten years ago, close by that place, a rancher found a neatly disposed skeleton in a crevice with glass beads, brass bracelets, spurs, a bridle, and a clay pipe, stones packed down on top. There must be dozens or even hundreds more within a radius of twenty or thirty miles in that country, but few turn up. They were well hidden; the Comanches had a flat and overriding conviction that a man needed his body whole in the next world, and it was only when panicked that they ever deserted their dead, let alone their wounded. From childhood one of their basic and repetitious rehearsals was the swooping horseback recovery of the limp bodies of companions.

South and east of where I was, across the river, the land rolls up tumblingly into the mass of Ward Mountain, where a Comanche of a likable kind once fought a fight. J. C. McConnell talked to white men who had been there, and wrote it down. . . . The People had run two Methodist preachers down the highway into Palo Pinto town without catching them, and citizens leaped at the chance for a cross-country chase. Ward Mountain was where they caught up— as often, in such high, rough country that they had to battle afoot. A man named Taylor, his aim confused by the dancing, squalling, retreating redskins, finally shouted after them in fury: "Damn you, why don't you stand still and fight?"

My Comanche heard, stopped, and looked around just long enough to holler back in good Fort Sill English: "Damn you some, too!"

And danced on . . . I always hoped he survived, though not many of them did for long. Their way dedicated them to self-destruction; with a paradoxical kind of innocence, a fierce lack of knowing what else there was they could do, they kept on playing the old Plains game of warfare against people for whom it was no game and whose weapons were not toys. Risk for The People was glory; in little stripped-down bands they slashed down at the frontier again and again and again in the sixties and early seventies. Companies of rangers made up of men like Charles Goodnight slashed back, but often at shadows, and for a long time the Comanches' ultimate doom was not certainly envisioned even by the whites. Many of the younger settlers rode off to the Civil War, and after they got home again the Northern officials in Oklahoma still ignored or maybe helped the Comanches in their raiding. The frontier's population thinned down to the purely tough ones, and some of those pulled back a way for years. So constant was the skirmishing that most of it went unregistered.

The People earned plenty of glory among themselves and in their own terms, but even while they raped and stole and killed and scalped and kidnapped in a totally glorious fashion, they were losing steadily, and after a while they knew it. They weren't numerous enough to absorb the losses; their women, from a hard and horseback life, miscarried constantly and casually and bore few sons to replace the young men who ended up in crevices, stones tamped down above them. Besides, it was happening with speed. . . . In '75, after the frontier whites and the smallpox and the other diseases and Mackenzie had finished with them, only about 1,600 Comanches were alive, abject government wards, where brief years before 10,000 had hunted and fought.

Those who went, went the way they chose. Listen to old Ten Bears of the Root Eaters, at one of the brave peacemakings whose meaninglessness he divined:

They made sorrow come in our camps, and we went out like the buffalo bulls when the cows are attacked. When we found them we killed them, and their scalps hang in our lodges. The Comanches are not weak and blind, like the pups of a dog when seven sleeps old. They are strong and far-sighted, like grown horses. We took their road and we went on it. The white women cried and our women laughed.

. . . There are things which you have said to me which I do not like. They were not sweet like sugar, but bitter like gourds. You said that you wanted to put us upon a reservation, to build us houses and make us medicine lodges. I do not want them. I was born upon the prairie, where the wind blew free and there was nothing to break the light of the sun. I want to die there and not within walls. I know every stream and every wood between the Rio Grande and the Arkansas. I have hunted and lived over that country. I lived like my fathers before me and like them I lived happily. . . .

Do not speak of it more. . . . If the Texans had kept out of my country, there might have been peace. But that which you now say we must live in is too small. The Texans have taken away the places where the grass grew the thickest and the timber was the best. Had we kept that, we might have done the things you ask. But it is too late. The whites have the country which we loved, and we only wish to wander on the prairie until we die.

Most of them did wander on the prairie until they died, and because of the kind of activity the wandering entailed, their dying didn't take long to accomplish.

They threw off a few sparks doing it, though. The Nɜmɜnə,
The People . . .

~~~~~~~~~

PROGNOSTICATING DESPITE MYSELF, I decided that the cold
front must have slowed to a stop somewhere to the north,
so I loaded up early in the afternoon and pushed on under
a blue sky pierced high by yellow thunderheads. Up a creek
canyon, searching afoot for an Indian rock shelter that someone had told the old gentleman in Weatherford about, I
managed to let a $200 borrowed camera jolt from its case
into a pool. When I fished it out and tried it, its shutter
went *clud*, foretelling the expenditure of money.

The canyon was worth seeing, though—a tawny, weather-
stained gash in the foothills of Ward Mountain with a clear
creek, and on the flats above the canyon wall a stretch of
primeval woodland. Maybe it had been too hard to reach
to cut out the lumber trees, or maybe by some quirk of in-
heritance the owners were absentee and indifferent; patches
of land turn up in the Brazos country from time to time
whose titleholders' whereabouts maybe the tax-collecting
courthouses know, but hardly anyone else. Towering burr
oaks and live oaks stood there above silence, and cedars of a
size I'd never seen before in that country: one, lightning-
split, must have measured nearly three feet through the long
axis of an elliptical cross section. Brambles overarched trails
that no livestock had used for years; squirrels played on high
branches, and from underbrush deer I couldn't see coughed
at me and ran away with a sound of kicked leaves.

The rock shelter, when I found it, sat in a scooped niche
of the canyon wall, a queer little circular sty with unmortared
walls built up of flat slabs that any Boy Scout might have
laid, but none had, and a fallen-in roof of larger slabs, one

of them grooved for corn grinding. It was like the others of
its kind I'd seen. A couple of people might have been able
to squat in it by a tiny fire when it had been whole, but why
they'd have chosen to do so, with villages near and the woods
for shelter too and even caves, I've never seen explained.
High water had scoured it; I found no midden.

Back on the river, I lost interest in archeology. Swirling
high currents swept the thunderheads out of the sky like
minor actors exiting before the stars show up onstage. For
thirty minutes a hot hush hung. . . .

Finally, from the northwest, an arched crescent of blue-
dun cloud, sky-wide, rolled hugely high and fast down at us,
the atmosphere clear before it and clear behind. Not having prognosticated worth a damn, I scuttled for the flatter
shore and had the tent up lopsided but solid under a half-
dead elm by the time the first big slam of cold hit, with a
sweep of leaves and sand and the fresh uplift of body and
spirit, probably barometric, that they always carry even
when you don't want them.

Unuplifted, the pup kept jumping back into the canoe
with the apparent faint hope that if we continued our float,
all that bluster would cease. He got sand on my shotgun,
and I had to switch him before he would face the fact of
our staying there. Working, carrying gear from where the
canoe was moored unhandily between a cutaway bank and
submerged willows, then chopping a thick branch of the
elm into chunks for a fire, I watched the sky.

From the southeast, rearing to meet the blue-dun cloud's
charge, a white roll of exactly similar shape moved up. In
the dusk, when I'd finished setting up and was squatting in
the tent opening by a good fire, they met with thunder and
the last red tints of sundown flame-edged their fight. . . .

Big drops of rain spatted down diagonally through the violent air, and the old elm in the fire hissed and spewed and stank and radiated; lightning took over the sun's work and made the early night for a time flickeringly white, and loud with thunder.

It was a fine show. Out, natural drama big and little sops up much of that interest that in towns we daily expend upon one another's small nobilities and bastardlinesses, and for me no surer proof of our unchanging animality exists than the response we give to storms. There is nothing rational about it. A man is a fool to welcome bluster and wet and cold, and yet he often does, and even indoors he is seldom indifferent to their coming. It is hard for him to talk about them without using the old personifications which, they say, first spawned theology; it is hard to write about them without leaning on the insights of poets who, sometimes self-consciously, have prized violence in nature. Maybe bare-nerved Shelley:

> . . . . *Thou dirge*
> *Of the dying year, to which this closing night*
> *Will be the dome of a vast sepulchre,*
> *Vaulted with all thy congregated might*
> *Of vapours, from whose solid atmosphere*
> *Black rain, and fire, and hail, will burst. . . .*

Not west the wind in Texas, though, but north . . . Nothing but a bob-wire fence . . .

Or maybe just "Blow, winds, and crack your cheeks!" There was no self-conscious prizing of violence in that—he prized everything.

I baked a slab of biscuit bread, dry and toast-tasting, beside the fire, ate it with thick slices of broiled bacon, and went to bed. The rain thickened, then slacked, then came down again in floods; the night crackled and roared with change and iron cold. Drunk with coziness, the pup wallowed beside me and groaned, and I remember wondering, before I slept, a little more about the relation of storms to man. . . . If, being animal, we ring like guitar strings to nature's furies, what hope can there be for our ultimate, planned peacefulness?

But night questions don't have answers.

CHAPTER NINE

BEHIND the wide blue roll of cloud the Canadian air moved down frigid but crisp and clear, and in the mornings by the fire, when I would set my coffee cup aside nearly empty and pick it up again a few minutes later, the sugary dregs would have become mush ice. Yelping flights of geese, convinced now of winter's imminence, V-cut the blue sky. At the caprice of the little man at Possum Kingdom, or of his bosses, the river dropped three feet; channel became a study, and the pup developed a stubborn habit of leaping ashore at shallow and difficult places. In John Hittson Bend dropping-splotches painted the high red-and-gold sandstone cliffs white below ledges. Eagle's nests? Falcons? I should check, some spring, and get my head ripped open by a defensive parent. . . . One day the big cold wind blew from morning until late afternoon, and under its bleak sweep there were only I and the pup and the canoe and the river and frost-dead leaves whipping across the air, and from time to time a great blue heron gliding away from a perch before us with a cry of protestant rancor. A dozen dead foxes lay heaped on the bank at one place, victims of the new squeak-squawk callers that lure them at night within reach of spotlights and shotguns; the hound people, ritualists, hate that innovation. . . . In a sand-bottomed canyon once, a stallion and two mares and a big colt, alert under the season's spur, came pounding down the beach at the strange thing that was the boat, then threw sand high stopping and pounded away as the strange thing broke in two and I began to lead it through a shallows.

Change. Autumn. Maybe—certainly—there was melancholy in it, but it was a good melancholy. I've never been partial to the places where the four seasons are one. If the sun shines all year long at La Jolla, and the water stays warm enough for swimming over rocks that wave moss like green long hair, that is pleasant, but not much else. Sunshine and warm water seem to me to have full meaning only when they come after winter's bite; green is not so green if it doesn't follow the months of brown and gray. And the scheduled inevitable death of green carries its own exhilaration; in that change is the promise of all the rebirths to come, and the deaths, too. In it is the only real unchangingness, solidity, and in the alternation of bite and caress, of fat and lean, of song and silence, is the reward and punishment that life has always been, and the punishment itself becomes good, maybe because it promises reward, maybe because after much honey the puckering acid of acorns tastes right. Without the year's changes, for me, there is little morality.

If you tell me that that is a poisonous northern puritanism and has no validity for the sun-warmed mass of the world's peoples, and remind me that the Greeks sired our cycle in a climate much like southern California's, I won't argue. I'm only talking about what is mine.

Looming over the outer edge of a bend called Poke Stalk is a line of high bluffs, an escarpment where the mountain country falls abruptly away to farming land. I camped beneath them that night near a place where, in an October years before, Hale and I had stopped and had eaten fat bluebills out of season, shot by kids upstream who had run off with their guilty consciences and left the ducks on the water when they saw us paddling down. Skinning them out that night, we broiled the breasts over drift-mesquite coals and burned the evidence, feeling guilty, too, but having eaten well. . . .

The wind died at sunset. The night, its wisp of a moon not yet out, was clear, with stars, and so still that I found myself resenting the fire's hoarse whisper and snapping against a boulder that bounced its heat into the little tent. Screech owls, rare in that country since the big drouth, were quavering tentatively to one another near where I'd seen a deserted flagstone house across the river. Masses of tangled dead timber overhung the tiny flat I was camped on; six inches from one of the rear tent stakes the earth fell away into an eroded pit eight feet deep, eaten out by the river in flood.

A truck's working-groan to the east, where Two Eighty-one climbed the scarp . . . Southward, a freight train threaded the T. & P., and sounded faintly the Cadillac honk of its Diesel, importunate, lacking the lonesomeness of the old steam wails we had once listened to from there. The day's wind and bright light and paddling had washed me with clean fatigue, and my muscles felt good, in tone. A week it had taken, seventy unhurried miles, longer than it had used to, but I was older now. The skin of my hands from work and from the alternate wetting and drying and the

cold had chapped hornily, and at the knuckles of my thumbs
and forefingers had broken in bloody stinging cracks. Cuts
and little sore knots where sandbur tips had embedded
themselves finished the disfigurement. . . . If one had a
modern-tragic viewpoint like—oh, Graham Greene's, one
might make symbols out of those fingers. But one didn't.
One felt damned good. One was for the moment a simple
puritan, soaking reward from the glow of a fire on one's front
while at one's tail the creeping cold of night only italicized
(puritanically?) one's simple comfort, and in the embers
one's simple supper, a potato, lay baking. . . .

The pup wanted play. It was his main trouble and the root
of the insubordination that had invaded him. After gnaw-
ing neurotically for a time on the blanket, which since the
norther was becoming important for warmth at night on
top of the sleeping bag, he tried to make love to it, and
yipped with rebellious despair when I made him stop, and
came to chew on my raw hands.

After eating, I walked around behind the tent to look at
the night and, forgetting the big pit, fell into it. I landed
flat in slimy mud, stunned, a tangle of old barbed wire six
inches from my forehead, and when I'd pulled up onto all
fours, still a little faint with the feeling you have after falls
and wounds, the pup scrambled down to me and began to
lick my face. I pushed him away, and a whole memory came
back to me of a lost two or three months after the war when
I'd stayed at a ramshackle hacienda in the uplands of Vera
Cruz state, with the slightly crazy old recluse whose people
had owned the place since the seventeenth century. We had
drunk habanero one night, and had discussed loudly, and
I'd wandered out the back door to fall into an unroofed
cellar pit among broken glass, and had come back to con-

sciousness with a little dog licking my face. Like an old man's repertory of stories, experience begins to repeat itself after a time, even or maybe especially in its meaningless phases. On the fringes of the middle age and after, the déjà-vu is likely not to be illusory.

No worse off than before except for another layer of filth on my clothes, I climbed out of the pit and went to bed and slept hard, half hearing things that screamed on the heights above us and once, as though in a dream, the tearing, splintering progress of a frost-freed boulder that bounded down through brush and trees and came to its next eon's resting place in the river, with a splash. . . .

When I got up, the thinnest of horned moons hung in the east and stars were bright all over the sky. Under the cold air a rounded roll of fog followed the river's course exactly down its twists and bends, and when light came the day had a windless clarity that would have been worth undergoing ten blue northers to see. It was old Parson Herbert's sweet day so cool, so calm, so bright, and I even had a small catfish on the throwline. I skinned and gutted it by the waterside, and when I was back at the tent feeding twigs to the embers left over, under ashes, from the night's fire, a man of about fifty carrying a thirty-thirty Winchester came picking his way among the boulders of the shore. He wore a Stetson, brogans, and striped bib overalls under a denim jacket, and looked embarrassed when I told him good morning.

"I guess you got permission to be here?"

I had to answer no, embarrassed myself. Though the tangle of barbed wire I'd fallen beside in the pit served no purpose, it was part of a fence, flood-flattened, on whose unpublic side I had camped. There hadn't been any other level ground. I told the man what I was doing.

He stared at me, then smiled. "I was thinkin' it was somebody slipped in for a deer," he said. "Found one last week with just a ham cut off. It makes you mad."

I offered him coffee and he took it, black, refusing anything to eat but staying to talk while I fried and ate the catfish. He was not a loquacious sort, but he liked the look of what I was doing, and people will open sometimes to a stranger, met strangely, whom they find partly sympathetic and whom they will not likely see again. It is a principle that gets one into involvements in the third-class carriages of French trains. . . . He'd run away from home down the country a way when he'd been seventeen, and had come to work for a rancher in that bend, tending cattle, batching in the flagstone house across the river. He'd met his wife there one day, when she had come to the river picnicking with a party of people.

"Looked at her," he said. "Liked her. Guess she liked me. Still both do."

When he had just about consolidated his own small ranch there (cheap land or no, it's a tough thing to get done), the big drouth had burned in and had shrunk his few head of cattle to sway-backed racks of bones before he'd sold them at canner-and-cutter prices, and he'd thought he'd have to sell the place, too. But mohair goats and a long stint at the Fort Worth Convair plant that draws much of its labor from that region had scrooched him by, he said.

The passenger brought a rock and dropped it at his feet, hoping for play. With a slanting grin the rancher looked at him and reached down to pull his ear.

"Son-of-a-gun dogs," he said. "Run out here from Mineral Wells at night. Kilt me thirty-five goats oncet from sundown to sunup. Two of the worst was hounds, and I knowed who they belonged to, but he said they wouldn't run no goats. Laid a load of number two shot into one of 'em one night, and the next time I seen that fellow, he said: 'Know that blue dog of mine? Bobcat clawed him up turble, other night.' And I said: 'You don't tell me? Rough outfits, bob-cats . . .'"

I said I doubted that the passenger was going to get big enough to do much slaughter among people's livestock.

"Sha," he said. "Tell me. I've seen Pekes out there a-run-nin'."

Though he said he scarcely ever killed deer, he had a passion for squirrel shooting and for hunting what he called "short varmints." He said the things screaming on the hill the night before had been ringtails, which were more numerous than he'd ever known them to be and which he blamed for a local shortage of squirrels: in the spring, he claimed, they went into the holes and ate the young ones on the nests. Of the projected Brazos dams—one is to be slapped up against those bluffs—he said: "I've learned to get along with her pretty good the way she is. Don't know how I'll like her when she's a lake. Good bottomland, them fish'll be grazin' on."

He was one of the quiet, tough, unprofane types that that country still breeds from time to time, close in type to the best of the old ones, or to what nostalgia says the best of them were like. He had blue eyes with seamed corners, brown skin, a strong nose, and thin lips that shaped themselves stiffly, thoughtfully, around his words. . . . He told me about a field full of Indian debris, and corn-pounding holes along a high ledge, and a kind of cave where he'd once let a hermit live for five years, occasionally bringing him coffee and beans and flour from town. The hermit had always stayed hidden until he could see who had come, and at the river had kept a big chicken-wire box full of live cat-fish.

"Give me one oncet weighed thirty-two pounds," the rancher said. "Up and left one spring, never said why."

He took a look at the canoe, and said he'd always thought he'd like to do a little floating himself.

"Come on," I said.

He looked at me. "Dang if I wouldn't," he said. "Dang if I wouldn't."

But then he grinned and shook his head, and after drinking half a cup more coffee wished me luck and continued his patrol along the bank. I washed pots and scraped off some whiskers and rolled my gear into bundles ready for loading, then climbed for a look at the hermit's hole. It was under a block of conglomerate forty or fifty feet tall, in a grove of live oaks beneath the bluffs. Age-long surface drainage had chewed out a chamber between the earth and the boulder's cuspate base, and the hermit, whoever he had been, had laid walls of sandstone blocks at either opening of the cavity, mortaring with mud, leaving a door at the big lower end and a chimney hole at the upper. The domed ceiling, blackened by smoke, was tall enough to stand under; it was a snug retreat, and if I'd known about it the night before I would have stayed there, though the floor was littered with the droppings of exploratory goats. In the live oaks outside titmice were whistling *peter-peter-peter*, and down the hill the river sparkled blue, and I found myself thinking that you wouldn't have to be a really peculiar old misanthrope, at that, to want to live in such a place for five years, or for a lifetime. . . .

A river has few "views." It seeks the lowest line of its country, straight or crooked, and what you see when you travel along it are mostly river and sky and trees, water and clouds and sun and shore. Things a quarter-mile away exist for you only because you know they are there; your consciousness of them is visual only if you walk ashore to see them. For a man who likes rivers, most of the time that is all right; for a man who seeks sharp solitude, it's special. But sometimes, too, the shores close in a bit as room walls will, and you crave more space. . . . Now, without having thought about doing so, I clambered beyond the hermit's hole up ledges, hoisting the pup at spots, to the top of the bluff.

I was out of breath when I got there, but it was a fine spot and worth the climb. I knew it from before. People drive out to it from Mineral Wells for picnics, on a dirt road running past Baptist crossroads churches and log ruins. As you stand there on weathered solid stone, the lowlands roll south and east from below you to the horizon; your eye can trace fifteen miles or so of the river's course as it meanders over sand, slower and flattened, between tall bright cottonwoods and oaks and pecans, and where you can't see it you can guess it, and can guess too the things around it, knowing them. Though it's nothing much in comparison to the vistas you get in real mountains, after a week in the Brazos's winding trough, it dizzied me a little; it made fun of what I had been doing. Heights have that kind of humor.

Likely that bluff had a good name once before some dullard called it Inspiration Point. The nation's map is measled with names like that, pocks from the old nineteenth-century plague that made people build gazebos and well-tops of rough masonry with oaken buckets on ropes but no well beneath (unless it was a "wishing well"), and sing "Annie Laurie," and read Scott for his worst qualities, and long to own paintings by Bouguereau or Landseer or Alma-Tadema, and, disregarding the guts and soul in the old nomenclature of American places, rename them Inspiration Point and Lovers' Retreat (there's one of those up Eagle Creek) and Maiden's Leap. It was worse in the interior than on the East Coast, where the old names had rooted themselves before that frame of mind came along. It was worst of all in the South, because the South yearned hardest to believe Scott, but the whole hinterland had the disease; in the Midwest it got flavored with Hiawatha. . . . Though it has its own cachet now—yes, I like gingerbreaded houses, and old pictures of women with buns and with big breasts under stiff shirtwaists—it was, for me, a flouting of real ghosts and genii, an unimaginative lamina of Greco-Scotch-English never-neverism on the surface of a land that seemed too new to would-be-cultured sensibilities. You don't have to line up too solidly with the America shouters to resent it.

Now that the land looks a little older and we don't have to stare directly at the tobacco juice on the haired chins of those who made its past, the grandchildren of the Gothicists are likely to be enchanted to find that the streamlet below their house used to be called Dead Nigger Draw, but they have a hard fight with the real-estate men, staunchly Gothic all, if they try to cancel out its present title of Bonnie Brae. . . . And the effort, somehow, seems little more praiseworthy or genuine than their grandparents' was.

One digresses? Certainly.

That whole arc of country below the Point is ghost-laden. Violent, obscure history piles in on you as you look off over the lowlands. They were richer than the mountain country; therefore more people wanted them and came there. People make trouble; trouble makes history, or anyhow tales, since not much of the history is reliable. After the trouble, little of weight happened in that piece of country—no oil booms, no industry to speak of until the Fort Worth factories began to suck the people away—so that for a long time remembrance of the frontier was strong on the slowly eroding farms and the ranches, and in the little bypassed towns. It sat on the land. It still does, a little, if the land means anything to you.

Two miles below the bluff you can see a railroad bridge where the Texas & Pacific main line crosses to hill-hidden Brazos town, which weed-shot to existence in the eighties when the railroad came. It is a dusty spraddle of small frame houses now, with a brick post office and an empty store or two; a few countrymen eye you with faint astonishment if you drive out there, as well they may. No one goes there by accident since their highway bridge washed out and made them a dead end, and if anyone goes there except by accident he makes ripples in that quietness. An old man lived there for a long time who used to hint of dark and pleasurable past connections with the Jameses and the Youngers and Quantrill. Since his death I'm unaware of even any refracted drama in Brazos, Texas, though there is fair fishing by the stark piers of the vanished road bridge.

A mile down from there is the Highway 281 bridge by the mouth of Palo Pinto Creek for which the county was named; no one knows what painted stick it was that gave the creek *its* name, but that kind of haziness perhaps beats Gothicism. Like Keechi and Elm and the other creeks, it drains history into the Brazos along with silt and leaves and drift and water. It has a hundred hidden valleys; The People loved it. In the fall of 1837 the ineffable Bigfoot Wallace came there with a wilderness surveying party—he was twenty years old, huge, and a year out of Virginia whence he had traveled to take Mexican toll for the deaths of a brother and a cousin at Goliad. Up the Palo Pinto (mostly they called it a river then) he strayed from his companions and got lost, fought some Indians, sprained his ankle, lived in a cave. . . . In good-humored old age, when he liked to talk, he told John Duval that other Comanches had taken him prisoner one day, and back at their camp had tied him to a pole with firewood around him in preparation for a redskin-style auto-da-fé. Things looked black, but—inevitably—"just at this moment the old squaw I had seen in the lodge rushed through the crowd of painted warriors, and began to throw the wood from around me. . . ." With like inevitability, he was adopted into the tribe, and stayed with them for three educational months before slipping away and going back to the settlements.

The fact is, there was probably truth in it. He was nearly everywhere that counted, Bigfoot Wallace, with enough vitality and humor to have seen four or five ordinary men through life. Though he was no half-horse, half-alligator sort of a liar, he sometimes told things a little big, but why not?

Port Smythe, M. D., on the other hand, modeled himself on the tradition of the clear-eyed scientific amateur when he visited the Palo Pinto in 1852, still before many whites had been there. As a kind of last bachelor fling, he rode horseback up the Brazos from the settled country to the south, hiring Indian guides to show him the way. He expected no trouble and found none, Latinized every scrap of weed that his horse's hoof bruised, and exclaimed over nature's grandeurs in unscientific tones that echoed Cooper and Scott: old, low, flat Comanche Peak down in Hood County was "the crowning Glory of the Landscape, . . . the Hoary Monarch of this wide domain," and his Indians could only be "the Sons and Daughters of the forest." Having attained the Palo Pinto, he noted:

. . . sundry specimens of Natural History, among which were the Raven, (*Corvus-corax*) Red Bird, (*Loxia-cardinalis*) the Humming Bird, (*Trochilus*—***) &c., besides innumerable Rattle Snakes, (*Crotalus-horridus*) Tarantula, (*Lycosia-tarantula*) and Scorpion, (*Scorpio*).

and, without climbing the bluffs to see where he'd been, rode back home again to write a pleasant, earnest journal of the trip, inconsequential from this range, though its newspaper publication may have lured some lackland South Texans up the river.

Up the Palo Pinto also, during the Civil War, settlers clustered against the Comanches, and while few details of that time have come down, a rhyme has that implies the details behind it:

> White's town, and Burnett's street,
> Stubblefield's fort, and nothing to eat. . . .

(Tip Seay rode out from that fort on a half-broken black horse one day, against good advice, and never rode back again. Maybe somebody repeated the good advice to his scalped corpse when they found it.)

From the creek mouth the river drops down and loops back north, making the great Christmas-stocking shape of the Dobbs Valley Bend, named for old Chesley Dobbs, who ranched there till his luck ran out and the Indians got his long hair (against good counsel, too, he'd ridden out homeward from Palo Pinto town), even though the tracks showed that his pony had given them a run. There seem always to have been those mournful post-mortem trail cuttings, since hoofprints and bruised bushes and tatters of cloth had voices for men both red and white in those days; I know a few for whom they still do, but not many. Chesley Dobbs was the one whose scalp they'd found at the Old Painted Campground, on Keechi. . . . Where the Brazos breaks south still again, forming the Littlefield Bend and piercing the invisible skin of Parker County, my merchant friend's bailiwick, stands a lonely, rusty-faced hill called Red Bluff, where the Comanches (I can't help it; the stories are there; I'm not telling even a fourth of them) hid once before making a reasonably bloody raid on Webb Gilbert's remuda and wounding Roe Littlefield in a place that nobody, for some reason, will mention.

Beyond that, Rock Creek comes in past the brick kilns at Bennett, draining the country where Fuller Millsap ranched and fought Indians and shouted but backed down from a shotgun duel with Charles Goodnight, and George McCleskey died at Blue Springs pumping bullets out of his Henry between the cabin logs even after his legs were paralyzed, and Old Lady Rippy reached in between her sagging breasts and hauled out a plug and bit a chew when The People tried to make her run so they could shoot her more amusingly, and cursed them in their own language, so that nonplused they went away, but got her later along with the crusty old man she was married to—howling like wolves down at his traps. . . . And Owl Head Johnson lived alone and got lynched for stealing hogs. . . .

When you see Rock Creek after a rain, you know what is happening to that country, and has been for a century. Above it, even in wet times, the river is likely to run fairly clear, since most of the tributary streams up to Possum Kingdom drain sandstone country without much rich dirt. But Rock Creek carries the runoff from the steeply up-and-down western part of Parker County which used to be an oak forest with grassed glades, and since the whites moved in with axes and moldboard plows and too many chattel ruminants, the western part of Parker County has been flowing down Rock Creek to the Brazos, and down the Brazos to the Gulf. After rain, the creek and the river below its mouth run thick as black-bean soup; it was the old men from up that way who could brag the loudest later, in front of the feed stores, about the farms they'd worn out. Now the S. C. S. tells them how to terrace, and a lot of them do, but that barn's door gaped wide for a long long time.

Rock Creek was a main avenue for Indian depredations into the richer low country. Dozens of people died up its valley, most of them interestingly, if your interests run so. But maybe Mrs. Sherman's story will suffice to give the tone of that warfare. . . .

~~~~~~~~~

THEY RODE up to the cabin while the Shermans were at dinner on November 27, 1860—dinner in rural Texas then and up into my young years being the noontime meal. There were half a hundred of them, painted, devil-ugly in look and mood. It was the year after the humiliating march up across the Red under good, dead Neighbors; the frontier country was not yet strange to The People, nor were they yet convinced they had lost it. They wanted rent-pay for it in horses, and trophies, and blood, and boasting-fuel for around the prairie campfires in the years to come. Horses they had taken in plenty—300 or so of them by the time they reached the

Shermans'—and they had just lanced John Brown to death among his ponies to the east, and the day before had raped and slaughtered and played catch-ball with babies' bodies at the Landmans' and the Gages' to the north.

Though the Shermans did not know about any of that, their visitors lacked the aspect that a man would want to see in his luncheon guests—even a sharper frontiersman than Ezra Sherman, who, in that particular time and place, with a wife and four kids for a responsibility, had failed to furnish himself with firearms.

The oldest boy, Mrs. Sherman's by an earlier husband who had died, said: "Papa . . ."

But by the time Ezra Sherman turned around, they were inside the one-room cabin, a half-dozen of them, filling it with hard tarnished-copper bodies and the flash of flat eyes and a smell of woodsmoke and horse sweat and leather and wild armpits and crotches. Behind them, through the door, were the urgent jostle and gabble and snickering of the rest.

"God's Heaven!" Sherman said, gripping the table's edge.

Martha Sherman said: "Don't show nothin'. Don't scare."

She had come to the frontier young with a brother and his family, but even if she'd only come the year before she'd have known more about it than her husband. There was sense in her, and force. Her youngest started bawling at the Indians; she took his arm and squeezed it hard until he shushed, looking up the while into the broad face, slash-painted diagonally in scarlet and black, of the big one who moved grinning toward the table. He wore two feathers slanting up from where a braid fanned into the hair of his head, and held a short lance.

"Hey," he said.

"Hey," Ezra Sherman answered.

The Indian said something.

"No got whisky," Ezra Sherman said. "No got horse. Want 'lasses? *Good* 'lasses."

"You're fixin' to have us kilt," his wife said, and stood up. "Git!" she told the big Indian.

He grinned still, and gabbled at her. She shook her head and pointed to the door, and behind her heard the youngest begin again to cry. The Indian's gabble changed timbre; it was Spanish now, she knew, but she didn't understand that either.

"Git out!" she repeated.

"*Hambre*," he said, rubbing his bare belly and pointing to the bacon and greens and cornbread and buttermilk on the table.

"No, you ain't," she said, and snatched up a willow broom that was leaned against the wall. But her eye caught motion to the left and she spun, swinging the broom up and down and whack against the ear of the lean, tall, bowlegged one who had hold of her bolt of calico. She swung again and again, driving him back with his hands raised, and then one of the hands was at a knife in his belt, and Two-feathers's lance came down like a fence between them. Her broom hit it and bounced up. The three of them stood there. . . .

Two-feathers was laughing. The lean Indian wasn't. The calico lay on the floor, trampled; she bent and picked it up, and her nervous fingers plucked away its wrinkles and rolled it again into a bolt.

"Martha, you're gonna rile 'em," her husband said.

"Be quiet," she told him without looking away from Two-feathers's laughing eyes.

"Good," the big Indian's mouth said in English from out

of the black-and-red smear. With his hand he touched the long chestnut hair at her ear; she tossed her head away from the touch, and he laughed again. *"Mucha mujer,"* he said.

The lean one jabbered at him spittingly.

Martha Sherman's oldest said calmly: "That's red hair."

It was. In the cabin's windowless gloom she had not noticed, but now she saw that the lean one's dirty braids glinted auburn, and that his eyes, flicking from her to the authoritative big one, were green like her own. Finally he nodded sulkily to something that Two-feathers said. Two-feathers waved the other warriors back and turned to where Ezra Sherman stood beside the dinner table.

"No hurt," he said, and jerked his head toward the door. "Vamoose."

"Yes," Ezra Sherman said, and stuck out his hand. "Friend. Good fellow."

The big Indian glanced ironically at the hand and touched it with his own. "Vamoose," he repeated.

Ezra Sherman said: "You see? He don't mean no trouble. I bet if I dip up some molasses they'll just . . ."

"He means go," Martha Sherman said levelly. "You bring Alfie."

"Go where?"

"Come on!" she said, and the force of her utterance bent him down and put his callus-crusted farmer's hands beneath his baby's arms and straightened him and pulled him along behind her as she walked, holding the hands of the middle children, out the door into the stir and murmur of the big war party. It was misting lightly, grayly. . . . The solemn oldest boy came last, and as he left the cabin he was still looking back at the green-eyed, lean, redheaded Comanche.

Two-feathers shouted from the door and the gabble died, and staring straight ahead Martha Sherman led her family across the bare wet dirt of the yard and through the gate, past ponies' tossing hackamored heads and the bristle of bows and muskets and lances and the flat dark eyes of fifty Comanches. She took the road toward the creek. In a minute they were in brush, out of sight of the house, and they heard the voices begin loud again behind them. Martha Sherman began to trot, dragging the children.

"Where we goin' to?" Ezra Sherman said.

"Pottses'."

He said: "I don't see how you could git so ugly about a little old hank of cloth and then leave the whole house with—"

"Don't talk, Ezra," she said. "Move. Please, please move."

But then there was the thudding rattle of unshod hooves on the road behind them, and a hard-clutching hand in her chestnut hair, and a ring of ponies dancing around them, with brown riders whose bodies gave and flexed with the dancing like joined excrescences of the ponies' spines.

Before she managed to twist her head and see him, she knew it was the redheaded one who had her; he gabbled contemptuously at Ezra Sherman, and with the musket in his other hand pointed down the road toward the creek. The pony shied at the motion, yanking her off balance. She did not fight now, knowing it pointless or worse.

"Durn you, let her be!" Ezra Sherman yelled, moving, but a sharp lancepoint pricked his chest two inches from the baby's nose and he stopped, looking up.

"Go on, Ezra," his wife said. "They'll let you go."

"Ain't right," he said. The lancepoint jabbed; he backed away a half-foot.

"Go on."

He went, trailing stumbling children, and the last she saw of them was the back-turned face of her oldest, but one of the horsemen made a plunging run at him, and he turned and followed the family. . . . The redhead's pony spun and started dancing back up the road. The hand jerked her hair, and she went half down, and a hoof caught her ankle; then she was running to keep from dragging. Snow was drifting horizontally against the chinaberries she had planted around her dooryard, though it was not cold; she saw finally that it was feathers from her bed, which one of them had ripped open and was shaking in the doorway while others laughed. In a shed some of them had found the molasses barrel and had axed its top and were drinking from tin cups and from their hands, throwing the ropy liquid over each other with yells. The old milk cow came loping and bawling grotesquely from behind the house, a Comanche astride her neck, three arrows through her flopping bag. . . .

Deftly, without loosening his grip, the redhead swung his leg across his pony's neck and slid to the ground and in one long strong motion, like laying out a rope or a blanket, threw her flat. Two of the others took her legs, pulling them apart. She kicked. The flame-pain of a lance knifed into her ribs and through her chest and out the back and into the ground and was withdrawn; she felt each inch of its thrust and retreat, and in a contraction of shock there relaxed elsewhere, and her legs were clamped out wide, and the lean redhead had let go of her hair and stood above her, working at his waistband.

Spread-eagled, she twisted her head and saw Two-feathers a few yards away, her big Bible in his hands, watching. Her eyes spoke, and maybe her mouth; he shrugged and turned toward the shed where the molasses barrel stood, past a group that was trying to light fire against the wet cabin wall. . . .

The world was a wild yell, and the redhead was first, and the third one, grunting, had molasses smeared over his chest and bed feathers stuck in it, and after that she didn't count; though trying hard she could not slip over into the blackness that lay just beyond an uncrossable line. Still conscious, and that part over, she knew when one on horseback held her arms up and another worked a steel-pointed arrow manually, slowly, into her body under her shoulderblade, and left it there. Knew, too, when the knife made its hot circumcision against the bone of her skull, and when a horseman meshed his fingers into her long hair again and she was dragging beside his panicked, snorting pony. But the hair was good and held, and finally a stocky warrior had to stand with a foot on each of her shoulders as she lay in the plowed field before the house, and peel off her scalp by main force.

For a time after that they galloped back and forth across her body, yelling—one thing she recalled with a crystallinity that the rest of it lost, or never had, was that no hoof touched her—and shot two or three more arrows into her, and went away. She lived for four days (another writer says three, and another still says one, adding the detail that she gave birth to a dead child; take your pick), tended by neighbor women, and if those days were anything but a continuing fierce dream for her, no record of it has come down.

In delirium, she kept saying she wouldn't have minded half so much if it hadn't been for that red hair. . . .

The oldest boy had quit his stepfather and had circled back through the brush and had watched it all from hiding.

No record, either, states how he felt about Comanches afterward, or the act of love, or anything.

It seems clear that The People were good haters. So were the whites, though, and that was a year before a war unconnected with Indians was to draw away many of the tough young ones. The Brazos frontier stewed; citizens and Rangers and soldiers joined into a pursuit to follow the party and its big herd of horses (500 or 600 by the time they left the settlements) to the Comanche winter villages in the northwest. Charles Goodnight was along, and Sul Ross, and Captain Jack Cureton, and nearly everybody else, and most of them left accounts of it which flatly conflict. What is sure is that they found Comanches on the Pease, and smote them hip and thigh, man and woman and child, and took back Mrs. Sherman's Bible and a blue-eyed, sullen squaw who turned out to be Cynthia Ann Parker, kidnapped twenty-four years previously on the Navasota. Her Uncle Isaac (Parker County is named for him, and he died there) journeyed up to Camp Cooper to identify her when the expedition returned. She lived for four captive years among relatives, scarcely ever breaking silence except to beg brokenly that they let her go back to her husband and her children and the free, dirty, shifting life of the plains. Since of course they wouldn't, she died in the damp windless forests of East Texas. But Peta Nocona had sired a son on her, Quanah, who was to be one of the great chiefs in the last years of the fighting, and who survived to wear black suits on visits to Fort Worth and to be friends with Theodore Roosevelt.

(That story trails on: Theodore Roosevelt gave Quanah land in perpetuity in Oklahoma, pretty land along Cache

Creek, and just last year—perpetuity, as is its wont with Indians, having expired—his children and grandchildren and the last of his wives came protestingly into the news again when the Field Artillery had the place condemned and grabbed it.)

Maybe the redheaded Comanche had been another one like Cynthia Ann, or maybe like Quanah the half-white son of another woman captured long before. The bag of fragmentary, jumbled, contradictory tales left over from the frontier is lumpy with mysteries like that, and no one will ever solve them now. The reason Cynthia Ann's story is famous, besides her relation to Quanah, is that it came to the surface again, and had an end, whereas most of the others didn't. Captive children, renegades white and black, Mexicans by the hundreds—The People weren't exclusive in terms of race. They'd been winners for too long to be a pure blood, anyhow; women go to winners. They were a spirit, another on the roster of the world's proud savages who had to win totally or lose totally, like Zulus and Araucanians and Moros and Pathans and Fuzzy-Wuzzies. All colonial and imperial histories are smoky with their fighting. There's more pathos in the defeat of gentle and reasonable peoples, but the fall of pride strikes more sparks.

If the river has meaning for you, you can see all of that from the sandstone bluffs where the mountains drop away. You don't have to strain to impose the tales on the landscape; they're there. . . . Margaret Barton at Brannon's Crossing with an arrow next to her heart which they were afraid to pull out, throbbing in the air with her blood beat, all night long . . . Bill Youngblood, whose cohorts gave chase and killed the Indian who had his scalp, and galloped to the graveyard just in time to put it back on his head—

their literal, Calvinistic application of the doctrine of cor-
poreal resurrection agreeing with the Comanches that it was
bad to go to your earthly resting place in more than one
piece, or for that matter less . . . Dignified Mr. Couts,
later the big man at Weatherford, who ranched in the early
days opposite Palo Pinto mouth and refused to take guff
from the four hairiest white bully-boys in the neighborhood;
they waited for him with shotguns between the spring and
the church door at Soda Springs one Sunday morning, and,
knowing them there, he walked on into them with a bucket
of cool water in his hand and a Colt's Navy in his waistband. When they opened fire, he got the first one through
the heart, the second one through the trigger hand and then
the shoulder, and the third in the hip. ("The reason I didn't
kill him as he went in at the door," he told Mr. Holland
analytically later, "was that he jumped up about two feet
getting in and I hit him that much below where I aimed.")
The fourth, comprehensibly spooked, piled his horse into a
ditch and smashed up his face and shoulder. Mr. Couts
counted the bullet holes in his hat and his black silk vest,
and the neighborhood was reasonably lawful for a time after
that. . . . In '66 he drove 1,000 longhorns to California,
rode back alone across the plains and down the Platte to the
Missouri with $50,000 in gold in his saddlebags, caught a
boat south, and opened a bank.

Most of those stories are recorded, though only a few are
recorded well. In what scholars call "primary sources"—
pioneers' memoirs and little county histories with a gen-
ealogical slant—they're likely to be a bit prejudiced and
fragmentary, with the choicest details left out either from
delicacy or because cowards and scoundrels have descendants. In the Texas brag-books and their ilk, a teeming spe-

cies, they're most often contorted beyond recognition. Only in the work of a few people who for the past score or so of years have been trying, literately and otherwise, to see shape in the too turbulent century behind us, do they come out straight—or fairly straight, since the old folks those historians talked to had written nothing down when things were popping, and only spoke of them later when memory was playing its dirty tricks.

There is consequently a mistiness. . . . Take Andrew Berry. The People caught him down the river a way from the Point with a wagonload of pumpkins, and after killing him scalped him and broke the pumpkins over his bloody skull. But one version of the story has him killed just below Lazy Bend, and another far down by Spring Creek, and a third, more dramatic but just as likely to be true, has two little redheaded sons along with him who were scalped and crowned with pumpkins, too.

The fact is, the stories have been retreating into fog for a long time, as maybe they should. Boosters in compulsory beards stage centennials in the little towns and resurrect the old bloodshed in pamphlets and festivals, and have high times dunking one another in reconstructed horse troughs. Some towns maintain annual pageants, and museums. But the significances are transmuted there, more often than not, by what Hollywood and television and the *Post* and who-not have said the general West was like, and by the Texas paranoia (petroleum and carved belts and bourbon and country clubs and nickeled six-guns and aircraft factories and the excessive regional glee of the newly arrived: mingle them with the old leathery thing if you can), so that the rough-edged realities of the past have faded dimmer each year.

Probably a man from that bump of the country who has

soaked the tales in runs a danger of overappraising their worth. In kind, they don't differ sharply from the lore most regions west of the Mississippi can muster. In weight—in, say, the number of people killed or the human glory or shame manifested in their slaughter—they're dustmote-sized when you compare them to the violences two wars in two generations have wrought among our race. I once saw 4,000 Japanese stacked like cordwood, the harvest of two days' fighting, on one single islet of one single atoll awaiting bulldozer burial, more dead than the Brazos country could show for its whole two or three decades of travail, and just as brave. Almost daily for years, Belsen or Dachau could have matched the flavor of Mrs. Sherman's agony. . . .

What it amounts to is that a short segment of the American frontier, distinctive in its way but not as distinctive as a local might be tempted to think, paused in the Brazos country, crackled and smoked for a few years like fire in underbrush while the Indians were being fought out of existence and the cattle were being harried north, and then moved on, carrying most of the vigorous frontiersmen with it.

Nothing that happened in this segment, then or later, made any notable dent in human history. From one very possible point of view, the stories tell of a partly unnecessary, drawn-out squabble between savages and half-illiterate louts constituting the fringes of a culture which, two and a half centuries before, had spawned Shakespeare, and which even then was reading Dickens and Trollope and Thoreau and considering the thoughts of Charles Darwin. They tell too —the stories—of the subsequent squabbles among the louts themselves: of cattle thievery, corn whisky, Reconstruction, blood feuds, lynchings, splinter sectarianism, and further illiteracy.

Can they then have any bearing on mankind's adventure? Maybe, a little. They don't all tell of louts. There was something of a showing-through; meanings floated near the surface which have relevance to the murkier thing Americans have become. It didn't happen just on the Brazos, certainly, but all along the line of that moving brush fire. There's nothing new in the idea that the frontier had continuing impact on our character, or that one slice of that frontier, examined, may to some degree explain the whole. . . .

But in truth such gravities were not what salted the tales I could read, looking off over the low country from the point atop the bluffs. Mankind is one thing; a man's self is another. What that self is tangles itself knottily with what his people were, and what they came out of. Mine came out of Texas, as did I. If those were louts, they were my own louts.

Origin being as it is an accident outside the scope of one's will, I tend not to seek much credit for being a Texan. Often (breathes there a man?) I can work up some proud warmth about the fact that I indubitably am one. A lot of the time, though, I'd as soon be forty other kinds of men I've known. I've lived much away from that region, and have liked most of the places I've lived in. I used to know who the good bullfighters were and why they were good. I'm familiar with the washed silent streets of Manhattan at five o'clock in the morning, and what Los Angeles promises in the evening when you're young with money on your hip, and once almost saw the rats change sewers swarmingly in Paris, and did see dawn wash the top of the old wall at Avila. . . . I've waked in the green freshness of mountain mornings in tropical lands, and have heard the strange birds cry, and the street venders, and maybe music somewhere, and have felt the hit of it like a fist in my stomach, going sleepy-eyed out onto a balcony under the green mountains and above flame-flower trees to thank God for life and for being there. And I'm glad I have.

If a man couldn't escape what he came from, we would most of us still be peasants in Old World hovels. But if, having escaped or not, he wants in some way to know himself, define himself, and tries to do it without taking into account the thing he came from, he is writing without any ink in his pen. The provincial who cultivates only his roots is in peril, potato-like, of becoming more root than plant. The man who cuts his roots away and denies that they were ever connected with him withers into half a man. . . . It's not necessary to like being a Texan, or a Midwesterner, or a Jew, or an Andalusian, or a Negro, or a hybrid child of the international rich. It is, I think, necessary to know in that crystal chamber of the mind where one speaks straight to oneself that one is or was that thing, and for any under-standing of the human condition it's probably necessary to know a little about what the thing consists of.

And Mrs. Sherman and Bigfoot Wallace and Charlie Goodnight and Old Lady Rippy and the rest of them, haunting the country they'd known below the Point, were a part of my thing. They weren't all of it, but they were a part. In mere fact, they were. Much of the good and bad and beside-the-point of what they'd been was stuck in me as certainly as the canyon wren's song, as surely as were the memories, looking down toward Brazos town, of the times we'd misread the wild zigzagging channel in those sandy stretches and had ended on bars and had had to get out to tug the loaded boat over, up to our knees in shaking, sucking quicksand. That it all meant much was doubtful, and that I'd ever understand a half of what it did mean was more doubtful still, but the effort seemed worth while.

Such, as Port Smythe, M. D., might have written if he hadn't been too tired for climbing when he got there, were the Conflicting Sentiments with which my Bosom was inspired as I gazed out from that Noble Eminence.

I inched and skidded back down the bluff, tossed my gear and my dog into the aged Old Town, and took off paddling down the river toward the T. & P. bridge. . . .

PART TWO

CHAPTER TEN

*⌇ I should not talk so much about myself if
there were anybody else whom I knew as well.*
Walden

THERE was an island, long and slim, built up of the varie-
gated Brazos chert gravel, which, when wet and shining,
looks like the jewels in a storybook treasure chest. Its top
was padded with white sand and bordered by big willows
and small cottonwoods. Toward the blunt upper end, where
spring's drouth-breaking floods had worked to most effect,
lay a bare-swept sandy plain, and the few trees along the
shoreline there were bent downstream at steep angles.
Against stubs and stumps down the length of the island the
same force had laid up tangled jams of driftwood—ash and
cedar elm and oak, good fuel. Here and there where silt had
accumulated, Bermuda grass or weeds bristled in patches.

Because I liked the look of it, I stopped there in the middle of a quiet bright afternoon and made a solid camp on
flat gravel under willows, eight feet above the water but only
a few nearly vertical steps from the canoe. I was tired and
my gear needed tending, and it looked like the kind of place
I'd been waiting for to spend a couple of nights and to loaf
through a little of what the abstractly alliterative military
schedules used to call "matériel maintenance." Islands are
special, anyhow, as children know with a leaping instinct,

and when they lie in public domain you can have a fine sense of temporary ownership about them that's hard to get on shores, inside or outside of fences.

By the time I'd finished setting up and hauling my chattels from the canoe—all of them, since they all needed cleaning or fixing—it was nearly evening. The stronger of the channels flanking the island ran on the side where I was camped; I walked up the narrow beach and put out a catfish line just below where the water dropped out of a rapids, tying a rock to the line's end and throwing it straight out so that when the line came taut the rock dropped gurgling and anchored the line in a long bow across the head of the deep run, back to a willow stub beside me. Trotlines from shore to shore get you more fish and bigger ones, but they're also more labor. After I'd finished with the line I worked along the beach, spin-casting bootlessly for bass. Four Canada geese came diagonally over the river, low, calling, and in a moment I heard a clamor at the head of the island, shielded from me by the island's duned fringe and by willows. I climbed up through them to look. At least 200 more honkers took off screaming from the sand bar at the upper end of the bare plain. The passenger ran barking after them. Calling him back, I squatted beside a drift pile, and in the rose half-light of dusk watched through the field glass as they came wheeling in again, timid but liking the place as I had liked it, and settled by tens and twenties at the bar and in the shallows above it where the two channels split.

Nine skeptics, maybe the ones that had seen me at first and raised the alarm, circled complaining for a time before they flew on elsewhere. Black against water that held the west's reflected red, the others stalked about till their alertness had softened, then began to drink and cavort, lunging at one another, leaping into the air with their wings spread and circling two by two in a kind of dance.

Old John Magnificence was with me:

> *What call'st thou solitude, is not the Earth*
> *With various living creatures, and the Aire*
> *Replenisht, and all these at thy command*
> *To come and play before thee?* . . .

He was. I used to be suspicious of the kind of writing where characters are smitten by correct quotations at appropriate moments. I still am, but not as much. Things do pop out clearly in your head, alone, when the upper layers of your mind are unmisted by much talk with other men. Odd bits and scraps and thoughts and phrases from all your life and all your reading keep boiling up to view like grains of rice in a pot on the fire. Sometimes they even make sense. . . .

I thought of the shotgun at my camp a hundred yards below, but it would have been useless if I'd had it; they were a long way from any cover. And for that matter there was about them something of the feel that the bald eagle had had for me in the mountain country. I'd been a hunter most of my life, except for two or three years after the war. Young, I'd made two-hour crawls on my belly through standing swamp water for the mere hope of a shot at a goose, nearly always frustrated. Just now, though, it seemed to matter little that these were safe out of range. Watching the red-and-black shadow show of their awkward powerful play was enough, and listening to their occasional arrogant horn shouts. I squatted there watching until nearly dark, then backed down quietly to the beach and went to camp.

Supper was a young squirrel who had nevertheless

achieved an elder's stringiness, roasted in foil on the embers, and a potato baked in the same way. I'd been going lazy on the cooking lately, mostly because I had little appetite, and that little most generally for things I'd have disliked in town —bouillon, or coffee thickly sweet with honey, or the stewed mixed fruit that made my breakfasts. From such sparse eating and from exercise I'd lost weight—maybe twelve or fifteen pounds since Possum Kingdom, to judge from the slack in my waistband. I ate the potato and chewed a little on the squirrel and gave the rest of it to the pup.

Hearing the geese honk still from time to time, I knew it would have been easy enough, on that moonless night, to ease up the defiladed beach near them and sneak across the sand on my stomach for a sniping shot. All it would take was patience. But I was years past being tempted by that kind of dirtiness; the contradictory set of rules that one works out for killing, if he keeps on killing past a certain age, usually makes an unreasonable distinction between ways that are honorable and ways that aren't, and for me night pot shots weren't. . . . And I didn't think I needed anything as big as a goose.

Someone else's rules were less strict, or maybe his need was greater; when I'd put a couple of heavy chunks of elm on the fire and sat watching them, sniffing the faintly urinal sharpness of their burning, two rapid shots sounded far off down the river and a minute later geese were calling confusedly in the sky. Stacked alongside my own abstention it angered me a little, but on the other hand it was none of my right business.

From brief yards away, in a cottonwood, a barred owl cut loose with flourishes: *Who, who, whoo, whoo, whah, whah, hah, HAH, HAH, WHO ALL!*

Then, an afterthought, he said: YOU ALL!

Certain it meant specifically him, the passenger barked back once almost under his breath, growled a little with an angry ridge of short hair dark along his spine, and sought my lap.

~~~~~~~~~~~

ELM STINKS, wherefore literal farmers give it a grosser name, but it makes fine lasting coals. That morning I was up before dawn to blow away the ashes from the orange-velvet embers underneath, and to build more fire on them with twigs and leaves and brittle sticks of dead cottonwood. I huddled over it in the cold, still, graying darkness and watched coffee water seethe at the edges of a little charred pot licked by flame, and heard the horned owl stop that deceptively gentle five-noted comment he casts on the night. The geese at the island's head began to talk among themselves, then to call as they rose to go to pastures and peanut fields, and night-flushed bobwhites started whistling *where-you? where-you?* to one another somewhere above the steep dirt river bank. Drinking coffee with honey in it and canned milk, smoking a pipe that had the sweetness pipes only have in cold quiet air, I felt good if a little scratchy-eyed, having gone to sleep the night before struck with the romance of stars and firelight, with the flaps open and only the blanket over me, to wake at two thirty chilled through.

On top of the food box alligator-skin corrugations of frost had formed, and with the first touch of the sun the willows began to whisper as frozen leaves loosed their hold and fell side-slipping down through the others that were still green. Titmice called, and flickers and a redbird, and for a moment, on a twig four feet from my face, a chittering kinglet jumped around alternately hiding and flashing the scarlet of its crown. . . . I sat and listened and watched while the world woke up, and drank three cups of the syrupy coffee, better I thought than any I'd ever tasted, and smoked two pipes.

You run a risk of thinking yourself an ascetic when you enjoy, with that intensity, the austere facts of fire and coffee and tobacco and the sound and feel of country places. You aren't, though. In a way you're more of a sensualist than a fat man washing down sauerbraten and dumplings with heavy beer while a German band plays and a plump blonde kneads his thigh. . . . You've shucked off the gross delights, and those you have left are few, sharp, and strong. But they're sensory. Even Thoreau, if I remember right a passage or so on his cornbread, was guilty, though mainly he was a real ascetic.

Real ones shouldn't care. They ought to be able to live on pâté and sweet peaches and roast suckling pig or alternatively on cheese and garlic in a windmill or the scraps that housewives have thrown in begging bowls. Groceries and shelter should matter only as fuel and frame for life, and life as energy for thought or beyond-communion or (Old Man Goodnight has to fit somewhere, and a fraught executive or two I've known, and maybe Davis Birdsong hurling his bulldozer against the tough cedar brush in a torn shirt and denim pants, coughing yellow flu sputum while the December rain pelts him, not caring) for action.

But I hadn't set up as an ascetic, anyhow. I sat for a long time savoring the privilege of being there, and didn't overlay the taste of the coffee with any other food. A big red-brown butterfly sat spread on the cottonwood log my ax was stuck in, warming itself in the sun. I watched until it flew stiffly away, then got up and followed, for no good reason except that the time seemed to have come to stir and I wanted a closer look at the island than I'd gotten the evening before.

It was shaped like an attenuated teardrop or the cross section of an airplane's wing, maybe three quarters of a mile long and 100 yards or so wide at its upper, thicker end. Its foundation everywhere appeared to be a heavy deposit of the multicolored gravel, and its flat top except for a few high dunes of the padding sand was eight or ten feet above the present level of the river. All around, it dropped off steeply, in spots directly to the water, in others to beaches, and toward the pointed tail the willows and weeds stood rank. I rooted about there and found nothing but coon tracks and a few birds still sleepy and cold on their roosts, but, emerging among cockleburs above a beach by the other channel, scared four ducks off a quiet eddy. I'd left the gun in the tent; shots from here and there under the wide sky's bowl reminded me that busier hunters than I were finding game.

Let them. I considered that maybe in the evening I'd crouch under a bush at the island's upper end and put out sheets of notepaper on the off chance that more geese would come, and the off-off chance that if they did they'd feel brotherly toward notepaper. You can interest them sometimes in newspapers.

And maybe I wouldn't.

The shores on either side of the river from the island were dirt and steep, twenty feet high, surmounted by pecans and oaks with the bare sky of fields or pastures beyond. They seemed separate from the island; it was big enough, with a strong enough channel on either side, to seem to have a kind of being of its own distinct from that of the banks—a sand and willow and cottonwood and driftwood biome—though in dry times doubtless there would be only one channel and no island, but just a great bar spreading out below the right bank.

Jays, killdeers, wrens, cardinals, woodpeckers . . . With minute and amateurish interest, I found atop a scoop in the base of a big, drifted, scorched tree trunk five little piles of fox dung, a big owl's puke ball full of hair and rat skulls, and three fresher piles of what had to be coon droppings, brown and small, shaped like a dog's or a human's.

Why, intrigued ignorance asked, did wild things so often choose to stool on rocks, stumps, and other elevations?

Commonsense replied: Maybe for the view.

On the flat beach at the head of the island the night's geese had laid down a texture of crisscrossed toe-prints. Elsewhere, in dry sand, I found little pointed diggings an inch in diameter and four to five inches deep, much like those an armadillo makes in grassland but with no tracks beside them. A bird? A land-foraging crawfish? Another puzzle for my ignorance, underlined now by the clear note of the unknown sad-whistling bird from a willow a few steps from me. He wouldn't show himself, and when I eased closer said irascibly: *Heap, heap!* and fluttered out the other side. . . .

The trouble was, I *was* ignorant. Even in that country where I belonged, my ken of natural things didn't include a little bird that went *heap-heap* and

— — —, — — —,

and a few moronic holes in the sand. Or a million other matters worth the kenning.

I grew up in a city near there—more or less a city, anynow,

a kind of spreading imposition on the prairies—that was
waked from a dozing cow-town background by a standard
boom after the First World War and is still, civic-souled
friends tell me, bowling right along. It was a good enough
place, not too big then, and a mile or so away from where
I lived, along a few side streets and across a boulevard and
a golf course, lay woods and pastures and a blessed river
valley where the stagnant Trinity writhed beneath big oaks.
In retrospect, it seems we spent more time there than we
did on pavements, though maybe it's merely that remembrance of that part is sharper. There were rabbits and squirrels to hunt, and doves and quail and armadillos and foxes
and skunks. A few deer ran the woods, and one year, during
a drouth to the west, big wolves. Now it's mostly subdivi-
sions, and even then it lay fallow because it was someone's
real-estate investment. The fact that caretakers were likely
to converge on us blaspheming at the sound of a shot or
a shout, scattering us to brush, only made the hunting and
the fishing a bit saltier. I knew one fellow who kept a permanent camp there in a sumac thicket, with a log squat-
down hut and a fireplace and all kinds of food and utensils
hidden in tin-lined holes in the ground, and none of the caretakers ever found it. Probably they worried less than we
thought; there weren't many of us.

I had the Brazos, too, and South Texas, where relatives
lived, and my adults for the most part were good people who
took me along on country expeditions when they could. In
terms of the outdoors, I and the others like me weren't badly
cheated as such cheatings go nowadays, but we were
cheated nevertheless. We learned quite a lot, but not enough.
Instead of learning to move into country, as I think underneath we wanted, we learned mostly how to move onto it

in the old crass Anglo-Saxon way, in search of edible or sometimes just mortal quarry. We did a lot of killing, as kids will, and without ever being told that it was our flat duty, if duty exists, to know all there was to know about the creatures we killed.

Hunting and fishing are the old old entry points into nature for men, and not bad ones either, but as standardly practiced these days, for the climactic ejaculation of city tensions, they don't go very deep. They aren't thoughtful; they hold themselves too straitly to their purpose. Even for my quail-hunting uncles in South Texas, good men, good friends to me, all smaller birds of hedge and grass were "chee-chees," vermin, confusers of dogs' noses. . . . And if, with kids' instinctive thrustingness, we picked up a store of knowledge about small things that lived under logs and how the oriole builds its nest, there was no one around to consolidate it for us. Our knowledge, if considerable, remained random.

This age, of course, is unlikely to start breeding people who have the organic kinship to nature that the Comanches had, or even someone like Mr. Charlie Goodnight. For them every bush, every bird's cheep, every cloud bank had not only utilitarian but mystical meaning; it was all an extension of their sensory systems, an antenna as rawly receptive as a snail's. Even if their natural world still existed, which it doesn't, you'd have to snub the whole world of present men to get into it that way.

Nor does it help to be born in the country. As often as not these days, countrymen know as little as we others do about those things. They come principally of the old hard-headed tradition that moved onto the country instead of into it. For every Charles Goodnight there were several dozen Ezra Shermans, a disproportion that has bred itself down through the generations. Your standard country lore about animals—about the nasal love life of the possum, or the fabled hoop snake—is picturesque rather than accurate, anthropocentric rather than understanding.

But Charlie Goodnight and the Ezra Shermans and their children and grandchildren all combined have burned out and chopped out and plowed out and grazed out and killed out a good part of that natural world they knew, or didn't know, and we occupy ourselves mainly, it sometimes seems, in finishing the job. The rosy preindustrial time is past when the humanism of a man like Thoreau (*was* it humanism?) could still theorize in terms of natural harmony. Humanism has to speak in the terms of extant human beings. The terms of today's human beings are air conditioners and suburbs and water impoundments overlaying whole countrysides, and the hell with nature except maybe in a cross-sectional park here and there. In our time quietness and sun and leaves and bird song and all the multitudinous lore of the natural world have to come second or third, because whether we wanted to be born there or not, we were all born into the prickly machine-humming place that man has hung for himself above that natural world.

Where, tell me, is the terror and wonder of an elephant, now that they can be studied placid in every zoo, and any office-dwelling sport with a recent lucky break on the market can buy himself one to shoot through telescopic sights with a cartridge whose ballistics hold a good fileful of recorded science's findings? With a box gushing refrigerated air (or warmed, seasonally depending) into a sealed house and another box flashing loud bright images into jaded heads, who gives a rat's damn for things that go bump in the night? With possible death by blast or radiation staring at us like a buzzard, why should we sweat ourselves over where the Eskimo curlew went?

The wonder is that a few people do still sweat themselves, that the tracks of short varmints on a beach still have an audience. A few among the audience still know something, too. If they didn't, one wouldn't have to feel so cheated, not knowing as much. . . . Really knowing, I mean—from childhood up and continuously, with all of it a flavor in you . . . Not just being able to make a little seem a lot; there is enough of that around. I can give you as much book data about the home life of the yellow-breasted chat as the next man can. Nor do I mean vague mystic feelings of unity with Comanche and Neanderthal as one wanders the depleted land, gun at the ready, a part of the long flow of man's hunting compulsion. I mean *knowing*.

So that what one does in time, arriving a bit late at an awareness of the swindling he got—from no one, from the times—is to make up the shortage as best he may, to try to tie it all together for himself by reading and adult poking. But adult poking is never worth a quarter as much as kid poking, not in those real terms. There's never the time for that whole interest later, or ever quite the pure and subcutaneous receptiveness, either.

I mean, too—obviously—if you care. I know that the whicker of a plover in the September sky doesn't touch all other men in their bowels as it touches me, and that men whom it doesn't touch at all can be good .men. But it touches me. And I care about knowing what it is, and—if I can—why.

Disgruntled from caring, I went to run my throwline. Coons' fresh tracks along the beach overlaid my own of

the evening before; one had played with the end of the line
and had rolled the jar of blood bait around on the sand trying to get inside it. The passenger followed some of the
tracks into a drift tangle but lost interest, not knowing what
he was trailing, robbed by long generations of show-breed-
ing of the push that would have made him care. . . . In
my fingers the line tugged with more than the pulse of the
current, but when I started softly hand-over-handing it in,
it gave a couple of stiff jerks and went slacker, and I knew
that something on it in a final frenzy had finished the job
of twisting loose. They roll and roll and roll, and despite
swivels at last work the staging into a tight snarl against
whose solidity they can tear themselves free. Whatever it
had been, channel or yellow or blue, it had left a chunk of
its lip on the second hook, and two hooks beyond that was
a one-pounder which I removed, respectful toward the sharp
septic fin spines.

In the old days we'd taken the better ones before they
rolled loose by running the lines every hour or so during the
night, a sleepless process and in summer a mosquito-chewed
one. Once in Hood County, Hale and I and black Bill Briggs
had gotten a twenty-five-pounder, and after an argument with
Bill, who wanted to try to eat it, we sold it to a bridge-side
café for a dime a pound. Another time on the Guadalupe
to the south—but this is supposed to be about the
Brazos. . . .

Tethering the little catfish to the chain stringer by the
canoe, I got a rod and went down to the sharp tail of the
island to cast a plug into green deep eddies I'd seen there
while exploring. Without wind, the sun was almost hot now.
From a willow a jay resented me with a two-note muted rasp
like a boy blowing in and out on a harmonica with stuck

reeds, and in an almost bare tree on the high river bank a flock of bobolinks fed and bubbled and called, resting on their way south.

Cast and retrieve, shallow and deep, across current and down and up, and no sign of bass . . . The sun's laziness got into me and I wandered up the lesser channel, casting only occasionally into holes without the expectation of fish. Then, on a long flow-dimpled bar, something came down over my consciousness like black pain, and I dropped the rod and squatted, shaking my head to drive the blackness back. It receded a little. I waddled without rising to the bar's edge and scooped cold water over my head. After four or five big throbs it went away, and I sat down half in the water and thought about it. It didn't take much study. My stomach was giving a lecture about it, loud. What it amounted to was that I was about half starved.

I picked up the rod, went back to camp, stirred the fire, and put on a pot of water into which I dumped enough dried lima beans for four men, salt, an onion, and a big chunk of bacon. Considering, I went down to the stringer and skinned and gutted the little catfish and carried him up and threw him in the pot, too. While it boiled, I bathed in the river, frigid in contrast to the air, sloshed out the canoe and sponged it down, and washed underclothes and socks. In shorts, feeling fine now but so hungry it hurt, I sat by the fire and sharpened knives and the ax for the additional hour the beans needed to cook soft in the middle. Fishing out the skeleton of the disintegrated catfish, and using the biggest spoon I had, I ate the whole mess from the pot almost without stopping, and mopped up its juices with cold biscuit bread.

Then I wiped my chin and lay back against the cotton-

wood log with my elbows hanging over it behind and my
toes digging into the sand, and considered that asceticism,
most certainly, was for those who were built for it. Some
were. Some weren't. I hadn't seen God in the black head-
ache on the sand bar and I didn't want to try to any more,
that way. . . . Starving myself hadn't had much to do with
spirituality, anyhow, but only with the absence of company.

Philosophically equilibrated, I rolled down into the sand
and went to sleep for two or three hours, waking into a
perfect blue-and-yellow afternoon loud with the full-throat
chant of the redbird.

Wood . . . I went roaming with the honed ax among
the piles of drift, searching out solid timber. Bleached and
unbarked as much of it is, you have a hard time seeing what
it may be, but a two-lick notch with the ax usually bares its
grain enough to name it. Cottonwood and willow slice soft
and white before the first blow, and unless you're hard up
you move on to try your luck on another piece; they're not
serious fuel:

The fire devoureth both the ends of it, and the midst of it is
burnt. Is it meet for any work?

But the river is prodigal of its trees, and better stuff is usually near.

If food is to sit in the fire's smoke as it cooks, any of the
elms will give it a bad taste, though they last and give good
heat. Cedar's oil eats up its wood in no time, and stinks food,
too, but the tinge of it on the air after supper is worth smell-
ing if you want to cut a stick or so of it just for that. Rock-
hard bodark—Osage orange if you want; bois d'arc if you're
etymological—sears a savory crust on meat and burns a

long time, if you don't mind losing a flake out of your ax's edge when you hit it wrong. For that matter, not much of it grows close enough to the river to become drift. Nor does much mesquite—a pasture tree and the only thing a conscientious Mexican cook will barbecue kid over. Ash is all right but, as dry drift anyhow, burns fast. The white oaks are prime, the red oaks less so, and one of the finest of aromatic fuels is a twisted, wave-grained branch of live oak, common in the limestone country farther down the river.

Maybe, though, the nutwoods are best and sweetest, kind to food and long in their burning. In the third tangle I nicked a huge branch of walnut, purple-brown an inch inside its sapwood's whitened skin. It rots slowly; this piece was sound enough for furniture making—straight-grained enough, too, for that matter. I chopped it into long pieces. The swing and the chocking bite of the ax were pleasant; the pup chased chips as they flew, and I kept cutting until I had twice as many billets as I would need. Then I stacked them for later hauling and went to camp to use up the afternoon puttering with broken tent loops and ripped tarps and sprung hinges on boxes, throwing sticks for the passenger, looking in a book for the differences among small streaked finches, airing my bed, sweeping with a willow branch the sandy gravel all through a camp I'd leave the next day. . . .

I lack much zeal for camping, these years. I can still read old Kephart with pleasure: nearly half a century later hardly anyone else has come anywhere near him for information and good sense. But there's detachment in my pleasure now. I no longer see myself choosing a shingle tree and felling it and splitting out the shakes for my own roof, though if I did want to he would tell me how. . . . Nor have I passion for canoeing, as such; both it and the camping are just ways to get somewhere I want to be, and to stay there for a time. I can't describe the cross-bow rudder stroke or stay serene in crashing rapids. I carry unconcentrated food in uncompact boxes. I forget to grease my boots and suffer from clammy feet. I slight hygiene, and will finger a boiled minnow from the coffee with equanimity, and sleep with my dog. My tent in comparison to the aluminum-framed, tight-snapping ones available is a ragged parallelogrammatic disaster.

Nevertheless, when camping for a time is the way of one's life, one tries to improve his style. One resolves on changes for future trips—a tiny and exactly fitted cook box; a contour-cut tarp over the canoe hooking to catches beneath the gunwales; no peaches in the mixed dried fruit. . . . One experiments and invents, and ends up, for instance, with a perfect aluminum-foil reflector for baking that agreeable, lumpy, biscuit-mixed bread that the Mexicans call *"pan ranchero"* and the northwoods writers "bannock" and other people undoubtedly other names.

One way or the other, it all generally turns out to be work. Late that afternoon, carrying abrasive armloads of the walnut from where I'd chopped it to camp, I got as though from the air the answer to a question that used to come into my mind in libraries, reading about the old ones and the Indians. I used to wonder why, knowing Indians were around, the old ones would let themselves be surprised so often and so easily. Nearly all the ancient massacres resulted from such surprise.

The answer, simple on the island, was that the old ones were laboring their tails off at the manifold tasks of the primitive life, hewing and hauling and planting and plowing and breaking and fixing. They didn't have time to be wary. Piped water and steam heat and tractors might have let them be alert, just as I'd been among the stacked tomes of the Southwest Collection.

It was a good day, work and all. At evening I sat astraddle the bow of the canoe on the beach, putting new line on the spinning reel, when three big honkers came flying up the river slowly, low searchers like the first ones of the evening before. The gun was at hand. Even though they veered, separating, as I reached for it, they still passed close, and it needed only a three-foot lead on the front one's head to bring him splashing solidly, relaxed, dead, into the channel. I trotted downstream abreast of him as he drifted and finally teased him ashore with a long crooked piece of cottonwood.

Till then I'd had the visceral bite of the old excitement in me, the gladness of clean shooting, the fulfillment of quarry sought and taken. But when I got him ashore and hefted the warm, handsome eight or nine pounds of him, and ran my fingers against the grain up through the hot thick down of his neck, the just-as-old balancing regret came into it. A goose is a lot of bird to kill. Maybe size shouldn't matter, but it seems to. With something that big and that trimly perfect and, somehow, that meaningful, you wonder about the right of the thing. . . .

For a while after the war I did no shooting at all, and thought I probably wouldn't do any more. I even chiseled out a little niche for that idea, half Hindu and tangled with the kind of reverence for life that Schweitzer preaches. But then one day in fall beside a stock tank in a mesquite pasture a friend wanted me to try the heft of a little engraved L. C. Smith, and when I'd finished trying it I'd dropped ten doves with sixteen shots and the niche didn't exist any longer.

Reverence for life in that sense seems to me to be like asceticism or celibacy: you need to be built for it. I no longer kill anything inedible that doesn't threaten me or mine, and I never cared anything about big-game hunting. Possibly I'll give up shooting again and for good one of these years, but I believe the killing itself can be reverent. To see and kill and pluck and gut and cook and eat a wild creature, all with some knowledge and the pleasure that knowledge gives, implies a closeness to the creature that is to me more honorable than the candle-lit consumption of rare prime steaks from a steer bludgeoned to death in a packing-house chute while tranquilizers course his veins. And if there's a difference in nobility between a Canada goose and a fat white-faced ox (there is), how does one work out the quantities?

Though I threw the skin and head and guts into the river to keep them away from the pup, an eddy drifted them into shore and he found them and ate a good bit before I caught him at it. The two big slabs of breast hissed beautifully in foil on the fire after dark. When they were done I hung them up for a time uncovered in the sweet walnut smoke and then ate nearly all of one of them. The other would make sandwiches at noon for two or three days, tucked inside chunks of biscuit bread. Despite his harsh appetizers, the passenger gobbled the drumsticks and organs I'd half roasted for him, and when I unrolled the sleeping bag inside the tent he fought to be first into it.

Later, in half-sleep, I heard a rattle of dirty metal dishes beside the fire. I shot the flashlight's beam out there and a sage, masked face stared at me, indignant. Foreseeing sport, I hauled the pup up for a look. He blinked, warm and full, and dug in his toes against ejection into the cold air, and when I let him go he burrowed all the way down beside my feet, not a practical dog and not ashamed of it, either. The coon went away.

Later still, the goosefeathers began their emetic work and I woke to the rhythmic *wump, wump, wump* that in dogs precedes a heave. Though the account of it may lack wide interest, later it seemed to me that there had been heroic co-ordination in the way I came out of sleep and grabbed him, holding his jaws shut with one hand while I fought to find the bag's zipper with the other, then fought to find and loose the zipper of the tent, too, and hurled him out into the night by his nose. He stayed there for a while, and when I was sure he'd finished I let him back in, low-eared and shivering, but I preferred his unhappiness to what might have been.

It came to me then who it was that had slept with a dog for his health. Leopold Bloom's father. The dog's name had been . . . Athos! Old Man Bloom had slept with Athos to cure his aches and pains.

One can get pretty literary on islands.

~~~~~~~~~~~~~~~~~~~~~~~~~~~~~

CHAPTER ELEVEN

> ↝§ Mar. *Marry, sir, sometimes he is a*
> *kind of Puritan.*
> And. *O, if I thought that, I'd beat*
> *him like a dog!*

~~~~~~~~~~~~~~~~~~~~~~~~~~~~~

THERE was an old man, too. He lived beside the river in Parker County, and my Weatherford friend had told me to look out for him, that he knew things. I scudded down there one afternoon before a bleak, damp, cutting norther, past shores with a farming-country sameness in their look. Willows and sand and cottonwoods, and at a fence line before a field, dead limb tangles shrouded in grapevines . . . Lost fishlines were looped around branches above the water; old refrigerators and washtubs and barbed-wire reels cluttered the bars.

At about the place where I guessed from my friend's description that the old man ought to live, I parked the canoe and tied it, and with the pup climbed up through bright-leaved hardwoods to a pasture. Across its fence and a dirt road stood a neat, white, new cottage with no grass or shrubs, square-surrounded by a tight hog-wire fence. Fifty yards behind it was a double hewn-log cabin, boarded on the ends, in what looked to be good condition, with a galvanized roof and winter-bare rosebushes against its walls. White Leghorns scratched to leeward of a part-log barn, and a pair of milk cows stood waiting.

At the gate I stopped, and under the wind's cut yelled: "Hello, the house!"—formula in that country, where you don't barge into yards or bang on doors until you've used up remoter salutations and seen if there are any big dogs.

Nobody answered. I tried again, and someone shouted from behind me. I turned to see a man a couple of hundred yards away at a crossroads by the pasture's corner, driving a calf toward me. I walked to meet him, the pup swaggering feistily ahead and then gradually falling back before the strangeness of the calf, a six- or eight-month-old bull, black and scrub in shape, that stopped and shook its head and pawed the earth a time or two as the gap between us narrowed.

The man, tiny and wizened and old in bib overalls, whanged him with a stick and said to me as though in greeting: "No-good piss ant!"

I guessed he meant the calf, and asked if he were Mr. Willett.

Thick gold-rimmed glasses beaded down his little blue eyes; he wore a blue chambray work shirt under the overalls, and over both an old brown suit coat, and had on a big dirty Stetson pulled to a drooping point in front, with no creases or dents in its ballooning crown.

He said: "I'm half of it."

I said that my Weatherford friend had told me to look him up and talk to him about that part of the river. He grunted, hit the calf again, and drove him on toward an open fence gap. Emboldened, the pup began to shrill at the calf's heels, and I called him back.

"Half Angus, half Jersey," the old man said. "Took my cow to one of my boy's bulls. Don't know why."

"You never cut him," I said.

"Ain't caught the moon right," he said. "Besides, I like him bull. . . ." He spat brown juice. "Said I knowed the river, did he?"

"Said so," I affirmed, that laconicism being easy to drop into. . . .

He said, wiring the gap shut behind the calf, that even living on her for fifty-six years he didn't know a damn thing about her and, further, that he didn't feel like saying what he did know in no sore-throat wind like that; why didn't we go to the house? We headed for it. As we mounted the porch steps, a jet cracked sound above the low scuttling cloud cover; the house shook and its windows rattled. The old man swiveled his little eyes upward for a moment in token attention, said: "Them son of a bitches!" and held the door open.

"Bring him in," he said, seeing me glance backward at the passenger. "Don't reckon he'll tangle none with a tomcat."

The tomcat himself would have tangled with anybody or anything, except that he didn't want to move. Heat-stupefied, he lay before a fierce butane stove and raised his head and made a noise like far-distant summer thunder, and the pup backed timidly into a corner. After two weeks on the river the room's temperature was dizzying; the old man dropped into a rocking chair beside the stove and waved me to another. Tugging at zippers and neck buttons, I sat down. In a corner of the room was a single bed, and beyond its foot on a rugless floor stood a silent television set. To conserve that oven heat, the doors to other rooms were closed. . . .

"Looks like you'd have more brains," Old Man Willett said. "Horsin' around a river this damn time of year."

I grunted defensively.

"What you think you're gonna find?"

I told him, or tried to.

He grinned and said I wouldn't know what the crap to do with it if I found it. . . . A coffee can sat between his feet; rolling forward on the rockers, he spat darkly and perpendicularly down into it, threw the unheroic Stetson into a corner, and said he wasn't nothing but a damned old farmer. However, if my Weatherford friend was willing to pay me money to run up and down a river in wintertime . . .

"Pay me?" I said.

"Pay you, hell yes," he said, eye-drilling me. "Think I don't know how cracked he is on old junk?"

I laughed. He took it for confirmation, and started a kind of lecture on the local background. Many of the old ones had still been around when he'd come into that country, and he had talked to them. He had known old Sam Savage, and had heard him tell of the time when he and his brother Jim had been violently orphaned over on Sanchez Creek and carried away by The People into the wild country for so long that by the time someone at Fort Sill swapped a pony for them, their English was forgotten. He knew where Margaret Barton had died, and had positive opinions about Andrew Berry and the two little redheaded boys.

But the butane fumes had me drowsy and out of the humor for lectures, and for that matter it was mainly second- or third-hand variant versions of matters I'd mostly heard about already. We butted heads over whether or not the Indians had killed Roe Littlefield ("Reckon I heared right," he said. "Got a arrow in his crouch. Hoop-arn tip. Hoop arn hit might near always infected bad . . ."), and I steered him onto himself as a subject.

It was one he had thought about, and with some bitter humor. He'd wandered into that country in 1901 as a young man from Georgia, via work in the pine timberlands of Arkansas and East Texas, part of a continuing drift from South to Southwest that was then, with all its fits and starts, eighty or ninety years old. A year or so later he'd married the daughter of a man who had married the daughter of another man who had built, in the Comanche time, the hewn-log cabin behind the cottage. With his wife, Old Man Willett had lived in the cabin for nearly half a century, planting peanuts and cotton and corn and sometimes, when the drouths and the floods permitted, harvesting them. He had always had a beef steer or two around for meat, but distrusted ranching, and ranchers too.

"Take my boy," he said. "Made him some money in Dallas. Bought him a little stock ranch south of Ward Mountain, old sorry land that wouldn't sprout a cuckleburr. Ought to see him dressed up like Gunsmoke, Sundays. . . ."

They'd raised a family, and four years before had built the white cottage to finish life in—though he said he'd preferred the cabin. An oak fire, now, it put out a nicer kind of a heat than ara gas stove. Sweating, I agreed. . . . Then his wife had fallen into a long sickness which coincided with the latter part of the big drouth and ate up $12,300 in hospital and doctor bills (he knew the sum with exactitude because they'd had $7,300 in the bank when she came down, and later he'd borrowed $5,000 on his place), and had died. He'd burned her bedclothes, and lived alone now, his children scattered to the cities. His manner in telling it all was wry and factual. Life's shape as he saw it held those things; he had a dry narrow dignity that did not ask for sympathy.

Later, not in comment on himself, he said: "A man needs

it hard. I don't give a crap. He'd ought to have it hard a-growin' up, and hard a-learnin' his work, and hard a-gittin' a wife and feedin' his kids and gittin' rich, if he's gonna git rich. All of it."

"Appreciates it better, maybe."

"*Does* it better," he said, and spat.

He said he had to go and milk. We went out into the wind, the pup and the gray-and-white tomcat with us. It was blowing wet and steadily hard and colder than before. At the little barn Old Man Willett elbowed past the nuzzling cows and pulled down hay into the feeders and let them in. Sitting on an upturned nail keg, he gently and perfectly pulled the first cow's unwashed teats and squirted milk into a cracked china bowl, which when full he set down for the pup to slop at. Then he aimed a couple of squirts at the face of the old tomcat and milked the rest into a dirty pail, which he carried just outside the barn door and emptied into a long chicken trough. The chickens gathered, vocal, and the tom and a friend joined them.

"Figure besides them cats and pullets, I'm feedin' three coons and a skunk," he said. "Separate some cream maybe oncet a week for me."

I said it looked like a good bit of trouble, keeping two cows for a bowl of cream a week.

He looked at me. "Hit ain't the cream," he said. "Crap, I wouldn't have no notion what to do. Always milked."

While he was milking the second cow, I walked over to examine the log house. It was a good one, the great flat-hewn post-oak trunks that showed on the sheltered porch joined into a single surface by chinking and smoothed mortar, no rot in them even at the corners, which were held together with miter-dovetail corners, the hardest of all to make and

the best, since water that might fester the joint or freeze and
burst it drains always out and down. Each of the separate
halves of the house had a sandstone chimney on its outward
side, and behind them were two good-sized lean-to rooms of
gray planks. In front and back, roofed and floored galleries
ran the structure's width, making an H with the shady open-
ended dog run. I've seen others with the dog run enclosed and
made a room, and with additional rooms tacked somehow
onto the lean-tos or the rear gallery. Most of them began as a
single square cabin with a door and a fireplace and maybe a
loft for shirt-tail kids to sleep in, and grew with families. The
log house was an infinitely expansible dwelling.

Stacked bales of hay showed through its windows, and in
the dog run bags of feed were stowed. A good many cabins
remain in that part of the Brazos country, though few compared to that time when they were the only houses. The great
south-hooking finger of the Western Cross Timbers traverses
the region. Largely scrub brush now, in the beginning it was
thick with straight-boled post oaks that the men from tim-
bered regions to the east and north knew uses for. . . . They
left the marks of their origins in the way they built, mainly
in their notches. Deep Southerners from the big-pine states
cut simple, vulnerable half-notches and quarter-notches of
the kind they'd used with the long, straight, expendable timber of home. Those flat notches rot out fast, and the exam-
ples that are left are mostly on houses that were boarded over
a few years after building. Hill Southerners—Tennesseans
and Kentuckians and Carolinians—had the tradition of the
peaked saddle-notch, a tight joint suited to quick-tapering
mountain hardwoods and good with post oaks, too, since a
number of such cabins are still around. Pennsylvania Germans, apparently, shoved the use of the dovetail and the

miter dovetail on into the Midwest, and when you find a house with those corners in Texas, you know that an ancient Ohioan or Illinoisan had his hand in it, or someone who learned from him.

Impermanent types, the wearers out and movers on, slapped up cabins like corncribs with round unhewn logs and haphazard plain saddle-notch corners, none of which have survived. . . .

A dull treatise? I daresay, though the field has its interest, and a properly obsessed student can get off into odd corners of it: the alternative use of rived boards or froe-split shakes for roofs, and how floor puncheons were hewn, and the effect that minutely local geology had on fireplaces. . . . And how we used to dig Comanche bullets out of the logs of the old Rippy place before it burned (somebody got mad at somebody else and set a pasture afire, and lots of things went that time), though oldsters said the bullets we got dated only from last season's disgruntled deer hunters, and maybe they were right.

The easy skill with edged hand tools, with ax and adze and froe and knife, which went into the construction of those houses for a scant dozen or so years of the last century, before the big post oaks played out and the planks came in, is nearly inconceivable now. If you doubt it, take a look at a good set of corners. I never knew anyone who could do that kind of work on uneven logs of varying size without saws or elaborate measuring gear. Like all good handwork, it was a matter of feel, and that kind of feel is short among us these days. Once in a foreign country I sat at the window of a little hotel by a trout river and watched a man in the courtyard below chop out a pair of stilt-soled chestnutwood shoes in fifteen minutes with an ax, all but the hollows inside, every blow counting and his hand sliding up and down the helve in control of the angle and force of his strokes. Some such art as that must have gone into a set of miter-dovetail cabin corners.

But I guess it may not matter greatly. For the most part the countrymen who live among the few surviving cabins seem to think not, and burn and batter them according to the dictates of pragmatism, and sometimes of whim. The logs make good fence posts still. My Weatherford friend, a scholar of log houses and a resister of their destruction, ordered some cordwood from a farmer one fall and got a truckload of sawed-up timbers hand-hewn 100 years before.

"Solid, ain't it?" the old man said, coming up behind me.

"It's a beauty," I said.

"Trouble was, she got to thinkin' it was too old-timey," he said reflectively. "Daughter-in-law stuck that in her head." He thought. "Hell," he said. "Her old maw she recollected when they had to squnch down all night long in there without no lights or fire, and the men layin' outside a-waitin' for Indians. They kilt one oncet down behint the barn." He snorted, and spat. "*Too* old-timey!" he said.

It appeared to be the tail of a losing argument that he was unwilling to have let end even at her death. He pointed out a place where a few rotten shakes still showed beneath the galvanized roofing and a layer of shingles, and said that under the plank floor of the right-hand log room the old puncheons were still firm. Swapping cabin lore, we wandered back to the house's butane fervor; I managed to prop back a swinging door that led into the kitchen, and it helped a little. . . . We spoke of the river, and he asked me if I'd run into any quicksand. I said no, not the real kind I remembered.

"They ain't no more," he said nostalgically. "Hell, I lost a team of mules in twenty-five. Somethin' happened since."

I mentioned the thought of a friend of mine, who'd theorized that Possum Kingdom Lake was settling out all the finer particles that quicksand needed, leaving only the coarse firm stuff in the river below it. He considered that, and said maybe so, unwilling that an outlander should tell him anything about the river. . . . Of my sand island where the geese roosted, he said: "Hit ain't no island up there."

I said he'd better tell me what river it was I'd been floating down, then.

"Ha!" Old Man Willett said. "You must of found it on that-air map."

My books and maps, when I'd shown them to him, had curled his crusty lip. Holy Scripture, he said, was all the books that anybody needed. Now, reminded, he went to the windowsill by his bed and brought back a crack-spined Bible to the fire. He thumped it.

He said: "If they's any salvation, she's in this book."

I said it was a fine book.

He said: "Crap! Hit's the only book they *is*."

His eye shone, and I didn't argue. He started damning commentators and interpreters, water-muddiers. You could drink the truth in its purity if you went to the source. . . .

Calvinistic fundamentalism and its joined opposite, violent wallowing sin, settled that part of the world and have flourished there since like bacteria in the yolk of an egg. They streamed in with the gaunt unaristocratic Southerners who predominated in that settlement, and you may like them or not, but there they are. You may consider that, given the region's temperamental tone, only a punitive God can keep its people from slavering animality, and a trip to the illegal beer halls of Glen Rose on a Saturday night will back your stand. Or you may wish that the whole schizophrenic mess could be tossed out and replaced with some sort of Mediterranean moderation. . . . But it hasn't been, nor does such a solution seem likely.

Most of my own people came from South Texas, from the cattle-and-cotton regions along the Guadalupe, a piece of country with four or five different breeds of men and a consequent easygoing messiness of tone. There is nothing like having a few Mexican Catholics around to dull the spines of the Baptist prickly pear, and as a kid I liked it down there, and looked forward to summers with my grandfather in a gingerbread frame house among big live oaks. But I did most of my growing up in the Baptist country. There you breathed in the Old Testament, like pollen, from the air, and it produced its own kind of hay fever.

Not only Baptists, of course . . . There were a dozen or more sects, and several splinters off of each, and they all squabbled like cats on a midnight roof about such matters as total immersion and the scope of predestination. But they all saw sin in pretty much the same light, and they all went to the Bible for the word about it.

Old Man Willett said: "Listen. Can you show me any place in the Book where hit says anything about a nigger?"

Reflecting, I mentioned the un-Caucasic reputations of the Queen of Sheba, and Balthasar the wise man, and Ham.

But my fundamentalism wasn't fundamental, and I knew it, as did he. He grinned. "Yes," he said. "But do hit *say* they was niggers?"

I couldn't remember that it did.

"Crap no, you can't," he said. "Because *hit* don't. Nor nothin' about no whisky, neither."

Despite an uncertainty about what all this proved, I didn't

ask, for fear of finding out at too great length. It proved something, for he chortled as he bore the Bible back to its place by the bed, and was in a grinning good humor when he sat down again astraddle his spit can.

"You damn right," he said. . . .

His load of evangelism thus queerly discharged, we began again to talk about the river, and about those times when, the Indians gone, the sharp-edged saints and sinners had carried their inherent squabblingness up the cattle trails or, staying home, had grated violently upon one another. Somehow, the old man knew quite a bit about the savage Reconstruction-time lynching of Dusky Hill and her five daughters in the northern part of the county, but he wouldn't talk much about it. Someone he'd known had been involved.

"They was Yankees," he said obscurely when I dug for details. "Liked Yankees, anyhow. And the gals was you know what. . . ."

It was late afternoon. The weather looked no better. I said I'd best get down to the river and make my camp.

"Crap, stay here," the old man said. "I got room."

Remembering the wind's damp bite, I didn't feel like arguing about it. He had a telephone. I called my Weatherford friend and asked him to come out and eat with me at some café on the highway. At dark he came; since he and Old Man Willett hadn't seen each other in a long time, they spent a half-hour or so catching up on country talk while I went down and made the boat secure. The old man refused to come along with us to dinner, saying that restaurant food made his belly burn. . . .

"Proud," my friend said when we were on the road. "Snake-bit, too. They hit a gas field west of him there, but not a smell of it showed up on his place. One daughter takes a little care of him, but the other kids don't worry much."

As we ate and talked in a steak-and-catfish place by a bridge, I could tell that he was disappointed in my historical digging on the trip. I'd found nothing new. I'd known he would be, though, because there wasn't too much new to be found, and besides, it was a goodbye trip, with a main part of its pleasure in the rehearsal of old things. . . . But there was enough to talk about. By the time we'd finished eating, the wind was harder and colder than ever and held a spit of rain. My friend left me off in the red mud before the old man's house and drove home, and going in I crawled under heaped quilts into the bed made for me.

Having slept heavily, I woke early and lay there unwilling to slide out into the cold air beyond the quilts. At six thirty Old Man Willett came in and switched on the light. He was wearing flap-backed long underwear and slippers and seemed to be dancing a little with contained emotion.

He said: "You're a blowed Jew!"

The pup started barking without showing himself from under the blanket I'd folded over him on the floor. "Why?" I said.

"Hit's a-snowin'!" the old man cackled, and gave a caper, and disappeared.

Rolling up, I looked at the window and sure enough, hit was. Big wet white globs were whirling out of the half-darkness and flattening themselves against the glass and sliding down to stack up against the partition moldings. I got up and dressed and went out to the kitchen, where the old man was patting out biscuit dough and the radio, full-blast loud, was gloating over the fact that the weather was in a hell of a shape and likely to stay that way. I sipped coffee and listened and looked out the window at the snow-dimmed bulk of the log house, and the old man laughed every time he glanced in my direction.

"November ain't so bad," he said, misquoting words of mine from the afternoon before. "November's the nicest month they is, in Texiss."

Nevertheless, he fixed a noble breakfast—oatmeal and eggs and good smoked bacon and fat light biscuits and white gravy and strawberry preserves and cream so thick that you had to spoon it out of its Mason jar into cereal and coffee.

He was so set up that he refused to be much concerned over the fact that his unharvested peanuts would now almost certainly rot in the ground, having been more or less continuously wet since early October. I was unsure whether he most enjoyed my company or my discomfiture. He got plenty of both, for it snowed all the long morning and into the afternoon. We pondered the state of man (parlous, the Scriptural mores going rotten in aircraft factories—though once with surprising liberality he said that Convair had saved Parker County during the big drouth), and the intricate lore of the upper-middle Brazos.

At around two o'clock the thick melting snow stopped, and though the outdoors was mainly sodden red mud and a sullen sky, I decided the worst was over. I called Hale and caught him loose, and argued him past his wife's objections by promising to get him to Dennis bridge by the following night. They drove out followed by a friend in another car so that Hale's wife could leave his at Dennis, and when I heard the peremptory chord of his horn outside, I picked up my bundle of gear and told the old man, with a little embarrassment, that I'd like to leave him something for his trouble.

He eyed me with his button glare, and I wondered if I'd

stepped over the thin line of offense, never precisely knowable with country strangers.

He said: "I didn't *ast* you for no money."

Relieved, I took out three dollars. He said it was too much and backed away when I proffered it, so I put it on his bed, where it stayed. I said I'd be around again some time, to visit.

"If you don't git drownded," he said.

"I'm not counting on it."

"All right," he said indifferently. "Don't wait no ten years, though. I ain't figurin' to be here for the Second Comin'."

~~~~~~

OF THE ISLAND GEESE Hale said: "I'd have filled the damn boat. You can have five in possession."

"Four would have rotted," I said. "I can think of stuff I'd rather possess."

"They were meat," he insisted. "You could have given what you didn't want to that skinny little old booger."

"If they'd kept that long. And then he'd have loaded them off on a bunch of other people that never even noticed a flock of geese when they flew across the sky."

"Maybe," Hale said, probing at the fire with a green willow stick. "Just the same . . ."

He was a hunter and a fisherman clear through and always would be; for a long-time he'd been impatient with my tendency just to snoop around instead of giving the business of killing wild meat the taut attention it needed. He worked hard and for good money and spent a lot of it every year on tight-scheduled expeditions after antelope in the Big Bend or mule deer and elk in New Mexico or bass in Florida, and the flesh of all of them was jammed usefully, labeled and dated, into freezers at his home. It fretted him that maybe African safaris would have ended before he had the money and time to make one.

He was also a good friend and an old one and the best kind of company. It was night. We were camped sloppily on a loose-sand shore a mile or so below Old Man Willett's, with willows furnishing a leaky break against the continuing cold northeast wind. The river was high and wide and thickly brown, and made angry noises in the dark against snags and the roughnesses of its banks. Hale had brought steaks and some good whisky, which we were drinking out of enamel cups with honey and lemon and water while we waited for the fire to make coals.

He'd put out a trotline, a quarter-inch nylon cord from shore to shore with maybe twenty hooks, baited variously. The big cats bite most willingly in a rising muddy stream. I'd helped him set it, fighting the brown shove of the river and watching for the drifting logs that can toss a boat end over end, but had told him that if he wanted to run it during the night not to wake me. Now, restless, he emptied his cup and took the lantern, loud and functional again with white gas he'd brought, and went down to check it alone, absorbed in the bow of the canoe, pulling himself across hand over hand and examining the stagings as he went. Against the night the lantern made a clear bright circular picture of Hale and the canoe's curving bow and the hard-rushing brown water. I wrapped potatoes and stuck them in the fire and got the grill ready to use. Hale came back grinning, the lantern in one hand and his chain stringer in the other, with a six-pound channel cat and a couple of others that looked to be maybe three pounds each.

"*My* breakfast," he said. "Them as works, eats."

The steaks were plump; garlicked and seared over glowing oak, they came out fine, and when we'd eaten we had coffee and smoked and talked about the days when we'd gone out to the mouth of Falls Creek in Hood County with big black Bill Briggs, Hale's family's chauffeur and yardman and occasional cook. Hale agreed that they had been the size of telephone poles, the tree trunks that Bill had lifted and carried over to drop across the fire. Red, the river had been then most of the year, high or low, Possum Kingdom not yet up above to catch the silt and hide the fact that West Texas was washing away, down toward the Gulf. But the creek had been clear, with bass and good bream. A girls' camp stood there now.

The wind, quite naturally, as though it had intended all along to do so, started bringing horizontal thin rain, so cold that it seemed it should be snow; and in fact, I knew when a fleck hit my cheekbone and slid down to where beard stubble stopped it, it partly was snow. We tarped things and tumbled into the little tent. Hale had unrolled a fancy down bag on the windward side, which was sagging, its stakes unfirm in the sand. After I'd lain there for a while and was nearly asleep, I heard him cursing under his breath.

"What?"

"Leak," he said.

The flashlight showed a drip from the down-curving sag of a seam, and a dark stain on his sleeping bag. We rolled out into the night, all wet snow now, and pulled the stakes tight and pounded them deep into the sand, trampling it down on top of them and finding stones to put on the trampled spots. It was tight then, but the snow was piling up against it, and I knew that having started it would probably keep on leaking. I offered to flip a coin to see who slept on that side. We did. I won, and lay down again on the good side and slept well except when, from time to time, I woke to hear him thrashing and blaspheming in his bag. Once when I did I said: "Hale?"

"Yeah?"

"Hale," I said, "how come you don't go run that line? . . ."

In the morning it was worse, still snowing, the ground a mass of melting slush and patches of dirty golden sand showing through. I stayed in the sack, as was my policy with weather. So did Hale, and slept a little finally; it had not been so much wetness as the first-night-out insomnia that had bothered him, most of the water having run off onto the tent floor beneath his air mattress.

Finally at about eleven he woke up and reminded me that I'd promised to get him to Dennis by night. It wasn't far, but on the other hand we were bound to move slowly. . . . Outside, the thick wet snow plastered itself to us, and having lost my raincoat somewhere upstream I soon got soaked through a "water-repellent" jacket. While I gathered wood, fishing for it with numbed, hurting hands beneath mounds of snow, stumbling on numbed, hurting, wet feet, Hale built a fire. It took him thirty minutes to get it going even with gasoline, and when he did, a willow branch bowed down with slow grace and deposited a load of snow in its exact middle, and put it out. Later, when we had it burning again and a pot of sugared fruit bubbling on it, nearly ready, I raised my foot too high as I passed and dropped a thick glob of wet sand from my boot sole into the pot.

I looked at it, aware that seldom in my life had I wanted food as I had wanted that hot sugared fruit. Not even those beans on the island . . .

Hale started laughing. So did I, and remembered with a clarity that I hadn't felt till then exactly why it was that he was good company, out. It was an awful day. The tent pulled together into a collapsed double-pointed lump finally from the weight of the snow on it. My old shotgun, left in the canoe, gushed water out both barrels when I picked it up. A drifting snag had carried away Hale's trotline, entire. We got coffee and fruit at last, and stood by the fire steaming ourselves for a couple of hours, and then, the snow thicker than ever, hit the big brown river miserably, the pup a shivering sullen protuberance under the tarp.

The current was fast and shot us down. I remember a big buzzard roost somewhere, the birds hanging like sad black husks in leafless trees, with nowhere to go on a day like that. I remember Hale shooting at three ducks 150 yards away with his magnum twelve, and thousands of the little sad-high-whistling birds in the brush, never showing themselves, and a heron or so, and a place where we stopped and built another big fire and boiled eggs and ate chocolate with them and hung over the fire with sharp animal relish until we knew we had to leave. There was a volunteer watermelon patch at that place of the kind that sprouts where people have had picnics and spat out seeds, but the frosts had touched all the big melons and left only green mush inside them. Hale walked among them smashing them angrily with his gun butt. . . . I remember most clearly of all the feel of melted snow crawling down the hollow of my back and between my buttocks, and I told him, to put it on record, that if it hadn't started clearing by the time we reached Dennis I was going to pull out too, for the year.

But the snow stopped not long before we came in sight of the 1892, plank-and-iron, one-way bridge, and blue sky showed behind us in the west, and at last the yellow setting sun. Soggy, we went into the old ser sta gro there and braved the stares of another set of philosophers while I bought some things I needed.

Outside again, Hale grinned. "When you think up another good joke, you be sure and call me," he said.

"You picked the worst of it," I told him.

"Picked, hell. Was picked."

But it was a measure of how much like me he was in certain childishnesses that he looked wistful as he stood by his car beside the rusty cotton gin, the stringer with its catfish in his hand, and watched us move off downriver. Wistful was the only word for how he looked. The pup stuck his nose out from under the tarp and looked back at Hale until willows intersected the line of sight between us. . . .

I camped alongside the mouth of Patrick's Creek in a grove of big elms and oaks where in frontier days and after they used to hold revivals, baptizing by total immersion in the Brazos, horses and guns nearby, and would still if an un-fundamentalistic owner hadn't fenced them out. I was on the river side of his fence. The hills stand far back from the river there and the bottom is flat rich sandy loam, Southern-looking, the ground stoneless, just sand and mud and the rotting twig-and-leaf carpet of the grove's floor.

At dusk the brush was full of whitethroats. It was also full of the sad-whistling song that had puzzled me. Ergo, the sad whistler was a . . . Certainly. Old Sam Peabody, they claimed the song said, and so it did if you pronounced Pea-body in the Yankee way. I supposed the big numbers of them had come in from the north with the cold. The thing was, it was a winter sound in that part of the country, and one tends falsely to associate bird song with spring, and to learn what little he knows about it then. . . .

I felt relieved, and again like an amateur naturalist, kinsman to Port Smythe, M. D. At Patrick's Creek, whither our *Red-Skinned Vergil* conducted us at Night Fall, there fell upon our Ear the lugubrious Note of the White-Throated Sparrow, (*Zonotrichia albicollis*). . . .

But not much like one. I had no red-skinned Vergil, and all I wanted really, scratch-eyed and chilled, was fire and a drink and bread and bacon. I had them, and went to bed. Owls called, and far off someone was running hounds; scent would be good in the cold fresh-dampened bottom. A wet log on the fire was squirting steam out a tiny sap vein at one end and saying: *Old, Sa-a-am, Peabody, Peabody, Peabody.* Beside me the pup wallowed and made groaning sounds in his regular expression of belly-full contentment. The night before had chipped at his routine—Hale in the tent, and the miserable snow.

Now it was all right, he seemed to be saying. Now it was the way it was supposed to be.

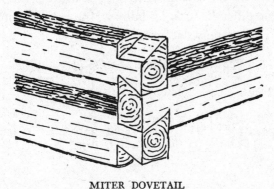

MITER DOVETAIL

IF it hurts it's probably doing you good. If it's pleasant it's most likely wrong. And that twisty road down which life leads you irretraceably farther each day is pocked with dust-disguised holes into which if you step, will you or nill you (most Methodists, for instance, will; pure Presbyterians don't), you break not your grandmother's back but your own soul's.

That certainty rose and spread like a smell from the meetings beneath the oaks and the elms, from brush arbors on the sun-seared, cicada-droning hilltops; the hammer rhythms of the old hymns pulsed it forth:

> *Far away the sound of strife upon my ear*
> *is falling, . . .*

or:

> *What have I to fear, what have I to dread,*
> *Leaning on the everlasting Arm? . . .*

or:

> *Whom on earth have I beside Thee,*
> *Whom in Heaven but Thee? . . .*

—that one an old man I know remembers watching his mother sing, with wonder as he watched and heard, since alongside her were ranged in ascending stairsteps of stature the vigorous ninefold issue of her loins.

Just beyond the circle of sacred emanation the saddled horses quivered their hides and switched their tails against long gray flies, and the oaken wagons sat loaded with fried fowl and cornbread and wet-wrapped jugs of buttermilk, and Henrys and Colts lay ready in oiled leather to meet the violence of the unredeemed, red or black or white. And inside the circle, if the sect was one that allowed such doings, old Alfred Tinsley, known as Bug Eye, lay down on the ground and wallowed like the hog he shout-confessed himself to be, and sweated out twelve years of bad whisky, worse language, and what strange women he'd been able to find. It struck home, that religion; it bit. And six months later the ecstatic angry job was there to do over again; fluid evil seeped ever in through the crack that Eve had made in the font, and had to be sloshed away. . . .

What other brand of godliness, though, would you have substituted for it—in that time, in that place, in that people? A gentle Brahmin reverence for Creation? The flickering-candle mysteries of Rome? The dignified static Episcopalianism of the Old Dominion? Those other ecstasies of fierce locust-eating saints, divorced almost from ethics, above them? Today's sectless well-wishing?

Besides, it made sinning more fun. Someone must have noted that somewhere, but if so I never saw his notation. If wrong is sharply wrong enough, its edge digs deeper down into the core of that sweet fruit, pleasure, than hedonism ever thought to go. Furtive, itching, hayloft love may have had it all over the silk sheets and mirrors of Paris. It was sensuality akin to that of the starkly simple liver, and not really separable from it. If anything could make savory the raw corn juice and septic girls of Dodge and Abilene, three months of choking down a steer herd's dust could—and the rowel of the deadly rectitude of one's people in Parker County, Texas. . . .

Up Patrick's Creek in '66, the Indians who'd just killed Bohlin Savage to the east and taken his sons found the home of his brother Jim, killed him too, and carried off his little girl as company for her cousins. Raw meat, all the prisoners in the chronicles complained of being forced to live on. It appears to have been much the same underdone protein that backyard brazier-masters pride themselves on these days, but it didn't look good to frontiersmen, whose descendants even now like their steaks pale gray clear through. . . . To rouse his appetite for it, little Sam Savage got to ride all the way to the Arbuckle Mountains on a pony with a squaw who carried in her lap the rope-severed head of one of the other Comanches. . . .

But you don't want to hear about that. You thought we were through with The People.

So did I.

Let's be through with them, then, though there's a lot more that could have been said—about the way smallpox could eat up a tented tribe; about how the buffalo went and their stacked hides stood higher than a horseman's head for miles in a row at Fort Griffin up the Clear Fork, awaiting shipment; about the last unwise magnificence at the Adobe Walls where a white buffalo hunter made a long long shot over a hill and had the incredible luck to kill the pony of Isatai the prophet; about how Satanta and Satank and Big Tree of the Kiowas massacred Warren's teamsters at Salt Creek and pricked the wrath of Yankee General Sherman, which brought Mackenzie, and the trials of Jacksboro, and old Satank shot down singing his soldier song ("O Earth, you remain forever, but we Ka-it-sen-ko must die") before they got him there, and Satanta a suicide finally in the penitentiary at Huntsville. A lot that could and should have been said about Kiowas as distinct from Comanches, though few whites seem to have minded the difference, and indeed in their thrust and in the completeness of their defeat there was little difference.

Sixteen hundred mangy, beaten Comanches lined up for dole meat at Fort Sill in 1875, their memory of arrogance tamped down in a crevice with stones on top . . . Let's be through with them, then. The frontier was. That other People had had its way, and could now swell west and north, or stew in its own juices where it was.

Milliken's Bluff (on down, drifting with the big brown river through the low country's tangled bottoms) that Milliken, dead at Goliad, never saw, but his Irish heirs took up his allotted bonus league of land there. Kickapoo Creek where a lone young bluebill flew from under a sand ledge and I shot it, and the pup, for the first time in his life connecting firearms and quarry, jumped into the strong-flowing ice water and brought it to shore and howled at me in rage when I took it away.

Horseshoe Bend on the left, all the sandy wooded land inside its big loop owned now (and maybe before, for all I knew) by one of those proud continuous clans that had begun ranching on that frontier and had moved on north or west, their push like Old Man Goodnight's, as the plains were cleared of Indians and the cattle markets were set up. They shaped imperial ranches in the big country and later, mostly under the pressure of wives who wanted to be able to spend the new cattle money in a civilized way, many of them moved back to live in Fort Worth or San Antonio— according to whether it was the Southern Pacific or the T. & P. that had threaded their particular empire onto the nation's railroad web. They built big nineties-style mansions in those towns, and their descendants live there still—some of them still rock solid, direct, functional, so that you can see in them how the empires got built; others gone rotten with whisky not sweated out in work and this century's easy oil money, spewing out in neurosis and wild sport and mismarriage the inherited restless force that shoved their grandfathers against the Comanches and the plains.

Race horses the bend held now, shapely big-eyed thoroughbred mares with their colts that watched the canoe pass from behind tight fences repaired after the spring's floods. Racing in Texas, when it existed, was a kind of property and a pride of those expansive families, kings in their way and in their time, but when old Mr. Waggoner died (his father made one start in Parker County, too, on Spring Creek) and a couple of others, no one remaining would keep riding fence against the citizens who thought that if it was pleasant it was most likely wrong, and racing was voted out. . . . Those Texans now who like to see their own fast horses run have to go outside the state to do it.

Are you washed in the blood of the Lamb?

Wind, big wind, slopping choppy spray at me from the full dirty river, slowing the boat so that the chips and sticks thick in the current floated downstream faster than I could paddle. At the bend's tip were bars, and beyond them big ugly sand boils that wrenched at the boat and would have spun it if I hadn't forced through. That is the pure sand country in there, and in normal times it's where the channel is hardest to read. You drift, and the river's torpor gets in you, and the green flowing water under the willows is as deep as the grip of your paddle. Then suddenly you know that unless you paddle gut-strainingly straight for the other shore, the current is going to run you up on the almost surfaced lip of a bar, with more green water just below it. . . . Sometimes, if you've drifted too far to try to get across the river to the new channel, you can stay free by jamming yourself into grasses and willows against the near shore and hoping to find the three-foot-wide secondary channel that's sometimes there, and sometimes not. And if, as often, you do get hung on the flat sand lip, just yards from floatable water with the current shoving you sidewise and trying to turn you over, the sand shudders and sucks obscenely at your boat and maybe the river will sweep you over into the green below, but probably not. More often the canoe shakes hoggishly to a halt and you can either pole, six inches at each huge thrust of the paddle and the planks crackling, or get out and wade towing, clinging at the same time to the boat for support against the hungry sand, swearing you'll watch more carefully, or just swearing.

But now the whole river was one wide sweeping channel, and there was only a need to watch the big boils and an occasional snag. Fat cattle to the right were eating good green grass, some of them whitefaces and the rest assorted scrubs, all that someone had been able to find in the rush for stockers to put on the new-sprouting pastures when the drouth broke. The big eroded gullies yawning out of that pasture onto the river had been fenced across with lengths of corrugated iron roofing stuck between steel stakes, and some of them had been crammed full of old car bodies to halt the historic Gulfward progress of the land. These imaginative expedients seemed to be doing the job, though they weren't as pretty a way as good grass cover or even dumped-in brush. But that isn't a part of the world where prettiness weighs much. West Texas runs functional, and when it does wax aesthetic it's as likely as not to end up with a front yard full of old tires painted red, white, and blue, with petunias planted in their centers. . . .

~~~~~~~

SANCHEZ CREEK, and old Francisco Sanchez who lived up it, Frank to the stark Saxons, and who knows how he came to be there among them? . . . Campbell's Island, a spreading, sandy hunk of public domain . . . The Hightower Bridge, pecan pickers rattling their buckets in a grove, and Spring Creek, brush-choked, and if there were room and time, we'd talk about all there was up there—about Dan Waggoner and his partner Mr. Brogden who had the old Muleshoe ranch, and T. J. Shaw the cabin builder from Tennessee, and J. T. Shaw his trail-driving son, and that Blackwell whom the hired boy killed, and the children William Wilson and Diana Akers carried off by the Indians, while their parents made sorghum molasses on the creek, to a night on Mount Nebo and a battle to the west (you try to keep The People out of it, even now that we're through with them).

Strange country then, a stretch I'd never floated where the live oaks begin to thicken and shale starts cropping out among the sandstone . . .

A fisherman, on a boulder . . .

"Hey," I said.

He answered, uninterrogative: "How you doin'."

"What do they call this bend?"

"Don't know," he said, as though glad of it, and without trust watched me out of sight.

CHAPTER THIRTEEN

&§ *Don Quixote perceiving that he was not able to stir, resolv'd to have recourse to his usual Remedy, which was to bethink himself what Passage in his Books might afford him some Comfort.*

ARE we going to re-redefine the cowboy? Shall we deny again the blue-glowing psychoanalytical myth of the television tube, give anew the lie to California's brave wide-screen miracles of amorous, bellicose pigslop? Shall we pin-prick the rotund gassy fiction of the code duello and the quick draw, and show the shotguns and the ambushes and the men who never fought at all, or needed to? Shall we—no half-horse, half-alligator types—sniff the bathless sweat of our fellows, and hear their hollers and the screams of red-eyed steers, and whale hell out of a runty ill-tempered mustang under us, and eat beans and biscuits and bacon, bacon and biscuits and beans, till we're loose with diarrhea or drum-bellied with its opposite, and sleep four or five bug-crawling, dust-coughing hours a night on the ground without being able to get the boots off our feet swollen with heat and fungus itch, and ford the rivers and ride the stampedes and worry about the Indians in the Territory and get sloppy-sleepy drunk at last in Wichita or Hunnewell where a pasty whore will stash beneath her mattress our wages earned so pleasantly, and maybe in return will give us a lasting souvenir? . . .

I think not. Men who know mountains more than I do about those things have set the record straight often enough, and if the general run of folks want to believe that John Wayne and Frank Sinatra and Ricky Nelson and the Gabor girls made high drama in the railheads of Kansas, they're going to keep on believing it. Read Andy Adams if you want to see cowhands right; read Teddy Blue Abbott, and Frank Dobie, and the groping-worded, utterly straight tales in *The Trail Drivers of Texas,* and J. E. Haley's work on Old Man Goodnight.

All that touched the Brazos country, of course—changed its tone, kept it awake as The People had. The Chisholm Trail passed through it from the south, and the herds stacked up on one another sometimes during high water at the Kimball's Bend crossing (down the river, farther than the trip would likely take me). The trail poured change and money and excitement and sin into Palo Pinto and Parker and Hood and Somervell and Bosque and the other river counties; Sam Bass robbed a stagecoach near Weatherford and had a fight with the law, and Belle Starr functioned there, and flamboyants with revolvers swaggered through or loitered, kicking up one kind or another of fuss. Some of it was even a little bit like Hollywood.

In return the counties poured cattle up the trail to the paying places, and young men, too. Of those, some came back sooner or later to marry good Baptist girls and raise more cattle and guilt-inspire their offspring as they themselves had been inspired, while others kept moving, restless from Old Testamentalism or from their rebellion against it or just from being born restless, in that migration that washed Reconstruction Texans up the whole wide belt of the West, where they taught other men to handle cows.

Chauvinism? A little, maybe, but not much . . . It was true. If it hadn't been for Mexicans, the South Texas Anglos would never have learned how to cope right with longhorn cattle. If it hadn't been for Texans, nobody else on the Great Plains would have learned how, either.

At Kimball's Bend now, bright tail-finned boats sometimes slice the water, trailing bathing-suited boys and girls on skis; it is a curl on the upper end of Lake Whitney. . . .

Of the people who stayed at home, farming or doing business in the little towns or raising the stock that went up the trails, there were many different kinds. It's no use trying to homogenize them for these pages; that process is pleasant, but it leads one into half-truth nearly always. . . . As people will, they became more homogeneous later when all the furors died down and they were left in the stagnant boomlessness of their little region, but just then they were still most of them from other places, with infinitely various reasons for being in Texas.

In general they were a yeomanry, as their offshoots still are, ethnically pretty much alike, angry in independence. But some had been of that yeomanry when they came, stock that had taken care of itself well and unplaintively for centuries, and others had moved down into it, bringing slaves and cherrywood chests and an un-Texan gentility of outlook, and others still had ascended socially with their westward shift, driven from the older states by poor-white desperation and a hot resolve not to take no crap from nobody nowheres no more. . . . There were Yankees in plenty and Southerners who lacked love for the South; many of them went to Kansas during the War but came back down gleeful when it was over, flanked by Negro Federal troops, to the imaginable delight of the region's beaten, returned Confederates. There were cattle kings and horse thieves and half-breeds and whole sons of bitches and preachers in droves and sinners in swarms.

There was a bit of everything, and the music they made rasping against one another, if not sweet, was noisy enough to ring down through the years—though, oddly, the records of that later time are even spottier than those of Indian days. When the records were being written, mostly in the first third of this century, too many people from the trail time were still alive; too many of the best stories, like a broken-backed rattler, still had a bite left in them. Once, a few years ago, when a writer showed up in the little South Texas town where my father's people lived, and began digging up details of the old filthy, bloody Sutton-Taylor feud of the 1870's, he had to be asked forcefully to leave. Families, friends till then, had gone to edging past one another in the street and glaring slit-eyed back and forth across the aisles of churches.

Of some aspects of the fight between the Truitts and the Mitchells in lower Hood County, T. T. Ewell wrote in 1895: "To enter into its details now would not be profitable." Or safe, he might have added, since—though he was chronicling twenty years after the major uproar—the story wasn't yet finished. Others later did enter into the details, or as many details as they could get hold of, but that comes in its place, down the river.

Take, for now, the sad and fragmentary tale of the sisters Mrs. McGee and Mrs. Bowen, also sketched with prudent caution by Ewell. In '72 these ladies were camped with their parents and a younger brother and a batch of kids, some probably theirs, up Robinson Creek, which runs into the river three or four miles below the Parker County line in

Hood. (Clear water flows slow at its mouth, shielded from the river's swirl by a big sand bar, and against its steeper bank you can cast a little silver spoon and let it sink wobbling without reeling in more than enough to keep the line tight, and in a moment, more likely than not, there is a bump and a bass. There was this time, anyhow. On down, the river still brownly high, the shores changing, all the rocks limestone now, aligned groves of diked, irrigated, city-owned young pecans on the flats above the banks, the blessed live oaks thickening on the hills, the unblessed cedar, too . . .) After the manner of the more feckless breed of drifting agriculturalists, the ladies' father was changing farms and hadn't yet built a house on his new place.

Does Ewell manage to imply that they weren't "nice" people? The ladies, though not widows, were both minus their husbands, and the lack is relevant, he seems to be saying, to what happened there on Robinson Creek. You need to be roundabout in your reading of such matters in those chroniclers, since at this range of years the spaces between the lines aren't wide.

What did happen, anyhow, was that at sundown one day, when the father wasn't around, nine or ten types dressed and decorated as wild Indians fell on the camp, shot Mrs. McGee dead with a pistol, perforated Mrs. Bowen so thoroughly with arrows that later she too expired, and coursed their young brother George with such zeal across the roughs that he escaped only by jumping his pony over what he later claimed to have been a twenty-foot-wide gulch. They didn't harm the mother or any of the small children, though they could have, nor did they take any booty, vanishing with the abruptness of their coming.

"It is generally believed," Ewell says straight-faced, "that the perpetrators of this crime were white men painted and disguised as Indians."

If it was believed, it was known, and known too who they were. The last real Indian raid in Hood County had been in 1869; it lay just far enough south and east of the protective edge of settlement that it felt relief before the other areas did. But "Indians" kept hitting all through the Brazos country far up into the seventies, long after the Comanches and the Kiowas were whipped and contained. They were whites, mingled just enough with half-breeds and tribeless, whisky-loving red men to keep things entirely confused, which is the way they wanted things to be. Mainly they were horse thieves, and though data is scant there seems to have existed an extensive, tightly governed gang that operated out of the Territory and drove its stolen stock up there as the Indians had, and maintained a network of spies throughout the frontier communities to spot likely loot and keep tabs on the counter-activities of more lawful folks.

People knew who the spies were and knew some of the raiders, too, but they were numerous and blood-mean, and for the most part their victims kept their mouths shut and went along with the diaphanous Indian fiction kept up by moccasin tracks and occasional whoops and arrows. The grandfather of my old Weatherford friend, a respected ranch-man, heeded his wife's plea for caution one night as they stood in their cabin and listened to a saw biting through the stable logs to which a thoroughbred stallion was chained. He knew by name who was out there sawing (once, when I was talking about the incident to another friend from Parker County, he started laughing; the progeny of one of the main thieves had gone the Bible road and constitute now a staid and weighty family), and he wasn't afraid of them. But he knew too that what his wife said about it was exact—that if he went out with his gun and ran them off or killed one of them, he'd have to spend ten years worrying about being shot down from ambush or "burned out," and the stallion wasn't worth it.

Law and order, in other words, were fairly faint ideals. The fake-Indian horse thieves had probably existed from the start—Robert Neighbors's murderer in 1859 was entangled in such matters—but they hit their peak in the seventies when everybody knew that no true Indians were still operating. Their talents were various; the iron cash boxes taken in a train robbery at Benbrook back in those times were washed to view just a few years ago by rampaging creek waters in a pasture close to the old homestead of one of the known gang members.

Further, the fiction lent itself patly to mob violence and personal revenge. It seems probable that Mrs. McGee and Mrs. Bowen were the butts of some such individual rage. Whose? Their husbands', almost certainly, from the way Ewell put it down, though what spiderweb of adultery and conjugal venom lay behind the attack no one now will ever know. Ewell knew, but one finds it hard to blame him— writing in Granbury, with that kind of people still around him—for not having set it down. There are all kinds of good reasons for the prevalent spottiness of history.

The group that dealt with the Hill family at Springtown in northeastern Parker County didn't stoop to masquerade. Maybe they lacked imagination. They seem to have been outraged Confederate Calvinists, grimly active brothers' keepers. They got Allen Hill, the father, during the Civil War, supposedly for his Union sympathies. The only grown boy, Jack, was shot in a fight over in the Palo Pinto country in '69 or '70. Of the Hill women and children, the following was later deposed to a county court:

Nance Hill, the oldest of the daughters, was supposed to have a bad character, a disturbing element in the community, and having gotten wind of the fact that she was to be waited upon by a posse of citizens of the Springtown community, endeavored to make her escape, but was followed, captured, and hanged by the enraged mob seeking her. This capture and hanging took place in 1872, near the line between Wichita and Clay counties, Texas. A few days after the death of Nance Hill and the return of those to the Springtown community who had hanged her, the mob spirit still prevailing, Martha and Katherine Hill were taken from their home and hanged at a spot about three miles Southwest of Springtown, in Parker County, Texas. Only a day or so after Martha and Katherine were hung; the spirit of the mob not having changed and its vengeance not being complete, the farmhouse of the Hills was burned, Mrs. Dusky Hill, with her daughters, Adeline, Eliza, and Belle and son, Allen, escaping at this time, but they were followed and overtaken when Allen and Belle, the two youngest of the Hill children, were driven back, while Mrs. Dusky Hill and her daughters, Adeline and Eliza, were taken to a point near the present sight of Agnes, Parker County, Texas, where they were shot and killed. The entire Hill family was thus wiped out with the exception of the two youngest children, Belle and Allen.

What lingers in the mind is that dangling appositive, "a disturbing element in the community." I guess they were. Vengeance is mine, said the Lord, but the good citizens of Springtown, Parker County, Texas, appear to have honed themselves into His cutting tools.

For what reason? Was Unionism still that repugnant, seven years after the War? Probably, though women seldom heat up enough about politics for it to matter. Did manless

Dusky put on the rural market her own and her daughters' only salable services? Maybe—though Weatherford a few miles south, a cow town, would have been a much better selling place . . . Whatever it was that she did (no one will ever know, and you can put that ending on story after story after story), she paid for it in the ultimate currency.

That same hilly belt (no, I don't know just where the stories are headed; I'm only talking about how a people was) and its violence had atmospheric connection with another tale I once pried up to view, unchronicled. I was talking, on a ripple-boarded front porch, to an old man down in Hood, and was trying to find out something about the history of a log house near there. He had been born in the log house and had spent his childhood in it, but he was ninety-four and his memory had gone piedald, with vast white misty gaps. In active years he'd been mostly a stockman. He remembered with clarity a cattle drive he'd made in the nineties to the Indian Territory, and how he'd raced horses with Cherokees, and to a silver dollar how much money he'd won.

But of the cabin he could recall only that an itinerant Irish mason named Regan had built its hillside storm cellar, where a spring still trickled through stone troughs for crocks of cream and buttermilk. When I would ask, maybe, if his father had built the place or had bought it built already, he'd smack his wax-white forehead with a white and withered palm and would say: "I'm sorry, son. It ain't no good no more, my head."

He said he knew a little about another cabin near there. I'd seen it, a ruin, its quarter-notched corners rotted out and the logs mostly collapsed into wormy heaps, though at one time it had been a comfortable place—double, a story and a half high with fireplaces top and bottom on both ends, and lean-tos and outbuildings. The old man, whose name was Rush, said that it had been built with slave labor during the War, by a family named Terrell.

"They knowed we was losin', the way I heard it," he said. "Wanted to get what they could out of them slaves before they lost 'em. Old Dad Lowry, the head nigger's name was. I used to talk to him later on, when I was a kid."

The Terrells around there had finally died down to two old bachelor brothers, sons of the cabin's builder, and their widowed sister. Once, Old Man Rush said, the brothers had gone for six years without speaking to each other, even living in the same house. "Old Iry he said one time: 'By God, I ain't gonna talk to you no more!' A-fussin', they was. And old Epp he said: 'Well by God, I ain't a-talkin' to you without you talk first.' And they didn't, not for six years, not 'cept through Allie, that was the sister."

"Where'd they come from?" I asked.

"Mississippi to begin with, seems like," he said. "Come here from up around Poolville or somewhere like that in Parker County. Old Iry he'd say at the table: 'Alice, would you ast Ephraim to pass the peas?' Would. Right in that house."

"Seems funny they'd move here from Parker County just when most people were moving the other way," I said.

"Does."

"I wonder why? Indians?"

Old Man Rush looked at me from tiny, triangular, pale eyes. "Son," he said, the white hand rising, "sometimes it seems like you pull down a window shade, right acrost my brains."

I never saw him again. But I stuck the bit about the Terrells away in some nook of my head as you do stick such things if you're built to care anything about them. Not that it's necessarily a good way to be built . . . One time a good while later I asked my Parker County historian friend if he'd ever heard of such a family, up that way.

He asked why I wanted to know. I told him. He shook his head wonderingly, and after thinking a little—he's not a man to keep old scandals alive, though he knows nearly all of them —he told me the story. The Terrells had been a patrician kind of family for northern Parker County, and what had happened had caused a stir. A Negro, someone else's, had come to the Terrell house one day at the beginning of the War, and had found Mrs. Terrell alone. The ancient Southern nightmare pieced out of masters' guilt found its occasional solidity; he raped her. With joyous speed, the light-hearted north-Parkerian mob took care of the rapist with rope and torch and afterward, charitable, made it clear that for them patrician Mrs. Terrell was a dirtied woman. Or maybe she herself thought so. . . . The family had had to move away, and until now, nearly a century later and their house in ruins and no Terrell remaining, perhaps no one else had known where it was they'd moved to.

Nor probably had anyone cared except a type or so like the historian and me. And maybe Ira and Epp and Allie, sitting at their morose dinner table in the old house built by slaves . . . If they'd known of the trouble, and possibly they hadn't . . .

What was it, I wonder, that could have made them start talking to each other again, could have made them break a silence that had lasted six long years? . . .

ANOTHER CREEK MOUTH, clear too as those limestone streams nearly always are, where I lingered throwing a cork bug beneath willows, though I didn't need whatever I might catch. Like someone in Tolstoy—Levin's brother, was it?—I'm fond of angling and proud of being able to care for such a stupid occupation. Even semi-chronic humanitarianism doesn't get in the way, with fish.

I caught nothing. Hard by the creek mouth was another of the too neat groves of young pecans, the ground beneath them graded level and irrigation dikes around the whole. Their few leaves were yellow and ready to fall, as were those of the cottonwoods up the creek, twirling a little in the breeze. Winter's pleasant sterile edge was on the air; in one of the pecans crows were rattling woodpeckerishly, prosperous omnivores, not dependent on any cyclical comings and goings of their food supply. Far enough away not to have noticed me, pickers were thrashing the trees with long bamboo poles and the ripe nuts were thudding onto tarps spread below, to be picked up and dumped into a cart behind a tractor.

On down . . .

CHAPTER FOURTEEN

At Thorp Spring the stone shell of old Add-Ran Male and Female College stares big-windowed off a hilltop, witness to gentler currents along the Brazos of the seventies than those I have recorded. Homicide and herdsmanship and horse thievery even in long retrospect hold color that grays the pastel ghosts of the townsmen who moved in behind the frontier or cropped up in the frontier's own second generation, wearing frock coats and full skirts and going to unvociferous churches on Sunday mornings, practicing law and medicine, and selling dry goods, and in talk and manner yearning back toward a staid Southern way of living which, by yearning, they were imposing on these rawer places. But slowly . . . Addison and Randolph Clark, if Campbellite ministers, were also realistic erstwhile rebel soldiers, and found it wise to write into their rules for the Male and Female College a ban against owning or using "fire arms, a dirk, a bowie knife, or any other kind of deadly weapon."

Near there, under a limestone hill, I camped for the night among boulders with my weapons deadly and undeadly. A fisherman visited me in the morning; I went to the shore for coffee water, and he was examining my canoe pulled up half loaded, while a scarred old pointer sniffed the passenger's messages on rocks and bushes, and drowned them out.

"Some boat," the man said in greeting. He wore a red hunting cap and despite the morning's edge a sport shirt without a jacket over it. Lean and tall and brownly falcon-faced, he looked to be a healthy sixty years old. In his hand were two steel casting rods with salt-water reels screwed on them and elaborate catfish arrangements of big sinkers and multiple hooks dangling from the tips.

I said the canoe was all right, though too high-ended for wind and with the fiberglass too heavy for one-man carries. He asked about my trip and I told him, and he smiled widely and shook his head.

"That's good!" he said. "By God, that's good."

His enthusiasm was unrustic, and his accent held a faint foreign flavor of precision, allied to the dialect of the country. His surname too, when he told me it, was foreign, Scandinavian, and after we'd talked a little he said he came from a Norwegian settlement on the Navasota down in Limestone County, not far from where Cynthia Ann Parker had been kidnapped. He'd drifted around and had worked in cities and other states and had ended here, single, as caretaker for a Dallas man who owned a farm above the limestone hill.

The pointer bristled as the passenger came rolling cockily toward us from camp, drawn by the sound of voices. "Shup, Pete," the fisherman said, and the pointer wagged its tail and went to play not-before-I-smell-you with the pup. . . . "Good on varmints," the man said. "The only trouble, he don't make no noise."

He said much of the land around there now was city-

owned. A big sand and gravel corporation had just bought
the place across the river for exploitation, and the pecan
grove I'd seen at the last creek was only one of a number
planted around that country on newly bought land by a Fort
Worth family with a share of the unbelievable money those
cities have in them nowadays. He had no tight link to the
region himself, and thought with gentle detachment that the
changes were mainly for the better.

"You take an old sorry place with the fences all down and
the floods washin' away the bottoms and the brush takin'
the rest, it most always belongs to somebody that had a
daddy it belonged to, too," he said. "Sha, you ought to see
what we've done, up on the hill."

But he said the locals had a point, too, fighting off change.
It was hard as hell to get yourself left alone nowadays, as he
thought he ought to know as well as anybody. . . . The
flexibility of his insight was of the kind that comes sometimes from not owning anything or anybody and therefore
not being obliged by your interests to shape your thought
narrowly. People of that kind are good to be around, though
they're fairly rare even among have-nots, since the quality
depends on some brains and an absence of envy.

Fishing was where he channeled his passion—catfishing,
rather, for it's a restrictive branch of the sport. He'd been on
the river since before dawn that morning and was quitting
now, fishless. But because a calendar he went by and his own
theory about the stage of the river—falling a little, still tur-
bid—had both favored bad luck, he was satisfied. Hook-and-
line catfish around there, he said, ran up to twenty-five
pounds or so, and others bigger. He had found a dead one on
a bar once which he couldn't lift.

"I guess they grabble those," I said.

"You mighty right they do!" he said. "Get all the breedin' stock. One of them he said to me one time: 'You can't catch none of these fish we take, not on no rod and reel.' I told him: 'No, I can't, but I sure can catch their babies.' "

I mentioned "telephoners."

"Them," he said, his mouth tightening, and wouldn't talk about it.

"Them" get hold of old Southwestern Bell or Ford magnetos and rig them to wires so that when cranked they send sharp current through the river's pools and stun smooth-skinned fish, which float to the top and can be picked up from a boat. Others, less capable mechanically, use sticks of dynamite which kill everything, or sometimes rotenone. . . . It is a part of the old ones' tradition of getting what meat you can when you can, linked now to technology.

He said grudgingly, when I told him good fish had been twisting off my throwlines, that I could get around that by tying swivels at either end of each staging. But he didn't like set lines.

"I want to feel 'em," he said. "It's no use havin' that goin' on down here in the dark while I'm up yonder asleep. I like to feel 'em."

~~~~~~~~

At Granbury, the only town of any size on the river from Possum Kingdom down to Whitney, I parked where the old bridge used to cross, and walked up a dirt street to the highway. A ser sta gro stood there, run by a taciturn middle-aged couple who, when I said I was going to walk on into town for some bits of hardware to replace things I'd broken or lost or used up, offered not only to watch after the passenger but to lend me their car. Their name too, on the sign outside, was Continental, which maybe explained their gentle open-handedness.

I drove to the square. The town is the county seat of Hood and has a stone Victorian courthouse of the kind the genteelly yearning folks put up in the seventies and eighties to express the firmness of their presence and their way. Around it old men sit now and chew tobacco and smoke and talk, and the stores and other buildings that face inward at them from four sides nearly all are older than they are. If you looked closely, you might find one or two with contemporary veneers of those shiny, vitreous, half-inch-thick materials beloved of ten-cent-store and movie-house architects these days, but I doubt it. Most are basically of the old rough-squared or rubble limestone construction, its courses often waving and wandering up and down with the size of the rocks that came to hand, that to me is twice as handsome as any laborious ashlar. Even back then, though, with an organic taste practically forced on them by the accessible local stuff, the builders disguised the rubble when they could, using it for backing and for rear walls, and buying brick or alien cut-stone for façades.

Are we biting again at gazebo builders, Maiden's Leapers? I guess so. The yearners were predominantly gingerbread Gothic in taste. I'd rather not bite too hard, though, for I like their courthouse, and like too their little red-brick bank, graceful in Victorian ugliness, with stone-lined Moorish-arched doors and windows (it's a drug store now) and its solid rear tied to the region by textured walls of fieldstone.

Masonry in that country now, when not concrete-block, is likely to be big polygonal flags laid on edge in jigsaw style, three inches thick, clinched to a frame structure underneath.

When one of the flagstone specialists wants to achieve special tone, he goes up to the Palo Pinto country and brings down some slabs of red sandstone to dot here and there among the white. The result dazzles, as it's intended to do. . . .

The stone hotel there stands sleepy, its name painted in red-and-white letters across its lobby's pane, changed certainly in few ways from those times when horses stood three-legged in the sun outside and the square rattled with the activity that went then—Fort Worth being a day or so away rather than a half-hour—with county seat-hood. A few of the buildings must certainly have stone memory of the day in 1875 when old Nelson Mitchell, known as Cooney, less guilty than his youngers but more available, was hanged in Granbury town. Names on some dig back into the shallow antiquity of the Brazos country, like the feed store of P. H. Thrash and Sons: in Ewell it is written that The People killed Jere Green in P. H. Thrash's pasture, in the sixties.

Nor could the hardware store, high-ceilinged and gloomy, have changed much since hame-strap and hand-pump days, but it was a good one and had the lantern chimney and pliers and ball of cord and other things I needed. At the ser sta gro again the owner, when I'd bought some staples from him and thanked him for his kindness, said: "Well, I always figure I can tell a man that means well when I see him."

I hoped he could, and hoped it was to him that they meant well. Back on the river, it felt odd to be coasting along under carpet-grassed picnic flats with barbecue pits and chairs and landings, and flights of steps leading up to houses on the hill. Granbury withstands the river's periodic ire by holding to the high ground. Beyond the houses, lining down into the country again, feeling benevolent toward people because of the couple at the ser sta gro, I came to a dirt bluff where the chromed nose of a hot rod showed against the sky. A young man moved up beside it, sideburned, dressed in bright blues, walking with the rolled jerking of his shoulders, akin to a pigeon's head movements, which afflicts a good many athletes and self-made men and people who want to look like athletes or self-made men.

"Well, look at the local hero!" he said, staring down. Someone snickered behind him and moved up to see—this one shorter, barbered hybridly with his hair burred on top and long and wavily greasy on sides and back, with ducktails.

I looked at them. They looked back leering, but said no more, maybe because I was dirty and gaunt and browned and had a shotgun's stock sticking up beside my thigh. A turn sliced them and their haircuts and their purple car off from view, and then there was nothing but the river and the willows and the big hardwoods, and on the hills the cedar— juniper, really, though no one calls it that.

Below Granbury the Brazos snakes among such hills for forty-five bridgeless miles to show itself again to public view at Highway 67 in the little county named Somervell, which broke itself off from Hood in the seventies on the grounds that Granbury was too far away to ride horseback for legal business. (The Somervellians are still a bit that way, otherwise-minded.) A part of Hood and most of Somervell make a kind of northern tip for a broken belt of cedar-covered limestone hills which skips south through a dozen or so counties and then curls spreading west into the vast Edwards Plateau. Once, before Anglo-Saxons hit it, much of that limestone belt was a rolling prairie thick in grass. But its topsoil wasn't deep and used away quickly under the bite of plows and herds. The cedars crawled up out of the draws as the only feasible expression, then, of nature's abhorrence of bare ground, until finally in some places, as far as you could see from the highest hilltops, there was only a green-black unreflecting expanse with a few flashes of white stone where even cedar couldn't grow. It was a poor part of the state. Its people —those who stayed, or those who came in because they couldn't afford to go to better land—shaped themselves to the world of the cedar hills, as people will shape themselves to country when they have to, and built a stoic economy around it—chopping fence posts, herding goats where sufficient hardwoods remained for browse, still farming a little and disastrously in creek and river bottoms, making white whisky, running ser sta gros. . . .

Lately city money, working hard and backed by Federal aid, has found the way to bulldoze off the cedars and with a few years' gentle care to nurse back native grasses and paint a semblance of the primeval range. Without having yet gone far, that process is the chart of the future. As we roll on happily toward that saturation census point that everybody used to lament in the Japanese, land—any land—gets too precious to waste. Though in most parts of the cedar hills the stoic economy and the Sam Sowells and the Davis Birdsongs still exist, drouth and discontent and wars and purchases are driving them out. Aircraft factories and beer halls and California and the general American driftingness absorb them.

Not that all those things are clear from a boat on the Brazos. A river in a sense makes its own country along its course, renewing the lowlands with silt, pampering on its banks trees and shrubs and grasses of species diffcrent from those on the ruined slopes of its watershed. But you can't miss the cedar hills bulking on one side or the other, and sometimes on both.

Their people differ from the other people of the upper-middle Brazos mainly in degree, but the degree does make a difference. The cedar people have more hill Southern in them; their dialect is stronger, as are their pride of poverty and their touchiness and their suspicion of other kinds of folks. And their fierce equalitarianism—an implicit attitude of "I'm as good as you are" which sometimes produces comedy and sometimes danger and sometimes, working on good material, dignity . . .

I knew a cedar-hill man who served as foreman on one of the new cleared ranches built by city men in that region. He was a good foreman and liked his job and liked his boss. An oilman who visited the ranch offered him twice his salary to come to Oklahoma and run a ranch that he had there. He turned it down. But finally, when the offer got to three times his salary and his wife was shoving at him to think of the kids and even his current employer admitted—wryly—that he wouldn't blame him in the least for going, he agreed. He called Buck Peebles, a silent wiry type who hauls cattle and household goods and Mexican shearers and goats and anything else that's willing to ride on his old truck and pay for the privilege. They loaded on the furniture and the kids and the wife, and drove 200 miles up to the new place.

The oilman was waiting for them, anxious that they like him. Good men are hard to come by. He was courtly to the wife and showed them their house, a stout and handsome one, two-storied with oaks around it and a fenced yard and a deep sweet-water well and a rich garden patch. He chucked the kids under their chins and called them by their right names, all five of them. The ranch itself spread velvet-grassed to the horizons, and below the house a flowing creek wandered, dammed at one point into a ten-acre lake stocked with fish, around which registered whitefaces and fat quarter horses grazed. The kids scattered like a flushed covey, shouting. The foreman listened and looked and tasted the water and kicked the garden's loam with his toe and dug his thumbnail into the house's hard coat of white paint, and said practically nothing. Finally they came out front again where Buck Peebles, unheeded by anyone upon arrival or now, was leaning against his truck's fender and smoking a patent drug-store pipe and peeling, with a sharp stockman's knife, the bark from a green oak switch.

"Might as well start moving in," the owner said. "I'll get somebody up here to help you."

"I don't know . . ." the foreman said.

The owner glanced up. "What's the matter?" he said. "You don't like the house? I'll have it changed, any way you want."

"Ain't that," the foreman said.

The oilman, unsettled, said he didn't understand. He thought it was a pretty good ranch. He *knew* it was.

"Ain't that," the other man said. "Hit's a hell of a sweet place and that's flat true."

"Well, what is it then?"

"Since you ast . . ." the foreman said without hostility, jerking his head toward the wordless, whittling shape of Buck Peebles: "Since you ast, I guess what's the matter is I don't want to work for nobody that's too good to speak to no God-damn truck driver."

And with a lift of his brows he moved his family back into and onto the truck, and Buck Peebles drove them the 200 miles back down to the cedar hills and the old job.

Like the rest of the upper-middle Brazosites, the cedar people are heavily Caucasian. But, as in other things, more so. The concept of race has a rawness just now, with good reason, but it still has a relevance, too. It has relevance all through the ragged griffon shape of the former Confederacy, and though the upper-middle Brazos was but fractionally Confederate, it has relevance there.

Almost no Mexicans came that far up the river in the old days, and only a few Negroes, brought by more prosperous families like the luckless Terrells. Mainly grazing land, that region lay north and west of the soils and rain belts where the true cotton complex of things could be reproduced; plantation-type labor was not economic. A thick preponderance of the whites who came were of the Southern independent and tenant-farming classes, people who'd always tied their own shoelaces and plowed their own fields but who, because of long competition and embarrassment, were fierce about the pigmentation of their skins. If they were "old" Texans, the war for independence from Mexico hadn't tended to salve that attitude in them.

There were more Negroes around during the fifties and sixties of the last century than there are today. Some of the ones in the old time were vivid, like Bose Ikard and the one I've never seen called anything but "Old Nigger Britt" (his lone-wolf vengeance on The People, before they got him, was spectacular), but most were a minor tide who, with emancipation and the legal injection into them of free will, moved back to more hospitable places, like coastal sea organisms which, having probed the temperatures and the plankton north and south, settle in a belt where they can survive.

The *Texas Almanac* tells some of it. Palo Pinto County, the good-sized resort and army town of Mineral Wells holding most of its people, has a population made up of "94.0%

Anglo-Am., 2.2% Latin Am., 3.8% Negro." (The Latin Ams are recent arrivals, shearers and artisans who make up little colonies in the towns or have been brought in for ranch labor; all Caucasians are lumped as Anglo-Ams, though that seems unfair to the occasional clots from less rough-edged cultures. . . .) Parker County, richer than the others in many parts and therefore more Southern, has nevertheless "97.0% Anglo-Am., 1.8% Latin Am., 1.2% Negro." Hood, less urban and shading into the cedar country, runs 99.3, 0.2, and 0.5, and Somervell, a cedar stronghold, is quite succinctly "100% Anglo-Am."

Ike Atterbury told me once, without either bitterness or humor, since he is incapable of either, that it was illegal for Negroes to live in Somervell County. Just against the law. West of there lies a belt equally touchy where they used to put signs outside the towns advising anyone whose epidermal darkness wasn't the result of sunburn to keep moving, and farther west still the whole question of tolerance goes academic for the want of any menacing outsiders, beyond a few Mexican sheepherders, to have to tolerate or not tolerate. In the scoop-shaped projection of Texas at whose point El Paso lies, Anglo-Saxon and Hispano-Indian rather balance each other, and despite Miss Ferber seem to get along not badly. In recent years the popularity of racial tension has roiled up some controversy out that way, but it tends, like the *gente ranchera* themselves, to be toughly, wryly humorous. A rancher in the Big Bend told me a very funny story of that kind, but it was pretty dirty, too, and for that matter far from the Brazos and its starknesses.

Shall we then desert the raw subject of race without furnishing any anecdotes? I guess so; none of those that come to mind is edifying—neither the time when gentle

Bill Briggs wouldn't get out of the car in Bowie, Texas, nor the time when Jim Lemmon and some cohorts shot up the camp of the colored highway workers, nor . . . No. Let us return to our picturesque Anglo-Ams, or maybe just to one of them, a solitary tattered sort coasting along a river in a canoe. . . .

Camped on mud—the river had been falling—under scraggly willows, hoping a rise wouldn't come in the night, I dumped out the sack of staples I'd bought onto a tarp. A ser sta gro doesn't cater to loners or to childless nibbling couples; it sells things in quantity, and most of the containers held too much. I filled my plastic sugar pot and threw the rest of the five-pound bag in the river, invoking pardon from the shades of the frugal old ones. For meat, since the pleasant grocers had had none fresh, I'd bought a square frozen pack of veal patties. They were about as far from the hot-streaming meat of one's own killing as one could get—close to the ideal of a friend of mine, oddly a rancher, who likes all food disguised and geometrically reshaped, as different as possible from the living organism it once was. He says that doctoring screw-worm infections did that to him. The patties turned out to be fine-ground hamburger, called veal to excuse their pallid fattiness. But fried in butter with onions, an egg on top of each patty and a baked potato besides, they made reasonable fare. The passenger took his tartare, and wolfed them.

In the dusk, at an old crossing a quarter-mile below us, two brindle scrub cows and a black calf waded out halfway across the river and casually swam when it got deep, sweeping far downstream before they hit slick footing again. Fit successors, though rare, to the cross-grained longhorns that used to ford above and below there by the thousands . . .

As always on the river after people, it was good to be alone again, and to know that another long lone stretch lay ahead. Not very long, though—I'd be loafing if I spun it out to six days or a week. The trip's end was visible, but the idea of its ending was a hard one to get my mind around.

AT YET ANOTHER CREEK MOUTH I eased down on yet another fisherman, and scared him. He jerked as the canoe's bow came abreast of where he sat, then contained it and looked at me expressionless. He had the dark eyes and blocky jaws that in our part of the country seem usually to mean Indiàn blood, but he would nevertheless qualify in the *Almanac* as pure Anglo-Am. (O irony, isn't it, you People who lost? . . .)

I ruddered out of the Brazos's flow into the crystallinity of the creek, and he turned his head, watching. His line tugged. He pulled out a foot-long channel catfish. Lifting a fat tow sack from where he had it tethered in the water, he dropped the fish in. I said he seemed to be doing all right.

"Nothin' but a bunch of little sommidges," he said.

Between steep banks the creek ran back under overarched trees in a long pool, the mild current that fell into it over rocks at its head just strong enough to hold out the silt-thick river. I said it was a pretty place.

He said: "Hit won't be so God-damn purty after *they* git thew with it."

"Who?"

"Them," he said. . . . It turned out he meant the Fort Worth family, who owned pecan land up the creek and planned to dam it for irrigation. The creek, like most of the others, was an old axis of settlement in that country, and has ancient grist mills on it (one of the millers, wrote Ewell, had a whisky still, "which upset the religious and attracted the unrighteous"), and stabs up near Acton and the David Crockett grant of land—posthumously awarded to that tough and misrepresented Tennessean—where the Widow Crockett lived out her time and died and is buried and some of their blood still thrive.

When asked, the countryman said he'd grown up in the De Cordova Bend downstream, managing somehow to accent both the first and second syllables of Cordova in a way that no one not from that neighborhood can copy.

"Some of that's pecan land now, too."

"*All* of it!" he said as angrily as was consonant with Anglo-Am reserve. "Same damn outfit. Cut down all the woods. My brother he's worked for them scutters eight years. Could of had a good job with the highway construction and he ought to of took it. I told him."

I'd been there. It's a shining orchard project four or five thousand acres big, block-built by the present owner and another before him out of the tired homesteads that used to quilt the post-oak scrub within the bend's great fleur-de-lis. Row upon row, the young pecans march out across the sandy loam, alternating now with ranks of fruit trees that help pay costs until the time when the nut crops will reach commercial bulk. Pecans are a long-term investment, more for the profit of sons than of the father who plants them. In our razzle-dazzle, speculative economy, that kind of permanent planning for land stands out pleasantly. It contrasts too with the savage traditional wearing out and moving on.

But old sour Square Jaw sitting there, winking black eyes at the river in negative fury, had his own kind of point. Plantations of that efficiency—"operations," rather than farms or ranches—were the death of the old way. Whether the old way had been good or bad, it had been his way. This other wasn't. When the city money buys you out, you can live no more in the poor-proud privacy of a shack back in the brush on the land your people wore out long since, raising your kids to the proud bitter mores that you were raised to before them, shaping in their mouths the proud nasal dialect that your grandfather shaped in your father's mouth. Not even if the city money buys your neighbor out, you can't . . . The bulldozers scrape bare your privacy and you move away to work in the city, or you take a job on the old ground for the city money and its operations, and every once in a while a bathed and shaven and tailored type drives out to inspect that particular one among his holdings and tells you what you're doing wrong, and how to do better, in language that sounds like a God-damn radio announcer. . . . Unproud alternatives . . .

The dispossession must bring much the same feeling the Indians used to have, a century ago. . . .

I remarked, to be saying something, that there'd been changes just about everywhere. But either he'd detected city-ness in my accent or he disliked inanities or he'd talked all he felt like talking. He grunted. I pushed up the creek and began casting a bug for bass, and when I looked around again he had gone.

The pup was restless; I put him ashore and he scampered around on the thick leaf mat beneath the trees, stopping now and then to plunge his nose into it up to his eyes, sniff, snort, and scamper on. There were bass, but they were striking short of the bug, slapping at it with their tails or arching up from under it and plunging down to make it dance on boiling water. I changed it and finally caught a couple, small ones but vigorous against the long aliveness of the rod. Jumpers . . . I'm afflicted by a belief (Veblen would smile) that the fly rod is the only decent tool to use in fishing fresh water. I use the others, maybe most of the time, because more often than not the fish are in moods or places that the long rod won't reach well, but I always feel a little guilty about it, less than serious. Bait casting and more especially spinning are technological processes, dependent on the rotary machine that holds your line, and while there can be pleasure in the plunge of their weighted lures to the spot where you want them to go, it can't compare, for me, with the feel of the long, slow whip of the long rod laying its line on the quiet water beneath trees. Besides, fly fishing is more sewn in with the whole evolved ritual of angling. That this is archaism I'll admit, nor would I argue its right against a man who finds his joy in hurling treble-hooked bullets through the air, and winching his fish to boat or shore with an apparatus that practically thinks for him.

I kept the fish. Attached through the lips to the chain stringer, they'd stay alive for days in the cold autumn water, a kind of living meat locker. On shore the pup yipped and backed away, shaking his head, from a hole in the base of a tree. Something had bitten him. I called him to the boat and held him squirming between my knees and examined his head and foreparts, but could find no fang marks, not that snakes were probable after all those frosts. A late-surviving wasp, maybe, or a tree asp or a scorpion . . . He crawled into his blanket-lined nook beneath the tarp, safe there from unknown stinging things.

Above the arching trees it was a fine day, blue and yellow with puffy white clouds. Off to the right a redbird called:

— — — —
  —   —   —   —,

and farther on, a Carolina wren answered him in key:

— — — —
  _   _   _   _.

Sometimes in summer when one or the other of them gives that call alone, I find it hard to be sure which bird it is, but heard together thus, each was clearly what he was.

Another Specimen of Natural History eyed me from a low branch up the creek, a kingfisher, cocked to fly if I got too close. Casting still, I made a spaghetti mess out of the slack fly line next to the reel, wrapping it around my feet and the handle of the paddle and the shotgun's stock. I pulled at it for a while and then started cursing, never having been patient with my own ineptitudes. Just then the kingfisher dived at a minnow, made a big splash, missed, and flew back to his limb with a long high chatter of rage. There we sat, two ill-tempered piscatorial dubs, the only difference between us being that I saw some humor in the likeness. . . .

The day was Thanksgiving. Maybe, trying, I'd be able to get more wild meat than those two little bass and celebrate it right. Not that it was a holiday that had ever seemed to me to have much real connection with that part of the country. There hadn't been much of the Pilgrim kind of Puritanism in those parts. A sternness, yes, and the old tough Calvinistic web holding ethics together, or trying to . . . But the Pilgrims had been Englishmen making do as best they could in a wild land, and at times they didn't make do so well, and when they did they had the English grace to be grateful for it to God. By the time Anglo-Ams had hit northwest Texas, they were the end product of two centuries of frontier, and could make do almost anywhere or at least survive, and the controlled graceful Englishness had rubbed off somewhere. They tended to be either religious and abstemious, or crazy wild.

The pup threw up his breakfast in the bottom of the canoe. He was swelling about the head and had a hump-nosed, gross look and red eyes; his ears when I touched them were hot and welted and a quarter-inch thick. It had happened once before, when he'd assaulted a yellowjacket at home, and I knew from that time, having paid a vet three dollars to find it out, that there wasn't anything to do except wait till he felt better. I cleaned up his mess and tucked him back in his blanket.

On down . . .

CHAPTER FIFTEEN

THE Truitts and the Mitchells (we still haven't reached their exact home country on the river, but we seem to have edged abreast of them in time) furnish a fair example of the dangers of charitable action—or maybe, depending on the point of view that gouges your sympathy, of the dangers of getting tangled up with the frontier breed of Texans. Ewell wrote a little about the trouble, and so did the biographer of an East Texas lawman who got drawn into its latter calamities. Armed with what they had recorded and with old clippings, court transcripts, and letters, C. L. Sonnichsen, an eloquent specialist in feuds, went to Hood County a few years back when the old ones were dropping off life's tree like November leaves, talked to the few who were left that knew anything about it, and wrote it all down as thoroughly and straight as such matters can be written down in the myopic aftertime, blinking back through the chaparral of fear and hate and love and pride and plain bad memory.

It always seemed to me (the myopia has an advantage: that dimly seen things can be shaped as one wishes and

given the moral one wants them to have) that the trouble
was one in which the civilized new townsmen showed their
brushed teeth, showed they were the future. It was a lot of
other things, too, and was not at bottom a town trouble, but
I think it did mean that. Old Nelson Mitchell, known as
Cooney, was a countryman of the ancient, sharp-edged,
let-me-alone stripe, with long back hair like Chesley Dobbs
and a white beard, and the opposing Truitts had a Methodist
preacher among them. For the Granbury-recruited jury that
finally knotted a rope around old Nelson's neck—though in
the brawl for which they sentenced him he'd been unarmed,
and his son-in-law and a friend who'd done some shooting
were only sent to jail—for that jury, preachers had a symbolism. So undoubtedly, and unluckily for him, did long-
haired Nelson Mitchell.

He had been there a good while before the Truitts came,
and was there solidly, owning a big stretch of land in and
about the bend that is still called after him. He was a cowman. He raised three sons in his own rough upright mold,
and one day in the late sixties or early seventies the quick
generosity that went often with that way of being caused
him to do a thing he must have pondered over considerably,
later on.

He and his oldest, Bill, working cattle near Comanche
Mountain ("the Hoary Monarch of this wide domain"),
ran across a sorry encampment, a broken-down, foodless,
transportless, and by now hopeless family of the migrant
westerers who in those years were gushing into the country,
filling it up. They were gushing in a little bit late, not having
harkened quite soon enough to the word or not having been
willing earlier to play The People's games. Now they had
to take the leached leavings of the first-comers or the hard-

scrabble stretches the first-comers hadn't wanted, or else to leapfrog the first-comers out onto the plains where, disliked by ranchers and having no cattle tradition to work from, they blocked out the dry-land homesteads that bequeathed a Dust Bowl to their grandchildren.

"Hot God A'mighty!" maybe Cooney Mitchell said, looking them over—the scrawny, sad kids, the washed-out, hungry faces of their elders, the old wagon with one runty horse that couldn't pull it by himself and the other one lying dead and ready to stink beside the whole mess. . . . "Fixin' to have some birthday doin's?"

"Had a little bad luck," maybe the Truitt man said in stiff answer, for that is who they were.

"A little. Looks like they turned the whole damn thunder pot upside down on you."

"No need to talk that way," the other said.

"Tetchy booger," Cooney said to his son Bill, raising on his stirrups so that the breeze could play against his sweaty rump. To Truitt he said: "Alabama, you sound like."

"Mississippi."

"All right," Cooney said. What he did then—and some of his last words later, with the prickly new hemp around his neck and the wagon about to roll out from under him and leave him pendant from a limb, reminisced back bitterly to the thing he did—was to shoot the blasphemous force of his will into the sorry outfit under the oak tree and pick them up and move them over to his place on the Brazos, and to give them jobs and help them build a cabin, and to pay young James Morgan Truitt's preministerial expenses, including a suit of clothes better than any Cooney himself had ever worn, and so thoroughly to reconstruct in the whole family its crumbled self-respect and solvency that before long it'd bought the next place to the north and was suing Nelson Mitchell in Granbury court over where the boundary between them lay—or, some say, over whether or not the land, originally Mitchell's, had been fully paid for and was the Truitts' to possess.

And won the case . . .

Historical differences that take people into civil or criminal courts—or both, as here—usually leave a pretty good record of themselves. It is a by-advantage of the common law's slow-grinding, cumulative muddle. But there were a swarm of people in Texas in the seventies and eighties who didn't want to have a pretty good record left of themselves in legal papers. In the years after the War, when the surly throngs of Spanish kine in the brush went from being practically wild meat, free for any hungry man's taking and welcome to it, to valuable property salable for hard Yankee cash at the north end of the cattle trails, few cowmen's hands from the Big River to the Red stayed rosy clean. The old way of brands and cow hunts, based on barter and trust and too much meat, was loose. Mavericking and related activities offered temptation that even the righteous didn't withstand. The unrighteous, as Heel Flies or whatnot, had been hard at work with iron and rope and quill even during the War. Land titles had been forged. Vengeance for transgressions and self-defense against such vengeance brought murder. The Reconstruction tug of war between scalawags backed by Negro troops and Confederate mobs dressed in bedsheets or Comanche buckskins didn't help. In the old courthouses —frame or log, most of them, combustible heaps—facts and the names of men stacked up in unpleasant files, ready to smear that honor which in those days was a commodity, or to make second and third offenses more painfully punishable.

So they burned down the courthouses. Scores went in that way, and scores of the quaint Victorian ones that replaced them (whose own occasional replacement now by block-modern, air-conditioned structures we as quaintly bemoan) date back to that time and that reason. The unpleasant papers went up in slip-sliding bright embers against the night skies, and the arsonists could start stealing one another's beeves and land and killing one another all over again.

Granbury's courthouse went thus in 1875, after the land dispute between the Truitts and the Mitchells, after the bloody fight that came out of it, after old Cooney Mitchell was in the jailhouse waiting for the rope. (What did the subsequent brawl on the square between Dr. Turner and James Counts, "desperate men" both of them, have to do with that burning, Mr. Ewell? You don't say; you just put the two facts into one paragraph. . . .) Therefore no one now (I told you that phrase recurs) will ever know just what went on in either the land dispute or the old man's trial for murder.

What is sure is that the Truitts had won the land suit, regardless of its details, and that on the afternoon it was over the two factions unfortunately ran into each other on the road back down into the Mitchell Bend, not over a mile or so from where Cooney and Bill had found the Truitts in the beginning.

Or were the Mitchells lying in ambush in a creek bottom, shotguns cocked, as Sheriff Spradley was told? . . .

Or did they, as newspapers reported, purposefully overtake the Truitts six miles out of Granbury and open fire (with shotguns; they're in all the versions, and had a sight more to do with most Texas squabbling than Colt's pistols), and if so how many did they kill, and whom? The father and the

eldest of the three sons, as Sheriff Spradley heard? All three
of the sons, as the newspapers said? The middle brother, Sam
Truitt, and the youngest, Ike, as Sonnichsen decided on his
evidence?

And did old Cooney Mitchell, unarmed, caper about the
outskirts on his pony hollering: "Give 'em hell, boys!" as
the slaughter progressed, and did he when little Ike Truitt,
fifteen years old, was screaming with the pain of wounds,
yell: "Somebody put a stop to that boy's damn mouth!" so
that Bill, as the child knelt begging for pity, shot the top of
his head off? . . . The Reverend James Morgan Truitt,
M. E. Church South, said so, and maintained it in court
dressed in a black suit better than any Cooney had ever
worn, and made his point.

The Mitchells said (or the Mitchells' friends told Sonnichsen that the Mitchells had told them) that the Truitts
had done the overtaking on the road, and had ridden past
them singing a song about an old nigger man who had gone
out to steal himself a hog, but got caught. The Mitchells
held their tempers and their tongues. Out of sight around a
turn ahead, the Truitts turned their horses into the brush and
hid till the Mitchells had passed again, then overtook them
yet another time, still singing. The Mitchells said nothing.

Then little Ike (a problematical personality; here, though
still fifteen years old, he is all nerved up and meaner than
hell and carrying a derringer) rode back past them chanting
the song's scurrilous burden, and still couldn't make them
turn their heads or blink their eyes, and finally galloped his
pony up behind Bill Mitchell with his derringer out and
snapped it, a misfire, at the back of Bill's head. An old man
in the Mitchells' party, James Shaw, saw it and blasted little
Ike out of his saddle, and Bill Mitchell, watching the guns

rise, picked out Sam Truitt and shot him, and there it went. . . .

Was *that* the way it was?

The way it was, like the way so many things were, is a fog. All that is certain is that some Truitts were killed with shotguns and that Cooney Mitchell, Old Man Shaw, and a Mitchell son-in-law named Owens were tried for it, Bill Mitchell and another in-law having meanwhile hit the brush. Whatever Truitts had died, the Reverend James hadn't; dimpled here and there by large buckshot, he was the major witness. On the strength of Granbury's genteel respect for ministers' words, Owens and Shaw went to the state prison, and old Nelson Mitchell, known as Cooney, got the rope. Before he hanged, his youngest boy Jeff was shot dead trying to sneak poison to him in his cell so that it might not be of record that a Mitchell had been executed as a criminal. Cooney's cup was full and bitter. At the ceremonial itself, just north of Granbury, the sheriff asked the usual question.

"Hell yes, I got somethin' to say," Cooney told him. "Did you think I wouldn't?"

He said it. There was a big crowd to listen. He said he'd always paid his debts and no man could call him a cheat, and waited to see if any man would. None did. He said it was a damned lie he'd told anybody to shoot little Ike Truitt, though he'd needed shooting bad, and that it was that lie that had put him there on the wagon where he stood.

He called: "Jim Truitt!"

People on the crowd's fringes turned to stare at a man in a good black suit who held his eyes on the ground. Loudly and surely, Cooney Mitchell asked Jim Truitt to cast his mind back to a time when one starving pony couldn't pull a certain wagon any farther west, and asked him how about that? And how about a big Bible and a suit of clothes that somebody had bought somebody else? . . .

The Reverend James Morgan Truitt, M. E. Church South, didn't answer.

"All right," Cooney said, his white hair and beard wild about his face in the October wind. "All right. Easy does it, Shur'f, I'm putt near done."

He said: "All right. I just want to make a ree-quest. I ain't makin' it to Jim Truitt. I'm makin' it to somebody else out there that knows I've told truth. I want that somebody to look up my boy Bill, wherever he's hid out. I want him to tell Bill that the last single thing I had a God-damn word to say about in this world, was how I hoped Bill would never lay down and rest till he run down and kilt the liar that put his old daddy up here with a rope around his neck."

The sheriff said, embarrassed: "Cooney . . ."

"I'm thew," Cooney said. "Hit was a lot of talkin'."

And a pair of unstarving sleek mules pulled another certain wagon quite smoothly out from under old Nelson Mitchell, known as Cooney, and that was that.

Before long, people decided that Bill Mitchell either hadn't received the word or he didn't want to do anything about it. They erred. For eleven years, a fugitive and a saddle tramp, he drifted about the Southwest nursing sour remembrance, working for other men under a name not his own, probably riding up the cattle trails two or three times or more. James Truitt left Granbury and prospered elsewhere.

Then in 1886 Bill Mitchell, not having forgotten a thing, sniffed James Truitt down in a village in East Texas called Timpson, where he was preaching and running a newspaper and raising a family. Bill walked in, spoke not harshly to Mrs. Truitt to make sure he'd found the right house, and shot the seated minister through the head with a pistol, riding away afterward on a sorrel horse with a little coffee pot tied up behind on his bed roll. The coffee pot helped to trace and identify him, but even so it took the law's bulldogs twenty-one more years to grab him out in New Mexico and bring him back, and they got scratched doing it.

Maybe Granbury was a little bit nagged by what it had done to old Cooney, or maybe it was just that later on, to keep the courts from choking on fodder, a kind of amnesty was understood to cover the multitudinous murders of the seventies and eighties which hadn't been collected for on the spot. Anyhow, a court there vindicated Bill of the '74 killings, and it took five more years for the concerted labor of several people to get him sentenced to ninety-nine years for the murder of the Reverend James Morgan Truitt. He went to jail finally in 1912, aged sixty-four, served two stoic years, slipped casually over the wall one night, and hasn't yet been seen again.

WERE THERE, you ask, no edifying events along the Brazos? Was it all gore and bitter gall, blow and counterblow, hate spun out to hate's only logical end? Didn't a mother somewhere along the river's banks once stroke a child's head and spark in him a flame to build laws or glory or ease for his people? Didn't jolly old men beneath live oaks tell one another tales in which no single droplet of blood sounded its splash? Didn't sober, useful, decent people build for themselves sober, useful, decent lives, and lead us soberly, usefully, decently up through the years to that cultural peak upon which we now find ourselves standing?

Yes. It isn't hard (the Western movies do it over and over and over again, to everyone's edification) to impose on that

hind-seen world a pattern that makes it clear that the kind-
liest of possible Gods had it in mind all along to install us
in two-car suburban homes with air conditioning, television,
and automatic kitchens. All you need to do is play around a
bit with the weights of the scale—every storyteller's right—
and show the gentle, genteel, sober, useful, and decent people clinching a few victories over the old violence, as they
did over Cooney Mitchell. Everything that happened was
to the good. The composite hero won. His pink Thunderbird
speeds into the sunset toward a new brick house engineered
for patio living.

The trouble is, you need to see it that way. That the
gentler people did gain a kind of control is certain. That it
was time they did so is probable. That the control they
gained was deep and lasting, and wiped out the old evil
roughness, and left space in every man for the Jean-Jacques
Rousseau kind of good to rise up like milky sap, I've tended
always to doubt.

Neither a land nor a people ever starts over clean. Country
is compact of all its past disasters and strokes of luck—of
flood and drouth, of the caprices of glaciers and sea winds,
of misuse and disuse and greed and ignorance and wisdom—
and though you may doze away the cedar and coax back
bluestem and mesquite grass and side-oats grama, you're not
going to manhandle it into anything entirely new. It's
limited by what it has been, by what's happened to it. And a
people, until that time when it's uprooted and scattered and
so mixed with other peoples that it has in fact perished, is
much the same in this as land. It inherits. Its progenitors
stand behind its elbow, and not only the sober gentle ones.
Most of all, maybe, the old hairy direct primitives whose
dialect lingers in its mouth, whose murderous legend tones

its dreams, whose oversimple thinking infects its attitudes toward bombs and foreigners and rockets to the moon.

I don't think this means only Texans.

Another trouble, too—a deeper one—with the establishment of that pleasant air-conditioned pattern is that you need to be able to see old Cooney Mitchell as an evil. . . .

CHAPTER SIXTEEN

MIGRANT yellow-bellied flycatchers, or I niched them so, brightly fruited the bare trees along the river for a couple of hundred yards below Square Jaw's creek, and then there were ducks. The banks are dirt in that stretch, and where the spring floods had undereaten them fallen cottonwoods and willows lay out diagonally in the river in a continuous tangle, their roots still clutching treacherous earth. "Sweepers," someone has called them who got shoved by the current into the rasp of their dry branchlets and lost his hat and dignity and fishing rod. In spring and summer the big moccasins drape themselves there, and if you're of a mind for such sport you can coast along popping at them with a twenty-two. Now eight baldpates swam smoothly out of the tangle in a little flock as I approached, and twitching their tails like honkytonk waitresses steamed ahead of me downriver, barely beyond reach of the shotgun's pellets. I kept the paddle in the water to prevent it from flashing and scaring them, and slid it forward edgewise between strokes, remembering the old imitation-Chippewa days when we used to practice such things.

For a time, wanting meat for a holiday supper, Pilgrim or not, I tried to put on speed, but the eye of the drake that led them kept a precise gauge of the interval between us; when I moved faster they did, too. Jump-shooting on the river that way, you usually do best on singles and pairs separated from their flocks. Drained of the calm that numbers give them, they tend to wait till you've come abreast, then to flush explosively from under the shore. But these eight had the wary wisdom of a group.

It was a good day, wind-wisped, with cottony small clouds on the high air. The river, dropping slowly from the spate of snow and rain, had not yet cleared but was coffee-translucent under the sun. On the flat place in the bow that was the tarp-covered food box, the pup had curled himself to soak up warmth against the venom in his blood; sleeping, he snored thickly and jerked from time to time, but looked better than he had. . . .

Ahead, faintly then louder, sounded the *pum-pucker-um, pum-pucker-um* of an old electric well-pump at some farm, and the voices of shrill children. The widgeons began to zigzag, nervous between the human noise in front and the human apparatus behind. The interval shrank to just within shot range. For a moment I pondered, balancing vague honor against the idea of duck for Thanksgiving, knowing that when they flushed it would be away from me and almost immediately out of range again. Then—honorless—I eased the gun up and shot at a young drake swimming off to the left of the group. He died into an abrupt lump on the water. The rest flew, but one delayed, and to wipe out the pot shot's guilt I fired the other barrel at him as he rose. It caught him unsolidly; he dropped behind the others and below them and beat, losing height, for a quarter-mile down the river before he slewed clumsily again to the water.

If I ever quit shooting, it'll likely be because of unrecovered wounded game. . . . I grabbed up the dead one and set off pushing hard. The oiled maple paddle dug in, bending, and the canoe rose and began to skim and the sun felt good and the speed felt good and my muscles felt good, doing fast and easily and well the work they'd been training themselves to all the way down the river. The pup sat up, staring back at me.

But the widgeon waited till I was within sixty or seventy yards of him, then flew another half-mile down. I kept going, and he flew again, and again, and again, until suddenly it was late afternoon and I was scooting past the live oaks and willows at the mouth of Falls Creek, three or four miles beyond where I'd planned to go that day. The duck had winged around a turn below, still strong, and I was tired. I crunched the canoe's bow onto a drift-strewn gravel bar where Hale and I and Bill Briggs used to make camp a long long time ago, and carried the gear up to the sandy second shore, hitching my tent's fore-rope when I raised it to the arch of a low thick live-oak limb that at its outer end dipped to touch the sand before turning upward and fraying into twigs and dark tough leaves. Inland a few yards rotting stratified limestone rose, and on top of that, I knew though I couldn't see them, were the buildings of a girls' camp that in summer was plangent with the shrieks of small females divided unfemalely into tribes and packs and regiments. But not now . . .

At the creek to get a bucket of clear water, I looked to the billowing line where the darker river shoved past, and saw a flashing beneath the surface. Since on the willow-thick bank there would be no room to whip a flyline, I went to the canoe and got out the spinning rod. In the half-hour before sundown, I stood in one spot flipping a little spoon with a pork-rind tail out on the river and reeling it back into the creek, and on each single cast just after it darted back out of the river's coffee murk I had a strike. I didn't hook all of them, but must have caught ten or twelve while I stood there, good head-shaking jumpers, blacks of two and a half or three pounds that kicked and splashed and bulldogged back and forth sidewise before yielding to the rod's spring and the reel's steady mechanical tug.

They were gorging without caution on hickory shad; the largest one I caught was stuffed with them and had a five-incher's tail sticking up into his throat, there being no more room in his belly. It was one of those times, rare in my experience, when the forces that rule such things fall queerly into balance; "Frank Forester" and "Nessmuk" and the other old pleasantly corny Eastern outdoors writers would have said that the Red Gods were smiling. I strung only two of the bass, letting the others go back into the water without handling them any more than I had to, remembering the afternoon's wasted, wounded baldpate.

It was good fishing, a little too good. In angling, as in reading, suspense is a quality worth having. You savor the waiting quest of quarry or fact and like their possession the more for the time and—you tell yourself—the skill that went into attaining it. I do, anyhow. When the Red Gods grin, there is no wait and no skill; there are just luck and fish. It's like reading in an encyclopedia. . . . I used to have a book by a trout-fishing Englishman, one of those little specialized unutilitarian volumes that our parent breed does better than anyone else ever did, in which there was a description of one heavily lucky day on a chalkstream. Then the author with fervor wished that such days might be few. They had no challenge in them.

For supper, though, I was able to Give Thanks. The holiday ritual seemed to have little to do with the river, but for its honor I put in an hour or so of food preparation and came up with fried bass filets and beans and steamed brown rice and biscuit bread and a roasted widgeon stuffed with prunes, and there seemed to be little reason to envy the fare of anyone in town. It was all good—the better for being the harvest of gun and rod—and afterward I sat under the arched live-oak limb by the fire with the pup, drinking coffee with a little whisky and honey in it, listening to the Morse dots and dashes of steam whistling out the end pores of a damp log. That gets to be one of the river's symphonic sounds, like owls and the gurgle of snag-thwarted water and the eternal cries of herons and the chug of tractors in unseen bottom fields. Whimsically I wondered if maybe the steam sounds might not *be* a code, the channeled voices of the ghosts of puritans and Comanches and horse thieves and, maybe, Gothic gingerbread fanciers. It seemed as likely a way for communication between the worlds as table-tilting or those other phantasmakinetic manifestations. . . .

Or maybe they were the Red Gods, sour because no offering had been laid on their altar. Cleaning up, I took what scraps the pup wouldn't eat down to the gravel bar and threw them far out on the eddying moonlit surface of the river just above the old mill rapids, for catfish or Red Gods or whatever, but when I went back to the fire the whistle-voices were still gibbering.

One trouble with sportsmanship (I guess we were talking

about it) is semantic. Field sports aren't conservationism or any of the other ways of being a pleasant fellow which often get confused with them these days. Neither are they the roaring pursuit of meat for meat's sake, or killing for killing's sake. If words mean what they say, sport is ritual, the setting of borders, the slighting of ends in favor of means. It is method: the white line you don't step over in tennis, the goal posts' H through which the football must tumble, the wingshot, the trout taken from beneath alders with a cleanly cast Brown Variant on 3X gut.

Ritual isn't a New World strong point. We resist it. In Europe—in England, make it, where formalities are born—hunting and fresh-water fishing stopped being root economic activities a long long stretch of years ago. Their leisure classes spent pleasant centuries building stone walls along the limits of what one simply does or doesn't do with gun and rod. Innovation collides with reluctance or refusal. Izaak Walton had heard of reels, but had no wish to use one. Around the turn of this present century Lord Walsingham ("a thousand and seventy grouse to my gun in a day," he boasts of somewhere, and he meant every one on the wing, with a sweating loader helping him to keep the hot guns shouting) fought hard against smokeless powder, chilled shot, and choked barrels. He lost that one, but by and large today in England and to a lesser, imitative degree on the Continent, to own a repeating shotgun is to risk one's caste, and no one who is anyone fishes for trout or salmon with anything but artificial flies, or levels down on horned beasts with telescopic sights, or chases foxes except by those rules which, in essence, had been distilled by the early Middle Ages.

The fact that a single small class, until lately a ruling one,

sits astraddle most of the rights to European hunting and
fishing probably makes it easier to keep them sports. We
over here haven't had an influential class much interested in
ritual except along a skinny strip of the east coast, and haven't
wanted one, and furthermore aren't more than fifty or sixty
years away from the idea of wild game as family meat or as a
market harvest. The limitations we accept, unwillingly for
the most part, are legal rather than voluntary. They have
less to do with subjugating ends to means than with the
chunky fact that if we'd kept on killing things at the bloody
clip our grandfathers maintained, there wouldn't be anything left to kill by now.

We have a kind of sporting ideal, British in root. It shows
up on the covers of the November issues of outdoor magazines (showcases, most of them, for the technological in-
novations with which manufacturers keep hacking at the
fringe of the law's limitations) as pictures of a couple of
sunburned Anglo-Ams moseying with a dog and their battered pet shotguns through golden autumn cornfields, dropping a few pheasants from the air with sweet skill and
restraint.

Most of us who hunt and fish do espouse that ideal, if
only guiltily. As often as not, reality is more hoggish and
less organic. Americans regularly shoot from automobiles
and fast motorboats and even airplanes when wardens aren't
in prospect. Most would use machine guns or electronic
compensating gun sights if they could get hold of them. The
old Brazos's dynamiters and telephoners are merely sympto-
matic of what a good many other people would do if they
had the equipment and the nerve.

And, faced with the choice between a risky ritualistic shot
and a certain sitting one, with a Thanksgiving supper in the

scales, had not one American let the grandfather syndrome rule him and shot the sure thing?

For which did he feel more shame—for the unsporting shot that brought good dead meat to the pot, or the approvable gesture that maimed a wild thing to no purpose?

For the latter, certainly . . .

One was, then, no true sportsman?

Not on the river, it seemed . . . Not consistently. Not while out for meat and no more meat than his belly could hold.

Some grabblers whom Davis Birdsong knew—do I remember that James Lemmon, deceased, was among them?—once located an enormous yellow cat at the spot where Squaw Creek and the Paluxy come together into the Brazos. Though he would let them touch him without moving, there was no question of anyone's being able to wrestle him out from under the deep-hollowed bank where he dozed, nor did such offerings as a ripe dead kitten on a great hook attached to sash cord even make his whiskers quiver. Wanting him with that heat of desiring that has nothing really to do with meat, and digs back so far in the relationship of man to beasts and gets so tangled with "sport" that it disrupts all agreeable semantic theorizing, they puzzled. One, inventive, went into Glen Rose and got a blacksmith to make him a short iron harpoon. He tied it with a rope to an empty oil drum, and followed by his companions and the blacksmith and that considerable fragment of the town's population who'd gotten wind of the affair, went back to the river. Shrugging off help, he stripped and jumped into the water with his apparatus, dived bearing the spear back into the monster's dim cavern, jammed it into his side, and got his shoulder broken in two places as the big fish came out, well stuck. Whooping along the shore, splashing through the shallows and swimming when they had to, the rest of the crowd chased the bobbing, racing drum for a half-mile down the river. When it stopped and the catfish rolled up to the surface dead and they took him out, he weighed 117 pounds.

Maybe that's the shape of pretechnological American sportingness. There was risk, and the guts to plunge against the risk. There was ingenuity, and practically no ritual. There was joyous illegality. There was success, and a hell of a hunk of meat in the end. If it was a long way distant from that pink-coated, view-hallooing pursuit of the uneatable by the unspeakable that Surtees ironically loved and Wilde satirized, it was at least something in its own right. Is still, even . . .

And then you could take up hound people. God knows they do have ritual, and not any ruling-class kind either. Sport is quite a subject, if not much of a word.

The big live oak's branch hung solid above me. I reached up and touched its roughness. The foliage of the upper limbs, frost-proof, shut out the moon and stars and reflected faint green firelight down, enclosing the sandy patch of space that held me and the fire and the tent's black yawn. On the embers, small dead branches I'd torn off smoldered fragrant; their smoke, unlike that from other oaks, doesn't smart the eyes. . . . It's a good tree, the live oak, the one I like best of all with that unreasoning affection one gets for breeds and species of things. The feeling is tied up with the big mossy ones in South Texas we used to climb as kids, to coon along the high branches barefooted and then to sit up there, unseen and we hoped unsuspected, sucking hot clandestine corncob pipes and flipping acorns at our tethered ponies below. It is linked, too, with a good pair of years that I spent once in Spain where on parts of the Castilian meseta and thickly to its southwest, in Estremadura, the mottes of black-green live oaks they call robles stain tawny hills, and under them mast-eating half-wild swine run lean and wary.

Nearby, though directionless, a horned owl was communing (with relatives? with victims-to-be? with himself? with me?) in that velvet hoot-hooting so much less savage than the hooter. Thinking of robles had stuck a song in my head, a scrap from an un-flamenco Andalusian charcoal-vender chant:

> Carbón de encina,
> Carbón de roble,
> La confianza
> La tiene el hombre . . .

which in its turn was drowned in another song that a twist in the air brought me in the voice of the mill rapids just down-river. More whimsicality, I know, but rapids, and one's head, do have voices. . . . Baptistly, poundingly, this one was singing "Beulah Land."

It was a woman who'd taught me the carbonero song, a pretty one, sailboating on a Mediterranean bay. Yes, ma'am, I too have heard the mermaids calling across the blue foreign waters, and once or twice at least I thought I knew what they were saying.

On the river alone, though, mermaid thoughts seem not to stick you deeply. Each day's fatigue accrues into a drained satisfaction at night. Not seeing any mermaids, you tend not to feel their pull. Not feeling the pull, you forget its strength. Likely it would be different if you stayed out longer, for months or years. Saint Henry himself, if I've read aright one passage in him, felt the pull and the itch and the barb, and fought Pilgrim-puritannically against them. . . .

In vain to me are calling,

the rapids sang:

None of them shall win me (boom!) *from Beu-lah Land.*

On the fire the Red Gods squeaked, out of key. . . .

~~~~~~~

NEXT MORNING in the predawn a hoarse and hollow shriek awoke me. Half dozing, I wondered about it—a little like the hunting, hovering scream of the red-tailed hawk, except that no hawk would fly abroad so early. I lay wondering, and then when it repeated itself, clipped and end-upturning unlike any red-tail, I remembered a winter in an old house by a creek when the barn owls had yelled and talked all night long in the cold moonlight beside the stable, and it fell into its place.

Later, with light, a Carolina wren came flicking from perch to perch along the shore, singing at each stop. He paused for a few phrases on the handle of my ax stuck in a log. Though good objective naturalists have taught me rightly to resist the anthropomorphic translation of wild things' doings, what the wren did sing was: *Good morning, good morning, good morning!—*

— — —
— — —

Or maybe it was only that I felt in the mood to hear him say it. They can be a disagreeably blithe bird when you're not in the humor to listen to them. Russet, the wren sought bugs in a crack of the log for a moment, found something, and flitted on to sing again farther along the bank. I eased out of the bag into the cold, quiet, perfect air of morning, and dressed. The pup, cured but washed-out, stayed in bed.

Skim ice dulled the bucket water's surface and had hardened the small gravel of the bar when I went down, and frost lay white on the canoe's varnished gunwales. I kicked a thick long section of elm loose from its grip, and as I twist-heaved it up to my shoulder to bear to the fire, said aloud: "By God, there you go, Bill Briggs!"

But knew as I spoke that despite memory's magnifications it hadn't a third of the weight of some of those pole-sized trunks that he, pine woods bred, used to pick up without even breathing hard and carry to our fires in that same place. Where he'd fried those wondrous eggs . . .

We'd been about ten when we started going out there with him, in an old low-slung German car that Hale's father entrusted to us; it would go only forty-five before jumping out of gear, and would get hung sometimes on hump-backed dirt roads and would sprawl there, pawing air, while we hunted brush and stones to give it traction. In those times still, no one much cared if you crossed his back pasture to get to the river. At Falls Creek we would camp in slovenly style with quilts and tarps and jars of bacon grease and ketchup and cans of city water on the gravel bar by the river, where one of the old head rises should have caught us but none ever did. The river was red-muddy then more often than not. We would put out lines, and with rods would fish the clear creek's pools for a mile or so up.

"Aw, naw," Bill Briggs would say mildly when we wanted to do something we had no business doing, like—tired of fishing—swimming in the river when it was running strong, or—tired of fish—swiping a pullet from a farmer's flock, or —tired of chopping hard resistant driftwood—trying out our ax on the big shade trees above the bank. "Aw, naw. Y'all go run 'at line. Us ain' got no supper fish yet, you know?"

And though we would holler back at him sometimes, we did not often gaingo his soft injunctions. He had a quiet authority, stiffened at long range by the authority of Hale's father. . . . Periodically he would vanish for six months or a year or so, and when he came back he would have been cooking on the Pullman dining cars, where he was in demand, drifting about the country. Hale's family's house was base for him but he was migratory, urged by some interior thorn of sadness or homelessness or womanlessness (he never kept one long) to search from time to time across the continent's spraddle. He was huge, flat-faced, dark brown, and altogether gentle. Falls Creek is not one of the hotly Anglo-Am parts of the river country, and farmers would welcome us in his care who later, with right, looked at me and Hale by ourselves inhospitably.

On summer afternoons the gravel bar even under willows would shimmer with heat, and we would move up to lie on the sand under the live oaks, and to talk. I don't remember much of what we talked about—what kids used to talk about with Negroes, probably—fish and animals and how Hale's mother kept trying to teach Bill Briggs to wait on her bridge group with white gloves. And Bill's youth in the East Texas woods, tumbling great logs about for the sawmill from the age of fourteen . . . And what the white folks were like in California: there's a place for communication then that shrinks later as you align yourself with the way things are. . . . But mostly laughing matters, we talked about. He was fond of laughter, Bill Briggs.

The squabble about the big catfish we caught was the only one I remember our ever winning with him, and that was mainly, I guess, because he was arguing from a standpoint not of moral rightness but of appetite. He loved catfish. Hale and I had been running the trotline early one morning in a leaky boat that someone kept tied in the creek mouth, and had come to where the big fish was surging at the end of his staging. Scared of his spines, we had held onto the line with him thrashing half out of the water till Bill from shore had started yelling to drop him before his weight tore him loose, and had come running out through the water with splashing giant's strides and up to his nipples in red water had hugged the catfish to him regardless of spines or anything.

"Grocies!" he said while we argued that afternoon under the live oaks. "You ain' goan git mo'n enough grocies for one sminchy li'l ole breakfas', what them white folks'll give you fo' that fish. *Ef* they gives you anythang. Shoot, what I says, is le's *eat* 'im."

But we sold him to the highway café, for $2.50 as I remember; it bought us a sminchy little old breakfast or so, and we stayed out two days longer than we'd planned to be able to afford. . . . Because of Bill's great strength, Hale's father got the notion of backing him as a professional heavyweight. Bill didn't think much of the idea. To oblige, he tried it once, but just sort of grinned and backed away during the round or two it took his opponent, bigger and darker than he, to hack his face into strips and pound him unconscious. The next day Hale's mother's bridge group was served coffee and cake by a white coat with bloody purple meat and a pair of swelled-shut eyes sticking out of its top, and that was the end of a Black Threat.

I ran into him once on a street during the war, in Los Angeles. He had fattened, and was running a cafeteria for a defense plant. He liked it. I was a new lieutenant in a green uniform and pleased with myself about it, and he was pleased with me, too. I was so pleased that I said I was thinking about staying in the service after the war, a professional.

"Aw, naw," he said, wagging his flat face slowly. "Aw, naw. You go on home, like you belong to do."

Red, the river had been nearly always. That had been West Texas, washing down to the Gulf from the dry-land farms. Except that there was a kind of good-old-days romanticism in that thought, an unwarrantedness. Long ago, when the Comanches and the first tough whites knew it, the Brazos ran clear a good part of the time because the matted grasses of the plains to the northwest held their soil. It ran higher and steadier, too, because the scant rain falling on that wide grass was held and soaked in slowly and fed out constantly from the subsoil into the country's drains, all necessary use having been absorbed from it on the way. But, nevertheless, the old salty red-bed terrain far to the west had always bled down its thick pigment in times of spate, and its flavor. Port Smythe testifies to that, and others. If it weren't so, the Southwest wouldn't have a plurality of rivers called Red—or Colorado, which is the same thing.

Something was trying to boil to the top of the rice pot of my mind, the way things do. Something else Spanish. I finally put it together, another of the maxims of old Juan Ramón Jiménez, who, exiled, lost his wife and got the Nobel too late and died having said that it couldn't mean much, then. . . .

"*Pie,*" he had written—"*Pie en la patria casual o elegida; corazón, cabeza en el aire del mundo.*"

Foot in one's accidental or elected homeland; heart, head in the world's air . . . Shaking two ser sta gro eggs in the skillet in vain imitation of Bill Briggs, I supposed the maxim was a comment, from somewhere inside me, on the parochialism of what I was doing, of the things I was thinking about from day to day. You get off into corners. . . . One scrawny, salty bit of river on the edge of West Texas seemed at the moment, together with its unsignificantly bloody past and its bypassed present and the kid memories I had of going there, to be maybe less than a noble focus for a man's whole interest.

But where the feet stand has importance, as Spaniards know better than almost anybody. The Antaean myth has meaning still. And one river, seen right, may well be all rivers that flow to the sea.

Aloud, I quoted Juan Ramón Jiménez to the passenger, who listened gravely, then tried to make off with a tent peg, and got the end of a rope across his hindquarters for his trouble. From high up in the live oak a squirrel barked at us, bright-eyed. I looked at him, and at the shotgun three feet away from me, and back at him, and wished him well. I was finished with burgoo for that trip, if the ducks and fish held out.

A big wind was starting to blow out of the north above the hill, and navy-blue-gray clouds were scudding solid across the sky. Across the world's air . . .

Out of the wind, out of the world's air, came small shrieking female voices. Unpleasantly I remembered it was the long holiday weekend, and hoped maybe they would stay up at their camp. But minutes later as I slogged across an open patch of sand beneath the limestone rise, carrying a bucket of water from creek to camp, their advance guard in dark skirts and beanies and sweaters and white blouses poured over the cliff and onto a wooden descending set of steps. Partway down, the lead ones saw me and stopped. I supposed I didn't look like much. . . . We stared at each other, and behind them their stacked-up cohorts froze in tiers. One at the top of the stair called back over her shoulder to unseen legions on the hill: "There's a *man!*"

Down a way another said: "It's the caretaker."

I said: "No, I'm not, but I won't hurt you. Come on down."

Squealing, they turned and panicked back up the stair and out of sight. In a moment a woman, harried-faced, peeked down at me, and I repeated, trying hard not to look like an itinerant rapist but handicapped by three days' beard, that I was harmless. She frowned. Beside me the pup started barking, tainting my kindly aura. I kicked at him lightly but caught him hard in the ribs. Bellowing, he lit out for camp. The woman disappeared. I picked up my bucket and carried it on, feeling guilty and brutal and grubby.

In a few minutes, though, they all came down, fifteen or sixteen Campfire Girls and half as many parents and counselors, bearing thermos jugs and paper sacks of sandwiches. Snaking widely around my camp, they moved down the shore to where some of the ruined masonry of the old grist mill still shows, and parents as they passed walled white-eyed, sidewise glances at me and my stained chattels. One of the counselors was handsome, but did not look as though she thought I was.

All right. I would have preferred to hang there in that place until the big wind had blown itself out or shown its intention; it was huge, raising even under the hill and the live oaks sting-pointed puffs of sand and scattering fire sparks among my gear. Its cold lacked the cut of the true norther, but it was damp and I knew it would make things grim on the river, whether it was for or against me in its push. Not wanting to be the tramp who spoiled the picnic, though, I guessed I'd move on, and went down to the canoe to clean it and get it in the water.

Squeals, nearby . . . A clot of Campfire Girls had taken up with the pup, who leaped and tumbled enchanted among them. He led them near where I knelt scrubbing with a sponge at mud between the boat's ribs, and they ended standing in a little tense line and watching me.

"Do you *live* here?" one said.

I looked around. She was a darkish clean-skinned imp of maybe thirteen, poised for flight. I said I lived on the river, up and down, all over.

"All the time?" she said. "Who *are* you?"

Lohengrin von Schnickelfritz, I told her, but she seemed disinclined to believe. In a row, teetering, the others giggled; they were all of those years on the edge of puberty when everything unknown frightens, and fear itself is sweet.

"Karen!" an adult called from their picnic spot.

The dark little girl flicked her head around and called frowning over her shoulder: "He's all right. He's just *silly!*"

More tittering, more teeters . . . What did I eat? Snakes and snails and catfish tails . . . No, *really!* Well, really, I guessed, going on with my boat-scrubbing, I ate beans and rice and squirrels and ducks and fish and whatever else I could get, when I could get it. It was a hard kind of life. . . .

Karen pushed out her lip and stuck her hands on her hips and glared with the exaggeration of gesture that spoiled pretty little girls often have.

"So!" she said. "*You're* the reason there are only five ducks by the bridge now."

I said what ducks by what bridge?

She said with genuine anger: "*You* know! Oh, you . . ."

A parent named Potts edged shyly into the group and introduced himself to me, sent, I supposed, by the women to take the measure of my degeneracy. The little girls swirled away with the pup, noisy. Potts lingered, watching me and the boat and glancing up toward my camp. It looked great, what I was doing, he said.

"Well, it is if you like that kind of thing," I said.

"I guess I would," he said. "I never did much of it. It looks like fun."

There was a poignancy about him, spectacled in a green corduroy sport shirt that looked wrong against his pink-gray skin and the hollow way he held his chest. He kept picking, cranelike first on one leg and then on the other, at needle-grass spears in his thin green socks. He said he got most of his exercise mowing his lawn, and the winter before had built a picket fence around his back yard. . . . That was what he told me, or rather told himself in answer to the discontent that sat plain on him as he looked at me and the boat and the Brazos River.

He said: "There's never enough time."

Sluicing loosened mud from the propped-up canoe, I found myself wanting to tell him that for God's sake there was plenty of time always, and why didn't he come on along with me, telling whichever of the big-jawed women it was over there he belonged to that he'd see her in a week or so, or a year?

But she might not be big-jawed at all, and a man nearly always picks centrally the channel of life that best suits his boat. If free will exists, he does. The parent Potts seemed engineered for patio living, and probably would feel the cozier there for having seen me lean and filthy on the river, even if at the moment I looked romantic to him. I didn't feel romantic. But I liked him and his wistful openness, and we talked for a while longer before they called him to the gristmill place to help distribute sandwiches and drinks. They were feeding the girls early and leaving, he said; the sky looked bad. . . .

In that case, the tramp wouldn't have to leave. I went up to tighten my camp against the wind, cutting longer tent stakes from the willows and lashing a tarp upright on the side of the fire toward the hill whence the worst gusts hit. From time to time I caught glimpses of the passenger sitting up for outheld frankfurters or cookies, and another pair of the little girls came to eye my housekeeping and to ask questions. But none of the women came near; the handsome counselor went stiff in the face whenever I caught her looking toward me. I didn't mind much. Her voice when she spoke to the girls was like a man's, and the defensive urban offishness of all of them was different enough from the river people's occasional quiet dislike to be a little funny.

Karen returned, alone. In her hand she held an elbowed willow branch with a short line tied to it and a cork and a worm-wiggling hook too big for bream.

She said: "Do you really eat ducks?"

"Sometimes," I said. "I don't eat many, though. Have you caught any fish?"

She said she didn't know how. I took her down to the gravel bar and had her drop in her line and close her eyes tightly, then took one of the little bass from Square Jaw's creek off the stringer and put it on her hook. When it pulled, she began to hop up and down, and loped yelling, the fish still on the hook bouncing behind her, toward the place where the others were gathered. Squeals . . . The whole outfit swarmed at me and wanted to be shown how to catch bass, but Karen's reproachful dark eye was on me and I wouldn't.

She'd peeked. As they were leaving, adult-herded, she dropped out for a moment from the procession, winked, said: "Thank you for the *fish!*" and giggled, and skipped away. Behind women's backs the parent Potts grinned and waved, and then they were gone, leaving the world to me and the swollen-bellied pup and the strewn wads of brown paper and tissue and cellophane that danced along the shore under the wind. . . .

Arranging, I found a big planklike curved slab of cotton-wood from the unrotted shell of a trunk that whole must have measured four or five feet through, and leaned it against two stakes on another side of the fire, at right angles to the stretched tarp. The sky had gone a lighter, frostier gray and looked a bit like snow, so over the whole I rigged a sort of shed roof out of a poncho Hale had left with me. The resultant hodgepodge would have given old Kephart night-mares, but it was tight, and I sat there and heard the wind topple great dead trees somewhere in the woods up the creek.

The land across the river from that place is in the De Cordova Bend. Falls Creek comes in opposite the first hump of its trifoliate sprawl. The bend was named not from Span-ish connections but for Jacob De Cordova, a Sephardic

Jamaican who served Texas as "Publicity Agent for an Empire," lecturing through the world on her riches. He tested those riches for himself, amassing a personal million acres of land script, and died in 1868 in Kimball's Bend down the river, where alongside the Chisholm Trail he was looking over into the next era and trying to harness the river's thrust for textile mills. Stone ghost buildings stand there now.

Others stand in the De Cordova Bend, but not from his times. In the teens or twenties of this century, a Midwestern Dane named John B. Christensen, who believed in Scandinavians, built Utopia there. He bought land, parceled it out to the Norwegian-Texans he invited up from down the country, furnished them cows, and launched them on a course of ideal, rustic, those-who-work-eat semi-socialism. The country people around there sometimes refer back to the experimenters as "them communists," but they appear to have been a pleasant, quiet lot who had their own marketing association and commissary and token money for use inside the community; built their own houses and buildings of native flagstone; produced for sale chairs, wild-grape juice, dried herbs and medicinal plants, and post-oak charcoal; farmed at their peak (some 200 strong) about 1,200 acres; put out pamphlets and a newspaper from their own publishing house (the last time I saw it, the water-stained tracts still lay strewn about); and when the depression roared in and smashed their cottage industries, hoped religiously for a dam to be built on the river which somehow would change things a little. . . . Kristenstad, it was called. Its founder, who was its personality and force, died in '36, and not much of the experiment long survived him. The lump of land he had amassed probably made it easier for the bend's present owners to build up the acreage for their pecan operation. The dam the quiet Scowegians dreamed of will probably go in soon, far too late to do them any good, if it would have then. Maybe they could have opened rustic Utopian ski-boat centers. . . .

Across the river from the bend's other side, Charles Barnard built his log trading house in the 1840's, a New York Irishman and the only white around those parts except for occasional rangers and lone-wolf itinerants. Tame Indians clustered about the place (you can still find their manos and other trash there) and brought furs and hides, and the glittering-eyed People rode in from time to time for a little arrogant swapping. Charles Barnard once swapped them something or other they wanted for a wife, "a Mexican lady of the family of Cavassas," whom they were dragging captive along with them. Husband and ransomed consort both survived into Ewell's time, and people still alive remember them.

Old Man Rush did . . . "Old Tomassy," he said, wagging his waxen head as we sat on the ripple-boarded porch. "Old Tomassy. You art of done heard her skin a man with that tongue."

Charles was quite a type, too. In historical records a confusion exists between him and his brother George, another trader, though few people are likely to get very sweaty about it now. Charles did much that George got credit for, but George wrote his memoirs. At his post on the Brazos, Charles was host to Port Smythe, M. D., and to all the other expeditions and drifters that came into that country when it was empty. Of stone he built Barnard's Mill down on the Paluxy; it still stands, a hospital these days, nucleus of Glen Rose. He resented civilization and liked Indians, and moved out west for a time after white men came. But finding them where he moved to as well, he came back to the trading house, and the little town that grew up near him there was called Fort Spunky because of all its fights. Ewell characterizes him as bright and adventurous, and says that "except for an unfortunate thirst, which long ago mastered his intellectual powers and consumed his considerable wealth," he might have made a splash on the waters of his time. It is told around that Tomasa gave him decades of hell about that Celtic thirst, but that it did her no good at all; it probably only succeeded, as wives seem never to learn, in making his throat burn worse than ever. . . .

You wonder sometimes—say, looking across the brown-flowing Brazos at the tangled shore below a millionaire's pecan operation—about the impulse that leads city people into the absentee possession of land. You wonder perhaps especially hard if something in you believes that land is really owned more with head and heart, with eye and brain, than with pocketbook and title deed. It's easy enough to understand city people who live on the land they buy, or who even go there often. We will be nearly finished, I think, when we stop understanding the old pull toward green things and living things, toward dirt and rain and heat and what they spawn. Most of us still have it in us, whether as would-be squire or peasant or drifting, poaching gypsy.

The other kind of ownership, not living there, may sometimes come from the same impulse. An occasional brief glance at green things and growing things for whose existence one is responsible financially if not personally may assuage the pull a little. And I guess there are people for whom ownership of land is only ownership, an investment.

Sometimes it seems to be bred from a kind of anger. Not all city people were city people always, and many of them, as persons or as families, remember back to sour defeat by the land. Drouth and flood and bugs and money cropping have hounded many a farmer into town who didn't want to go. Later, maybe, having money, he or his children or their children return for another bout, and sometimes win. If, scientifically and with the surging horsepower of cash, you can bulldoze a whole countryside into gainful new growingness, you may have wiped out a little of the hurt of that old wound.

That is, if it hurts . . . A friend of mine once tried to talk his father-in-law, an oilman with an East Texas country background, into buying a farm or a ranch. It was a certain place to put money, he said, better than gold. And besides, he said (he is city-reared), there was something good about it; owning land was pleasant.

"Play hell," the old man said. "Listen, boy. When I was seventeen I was plowin' one day with two mules in a bottom-land field with a railroad levee runnin' right alongside it. It was hot. There was a slow freight train passin' on the levee. All of a sudden I looked at those mules' butts, and I looked at that train, and I stopped, and I took my hands off of those plow handles and walked over and got on that train. And I'm not goin' back now. Land! . . ."

Good or bad, sentimental or hard-headed, city ownership is an extensive fact now. For the land it's mostly good. Whatever one's view of businessmen in general, it's most often true that if a man has the shove to want a lot of money and the sense to have made it, he generally has the sense too not to abuse the thing in which he invests it.

For country people and the old way it's destructive. But old ways seem usually to be fated for destruction anyhow, under one ax or another, and maybe our old way most of all.

It was self-destructive. I mean the real old way, not the way it should have been. . . .

For the natural world it can mean either thing. Too efficient operations are rough-edged for wild creatures; fence-to-fence cultivation uses up all cover, and the fell insecticide one plane can defecate in a day can kill a million song birds. A good many owners, whether city or country in root, don't care. Others do, and maybe those who buy land (admitting it or not) because of a warm pull in them toward dirt and rain and heat and the things they spawn are likely to care most of all. One hopes so.

But, buying land for any reason, you need to remember a thing. A rooting, poking, dog-trailed child turning over stones in a creek bed, or a broke old man wandering back from a pulp mill in Oregon to toe-nudge rusty cans and the shards of crocks at the spot where his father's homestead once stood, or a drifter in a boat on a river, can all own it right out from under you if you don't watch out. Can own it in a real way, own it with eye and brain and heart . . .

The big wind didn't amount to much. It blew hugely, but brought no change, and I sat in my shelter all afternoon under its roar and read, and found in Deuteronomy an injunction:

Defile not therefore the land which ye shall inhabit, wherein I dwell: for I the LORD dwell among the children of Israel.

It blew big into the night, unnaturally, but did not depress me as that other wind had so short a time before—and so long, too. In the morning it had stopped, and I packed up and pushed on down.

CHAPTER SEVENTEEN

⟨ *I hear the steps of Modred in the west,*
And with him many of thy people, and knights
Once thine, whom thou hast loved, but grosser grown
Than heathen, spitting at their vows and thee.

AFTER the eighties the Brazos country needed rest. It pulled up its blanket of scrub oak and cedar and had itself a doze, a long one that is only now ending as the city money pulls away the blanket. The frontier had moved on and petered out, with most of its violence. The Brazos country ranched and farmed, or its people did—without knowing, most of them, any more about soft treatment of the land than their fathers and grandfathers had, so that they went on compounding the old error. They money-cropped when they could make the money crops grow; little Somervell County at one time had sixteen cotton gins (you ought to see the stands of needle grass in *those* old fields), and where nothing else would grow they ran cattle, too many of them always, so that the grass went from the slopes and then the dirt, and the white lime rock showed through and the brush spread, and we've gone into that before. . . . In the end the country's sleep was one of exhaustion.

The cedar country went perhaps more solidly to sleep than the other stretches along the river. It was tireder, and had less left to stay awake about. Hidden by the aromatic scrub that covered their hills and had to be fought back out of their leached valleys, the cedar people grew separate, grew different as people will in a generation or so of living on separate, different country.

Not much different . . . Country in a generation or so can't scallop the contours of a breed of people in the way it has in a thousand years in mountain places in Spain and Italy, where you can stop at a village which, though money-less nearly always, is rich enough in things that matter—in oil and wine and wheat and fruit and the flesh of animals, the valley around it providing—and then can wind on up the valley toward gray crags where the soil thins or disappears, and can find within four or five miles a grim unmortared rock pile whose people glare at you from doorways and subsist during the year's five or six leanest months on por-ridge stewed out of acorns or chestnuts from the wind-warped trees around them. In the one place there is music and tough humor and wholeness—in the other, sickness and silence and hate. For me, the kind of people that hard living carves are usually worth having around, but there is a point past which that doesn't work at all.

On this continent, place dependence doesn't get quite so intimate. Between a skinny grim New Hampshireman and a Cajun laughing on a bayou there is difference, and much of the difference has to do with place—with dirt and rain and heat and the things that grow. But a lot of it has to do with distance, too, and there isn't enough distance between points in my piece of the Brazos to matter that much. If a tuned ear can pick out a progression in the dialect, it's nevertheless still all West Texan, hill Southern, in its ring. If the Palo Pintans run a bit more to real ranching and the big Western openness of view that goes with it, and the Parker and north-

Hood Countians to prosperous sandy-land farming and to farmers' shrewd philosophy, and the cedar people to small marginal freeholdings and to slit-eyed exclusion of outlanders, those are certainly effects of country. But in no place along there does no ranching at all exist, or no sandy-land farming, or no small hard-scrabble freeholding, and a man would have to live more continuously among those people than I ever have, to speak with weight about real difference. There's more of it than there was in the beginning when all men started the joyful rape of the land with equal fervor and from like backgrounds; there's less than during the long stasis, the doze before the Second War.

What the cedar people are, mostly, is sort of more so. More Anglo-Am, more belligerent, more withdrawn, more hill Southern, more religious, or more hoggish in their sinning if they lack religion or backslide from it . . .

More tied to their country, too, in various ways . . . Since the country as they know it is so sorry, that's a paradox, but it's so.

Davis Birdsong was walking through the shinnery one day behind old Sam Sowell—I forget why; maybe he was going to chop some posts on the old man's place on shares—when Sam stopped short, then slowly, felinely backed up. Davis looked over his shoulder. Coiled in a bare spot, rattling his rear off, was a diamondback as thick as a two-bit post. Davis eased his hand back along the oiled helve of his ax.

"Le'm alone!" Sam Sowell said.

"What?" Davis said.

"Le'm be!" Sam said. "Hin bi' me. Hin bi' oo. Le'm be."

Davis said he needed more explanation than that before he was going to give up the idea of killing a rattlesnake, but the old man gave it to him. He said, as nearly as Davis could follow, that the snake from its looks had been around that country as long as either of them had, that it had given fair warning and hadn't struck when it could have, and that by God it had as much right there as Davis Birdsong or he, Sam Sowell.

"Looked like a old snake hisself, a-hissin' and a-spittin'," Davis said, telling it. "You kind of had to dodge, talkin' with Sam, if you didn't want no sharr bath."

Therefore they made an arduous half-circle around the rattler's sunning-spot, and went on with their trek.

Davis, though infected with that fungus which presently diseases roots, is himself inextricably a cedar man. He has trucked transcontinentally and lived in a trailer in Michigan and worked a stretch at Convair in Fort Worth and slouched through the nation's far dust traps in a mustard-colored army uniform, but he has always come back, having in a major sense never left, and for some years now has worked, quarrelsomely but hard, for a friend of mine who has built a grassy ranch on the cleared hills. He is good at land procurement, at finding another little neglected homestead to tack onto Bill's holding, and at persuading the reluctant ones who own it—townsmen often now, needing money and not the brushy unproductive land, but distrustful—to sell at a fair price. He is of their breed and they know him honorable, as men in that country from long storytelling and long watching clearly know one another to be whatever it is they are.

In general, I think Davis likes the changes that are taking place. He hasn't been fenced off from their fruits. The old way was cob-rough on him and his, back through his parents to his old grandmother, who was another thing and had seen The People in the time before the cedar. . . . He recalls years when his wife had to make her housedresses out of flour sacks, and the milk for his kids was short. That's past now. He prospers reasonably from the change, and his razor-minded son will go to college.

He likes a bulldozer, crushing agent of change. Likes lowering its bright-worn battering blade and aiming it at the thick gnarled junipers and knocking them down and leaving behind him a strewn path full of edge-standing limestone boulders clutched by the roots that, uptorn, still hold on. Likes "chaining" best of all, another bulldozer howling parallel to his fifty or seventy-five yards away, and stretched between them a fat cable or anchor chain that inexorably, with a racket like the world's own end, smashes out its mighty swath in eighty years of brush while little creatures flee. Likes clearing, cleaning, burning off the dried debris. Likes watching the doveweed and the sunflowers and the Johnson grass break through the bared ground the first year, and then the grain-rich native pasture stuff that, nursed, lays itself down on the hills' slopes in a rug that soaks up rain and opens cool seep-springs all along the draws. Likes too the fat cattle those pastures will maintain. Once, in an access of enjoyment, he leveled an excellent log house on one of the homesteads they were clearing; it made Bill sore as a skunk for a time. Davis will even knock down live oaks if not watched.

And yet his gaze can turn back, too. Not long ago he and I went to look over a lost 140 acres on a dry creek, far back in the cedar. After the road to it played out at a wash, we left the pickup and walked, and along the way we came on a place with junk scattered around and a concrete well curb and the tumbled fire-blackened stones of a foundation and a fireplace under a pecan tree. Davis stopped, and grunted.

"What?" I said.

"Nothin'," he answered, and leaning over stared down the dark eight-inch tube of the well, crisscrossed at its mouth with ragged spiderwebs. Davis said: "Went dry."

"You can't tell just looking like that," I said. "It might be a deep one."

"Used to run over like a sprang," he said. "Hit was artesian."

"You knew it."

"I reckon," Davis said. "I growed up where you see them rocks. . . ."

We walked on parallel to the dry creek, ascending, but the ghost place had reached him and he felt like talking.

"We didn't have nothin'," he said. "I mean, *nothin'*. Two mules and a wagon to rattle into town with ever' two weeks haulin' a load of posts. A ridin' horse, wind-broke. Some old pieces of arn you could farm with, a little. Choppin' cedar. Putt coal oil on ever'body when they got hurt or sick. Coal oil on a cut. Coal oil on a rag on your neck if you tuck down with flu . . . But you know somethin'?"

"What?"

"We didn't *live* bad," he said. "They was a garden patch under that artesian well and it'd grow might near anythang. I mean. And we kept a cow most of the time, and hogs. Good house. Plenty of wood to burn in winter. And old Maw she kept thangs right."

Maw was not his mother but the female grandparent who, alone against the lassitude of soil exhaustion and demoralization, had held stiffly upright those members of the clan within her touch until she had died a few years back, at ninety-seven. I'd only seen her a couple of times, but she had black eyes that burned you. . . . She was "good stock," in the old phrase, Tennessee-born and brought at the age of three to Texas where The People screech-owled in the moon-lit brush and you hunkered down clutching your mother's skirt in the lightless, fireless cabin while outside the men lay watching with rifles. Once, young, she passed a band of Comanches beside a trail near her father's house. They'd killed a paint mare belonging to a neighbor and were roast-ing its hind leg over a fire. They looked at her. She looked at them and walked on.

And if, later, the man she'd picked had chosen the wrong place to stay, and if dependence on that wrong, exhausted place had eaten at the fiber of her sons and daughters and grandchildren, those things weren't her fault, and she'd kept the erosion from going as far as it had with other families. None of her children had turned out to be whisky makers or brawlers or shifty-eyes. Only a couple of the grandchildren had. She'd seen what there was to fight and she'd fought it. She'd kept thangs right.

Are we then praising the Noble Pioneer Mother? No. Just praising Noble Anybody who could shore up a clan's pride against cedar and bitter indigence . . . And there were more than you'd think who could, with the help of Old Tes-tamentalism. That was always there. It's why one can't laugh too hard at Bug Eye Tinsley, wallowing on the ground. . . .

Meeting me, Maw had said: "Where your folks from?"

South Texas mostly, I told her, and before that Carolina and Mississippi.

"Flat country," she said with the reserve of her people to whom for two centuries or more flatlanders had been aliens. . . .

Davis said that that home place, which he hadn't visited

in twenty-five, nearly thirty years, had then had three pecan trees instead of one, and the well had flowed all the time, and so had the creek, with good fish swimming up it from the Paluxy as far as a little waterfall just under the house.

"Maybe hit'll run again, though," he said. "We git some grass around here."

We crossed a rusty fence, sprung from its staples, into the place we were looking for, and started up a hillside streak of crumbly white caliche and rock between cedars; even the mud-daubers' nests in parts of that country are limey white. . . . The trail narrowed and disappeared, overgrown. Davis paused, searching with his memory.

"Used to run here," he said, pointing to a blank thicket wall of cedar.

It still did, on the other side. The family who'd lived on *that* place, he said as we went on, had been named Applegate and had had eight kids. They hadn't owned the place or rented it, but whoever did own it had given up the idea of making it pay and didn't care who did what with it. For hauling and plowing and the other unhuman work of the place the Applegates had used donkeys. Little old Meskin burros . . . Maw hadn't entirely approved of the Applegates, though the donkeys had nothing to do with that. The Applegate girls would teach you things back in the cedar, was the trouble.

Davis said: "I guess you'd call 'em . . . poor folks."

In his pause and substitution was sad awareness that everybody around that country for a long time had been so close to being what you'd call the Applegates that it would hurt a little actually to call them it. . . . Like an old twenty-two Hale used to have that would speckle fire across your forearm when you shot it . . .

He stopped. He said: "Right about here is where we berrit Bud Applegate's thumb."

"Whose?"

"They had a little old post-haulin' wagon," he said. "Pulled it with them donkeys. Didn't have no regular wheels; Model-T rims, they used. Bud he was a little old kid and he was playin' around the wagon one day when the old man was a-cuttin' posts. Old Man Applegate he clucked to them donkeys and they started up and old Bud he had his thumb under one of them rims. Sliced it off like you'd slice a sausage."

And after Bud's stub had been fixed up fine with coal oil and a piece of somebody's shirt tail, all the kids—the eight Applegates and Davis and his brothers and sisters—had laid the severed digit in a little cardboard box and carried it into the cedar and held a funeral for it, with speeches.

Davis said: "I bet I could putt near go to it and dig it up, right now."

He lingered. He said: "I bought Louise a warshin' machine last week."

"Save a lot of work," I said.

"Yeah," he said, but kept looking around on the crumbling white soil beneath the cedars.

"God damn it!" he said finally.

"What's the matter?"

"Nothin'. Just God damn it . . ."

~~~~~~

HE HAS AN UNCLE named Herb who can witch water and has something wrong with his taste buds, so that he puts ketchup on peach cobbler and once drank a glass of coal oil for water, not knowing it until somebody told him.

"Then he said he'd noticed his stomach was a-burnin' a

mite," Davis said. "Twenty miles to town. That old wagon. We all sat up to three o'clock waitin' to see if it was a-gonna kill him and it didn't and we went to bed."

He has a friend whom he admires named Clarence, who went to Waco young and made some money finally in contracting, and bought a little place in the cedar hills where he comes for weekends, a city owner. Clarence drives a second-hand Cadillac and drinks Mogen David wine, and on Saturday nights he and Davis and Louise and occasionally a lady friend of his from Waco, a Miss Antelope of Apache derivation, drive thirty, fifty, sometimes eighty miles to country dances with fights and heel-stompings and all kinds of added amateur attractions. Once, coming home, they hit what Davis called a "bear cage" in the road—it took me a week to get "barricade" out of that one. It took Clarence longer to get his Cadillac fixed up.

Davis will work in cotton clothes under January's sleet for twelve hours in a row if he wants to get something finished, or in the frying glare of August, hurling prickly seventy-five-pound bales of hay onto the back end of a truck in a windless bottomland field. Air conditioning and the silver-blue lure of television have little pull for him, and he'll eat chicken-fried steak and beans every day for lunch if that is what is put before him, or alternatively mustard greens. He is thus an ascetic, though I'd dislike having to weave the logic of his kinship to Saint Henry. . . . Like many people in that country, he mistrusts the right names for things, the special vocabularies that go with specialized activities, so that pullets, cocks, hens, and capons are all just chickens, and in the strips of cow country even leathery experts may call chaps "leggins," and lariats "ropes," and corrals "pens," and a cantle "the hind end of the saddle." I don't know why.

Davis quietly knows himself to be as good as any man, and can show it if he has to, if at times in strange ways. One September during the early years of my friend Bill's owner-ship of land out there, not long after the war, Bill and I went out to spend a few days hunting doves. He hadn't yet built a house to tempt his wife into bringing the children for week-ends, so we were staying by ourselves in an old tin-roofed shack, a couple of miles across brushy pastures from where Davis lived in a new concrete-block cottage.

Early one morning Davis rattled into view in his pickup. Getting out, he stood looking at us where we sat on the edge of the sagging porch. He wore a straw hat curled cowman fashion and a suit of pinkish khaki.

"Mornin'," he said, tepidly, since he and Bill had dif-fered the day before over what pasture to put some goats in.

Bill said: "Nice day."

"Sha," Davis said. "I wouldn't take nothin' to live in that old snake trap. Wha'd you eat for breakfast?"

"Doves."

"Chicken eats better."

Bill said: "I'd like chicken better too if I couldn't hit doves anyhow."

"Be damn!" Davis said. "Oncet I kilt thirteen with one shell. Not no two whole boxes."

He doesn't discern the logic of wingshooting—because, of course, it has none. He said: "What I come for, somebody wants you long distance up at the store."

Rising, Bill said: "If you want to, we can play a nice long game of mumbly-peg before we go see about it."

"Sha," Davis said. "They done waited this long."

They rattled away. I washed the breakfast dishes in the trough by the windmill, cleaned my shotgun, and sat around listening to a tribe of chickadees quarrel in the ailanthus trees, and in a while they came back. Bill said the Jaycees in the city where we'd both grown up had been saddled with the entertainment of some foreign dignitary, and one of them, an official in a bank to which Bill owed money, or had owed it, had decided that it would kill time to show him a ranch.

"This one?" I said. It was not much to see at that time, a thousand acres or so and only partly cleared of cedar.

"Flat Top," Bill said. "But they don't know the Flat Top people and they don't know their way around this country, so I guess we're elected."

"You are."

"We are," Bill said.

"France," Davis said, his tone less unconcerned than usual. "Hit's a big Frenchman."

He doesn't lack curiosity, and an hour and a half later when a seven-passenger Cadillac eased to a stop at Bill's gate on the highway, Davis was with us. The bank official was driving, a plump fellow I'd known as a boy. Call him Seagrove. . . . He introduced us to a little mustached Frenchman named Ratineau, seated beside him. A newspaper photographer in the back seat looked boredly away.

Ignored, Davis stuck a hardened hand through the window at the Frenchman. "Birdsong," he said. "D. M. Birdsong. How do."

M. Ratineau blinked and was again charmed.

"I was borned and raised around here," Davis said.

"Yes," the Frenchman said.

"He doesn't understand much English," Seagrove said irritably. "We better get moving."

We climbed into the back by the photographer and Davis took one of the jump seats. I saw Seagrove's eye flash coldly around at him, and saw too that Davis hadn't missed it.

Driving, Seagrove said with wide gestures, gravely: "Ranch country. Much cow, sheep, goat."

M. Ratineau nodded politely and gazed out.

Davis snorted. "What kind of movie-Indian talkin' is that?" he said.

"Please?" the Frenchman said, turning.

Seagrove said: "I told you, he doesn't understand."

"What is he, anyhow?" Bill asked.

"Well," Seagrove said. "Secretary of something or the other. Treasury, I think."

"Commerce," the photographer said.

"I think Treasury," Seagrove repeated.

I tried out a stumbling, polite remark in French to the Secretary, and he spouted back happily. I had to ask him to slow down. He said he had a hard time understanding Texas English, and began telling me, too fast, about some unjust experience in a hotel. . . .

"Pretty talk," Davis said, listening. "But damn if it don't look stupid, comin' here without knowin' no English."

"That's a hell of a thing to say right in front of the man," Bill said.

"He can't understand," Davis said. "Fatso there done said so."

The photographer snorted. Seagrove's thick neck was pink. The Secretary asked if I was familiar with the combination of the little peas with the carrots, at luncheons.

Was I not.

"*Sacré nom!*"

Where it seemed I should, I murmured.

But at the big ranch, a show place used to celebrities, a foreman took over and drove Seagrove and the Secretary and the photographer around the pastures while Davis and I and Bill waited at the auction barns. When they got back, the little Frenchman had his picture taken aboard a palomino stallion with someone else's big Stetson down around his ears, and taken again holding a rope attached to the halter of a prize bull.

Then we left. It was hot in the car and no one spoke for a time, until the Secretary said to me: "One prefers vineyards. Listen. That bull. Thirty-five thousand *dollars?*"

"Yes."

"What folly!" he said.

Davis tapped his shoulder. The Secretary looked around. Davis said: "Like I told you, I was raised right here in these cedar hills. Now looky here what I can do."

Reaching down, he grabbed his right boot heel and then, with a quick thrust upward, placed his leg around his neck. "By God!" he said. "Looky here."

The wonder in the Frenchman's face became a smile, and then abruptly he let out a squeal of such genuine laughter that it made Seagrove in the driver's seat leap.

"You look too, Fatso," Davis said levelly from beneath his own knee.

Seagrove glanced around briefly, the heavy flesh about his mouth twitching with fury. But the photographer was laughing, and so was I, and M. Ratineau was wiping away tears while he sobbed to himself: "Ah, the droll! Ah, the marvelous peasant!"

And later, as the three of us stood by Bill's gate watching the Cadillac vanish ahead of an irate wedge of white dust from the road shoulder, Davis said: "That Secretary of France, he was all right. Wait till I tell 'em in Glen Rose."

"How would you know what he was like?" Bill said, pausing with the gate half opened.

"I could tell," Davis said. "But that Fatso . . ."

"What?"

"I got his goat," Davis said. "I guess I showed that jessie."

We passed through and Bill latched the gate behind us, grinning a little off center.

"Dog gone you," he said. "I guess you did."

~~~~~~

THAT RANCH IS A GOOD ONE NOW, 4,000 acres or so, ragged in shape because of the way it was built up, homestead by homestead, dollar by dollar that Bill could make or borrow. It's a "good investment"; he could sell it now for two or three times what he has in it. He'll cite that justification for its ownership to people who think in those terms, but he doesn't need it for himself. He spends all the time out there that he can, and wanders around the pastures alone for two and three days at a stretch, chewing the stems of the good grasses, studying out places for stock tanks or terraces. . . . He knows pretty well what the birds and animals are that wander there too. A city boy, he is the cedar people's successor, as the cedar people succeeded Cooney Mitchell and Cooney Mitchell succeeded Bigfoot Wallace and the Comanches, and because Bill has some notion of what Cooney and Bigfoot and the Comanches were, the good and bad of them, he isn't a break in the country's continuity as the big absentee "operations" nearly always are.

I think it's not sentimental to say that Bill belongs there, and if he has anything to say about it his children will belong there even more than he does.

The cedar people don't always leave happily. They drag their heels, and have to be waited for and bought out at the right times. The reluctance is not really rational and economic, though more often than not they say it is ("Land's a-goin' up. Sommidge wouldn't want it if it weren't . . ."), but is built on a dread of breaking the stringy line between themselves and the old ones.

Davis's Uncle Herb dragged his heels for years in regard to one quarter-section that had no link at all with his own personal old ones. It had come to him through his dead wife and was five miles distant from the place he lives on with four hounds and a few chickens, hauling his water in buckets from the well and achieving nocturnal illumination, despite a cheap R. E. A. line that passes a quarter-mile away, with kerosene lamps.

Bill and Davis wanted the quarter-section because it adjoined them. He wouldn't talk about selling. One time—I was there—they persuaded him to ride over to it with them and look around, but it was a mistake. When we had him there he stood bowlegged under the chinaberries before the place's ruined main house (remember the shack where Davis and Jim Lemmon and Bert and Ike planned a dummying, long before?) and told how his wife Stella's grandfather had exchanged fire with enemies from that same spot. On a nearby hill—"Yonder, see hit? Looks like a titty"—he said someone else of that collateral clan had once, on a certain night of a certain year because that was the way it had to be, glimpsed the flickering shaft of light that shows where gold lies buried.

He said: "I done tried a dozen times to witch it, with a gold cuff button. Couldn't do no good."

Davis said: "Herb, you know they was just a-tellin' that."

"Naw," Herb said. "Hit was there. You need a coin, is what you need."

He grew indignant, thinking. He said: "You take me God damn home, Dave Birdsong!"

And went . . . Sourly, in the pickup after we'd dropped him off, Davis said that he knew the old man was kin to him, and that he was a good old man, but that sometimes he crapped too close to the house. . . .

He did sell finally, though with stipulations written into the instruments. He said he wanted to be able to wander there if he wanted.

Bill said: "You can go anywhere on my place, any time. You always could."

He said: "I want it on the paper."

He wanted ownership of another old shack back in the place's cedar, worse ruined than the main one, with a rotten perforated shingle roof and one of the windows made out of an old Model-T windshield, the hood's arc faithfully reproduced along its lower edge. Not ownership of the land under it, just of the shack . . . The provision was typed in, and three months after that he went over with a double-bitted cedar ax and a wrecking bar and tore the old shack board by board apart. It took him a week. If you happened by he wouldn't keep up the work, but would sit down and watch you tight-lipped till you left. He carried none of the wreckage away, and when he'd finished what remained was a square of foundation stones and a chimney's shaft and a jumble of boards, rotten furniture, broken churns, and maybe a thousand Mason jars. And the Model-T windshield . . .

Davis said it must be more treasure foolishness. He said his Aunt Stella's uncle, who'd once lived in the shack, had been supposed to have money hidden somewhere.

"But it might not of been that ay-tall," he said. "Old Herb he takes a notion."

"Wonder if he found whatever it was?" I said.

"Shoo!" Davis said. "Won't nobody ever know. If he'd of found a million dollars, he'd of just hid it again somewheres else. Without even buyin' no electric lights."

The heap of lumber and glass and crockery sat there for a good while until Davis, burning downed cedar one winter, squirted distillate on it and set it afire. Now there are only the fireplace and the foundation and ashes and molten glass and blue-scorched rusting rods and straps of iron, and Davis says the first time he has the dozer down that way he'll shove it all into a draw.

So many tales, and every time you go to that country you hear a dozen more—good ones, if that's your kind of thing. Too many to put down here, too many for a book not just about the cedar people . . .

No room, then, for Herb's boy Clint, truck driver and rodeo rider, who though perfumed with dark charm is, like Jim Lemmon, about half mean when he gets mad, and who once, after a trouble with his first wife, sought her out at her parents' house where she'd gone, and kept the whole family up under bright lights all night (they deserved it, but there is no room) while he twiddled a thirty-eight by its trigger guard and nipped at a bottle and swore he was going to shoot them all dead by dawn, but with the first light outside started laughing hard at the looks on their faces and walked out and took up again his 30,000-mile truck route. No room . . .

No room either for tales of "burning out," of pastures blackened by revenge and houses gone the same way, or for what Davis Birdsong said to the air-force lieutenant colonel over long distance after a jet bang put a stair step crack across one wall of his house . . . Or for the cedar-country man who went to college and won a Rhodes and studied at Oxford and was a bright gleam of the Dallas bar, prosperous, only to drop it all one day on impulse and go back alone to the cedar hills and live in khakis, barefoot in the warm months, impartially inhabiting caves and abandoned houses, they say . . . Sometimes you'd see him hitchhiking with a brief case, hatless and bushy-headed and still in khakis, to litigation in some little county court, because the cedar people always wanted him when he'd take their cases.

Or for the big cockfight out in the brush in Bosque County one Sunday when two city ducktails tried to hold up the crowd for its betting money, and everybody ran for his car but not to get away, and even after the ducktails had roared off, shot to pieces, to a city hospital, the happy fusillade kept up in and around the cars where old enemies were shooting at one another, the cockfight forgotten . . . Chicken fights, they call them, partly from a distaste for right names and partly because of the old Anglo-Am tabu on the sexual homonym.

Or for the man who rides a bony horse into Glen Rose on summer Saturdays, barefooted but with big roweled spurs on his heels . . .

Or for tales of whisky, so central . . . No room for whisky, fuel for the northern peoples' empires? There must be. When empire had burned its way on through and far beyond the Brazos country, the Brazos people kept on using the fuel, imperially. The gentle, genteel people and the clear-sighted ones like Maw among the older stock have been fighting it ever since, with varying success.

It's hard to blame them, even if you're a drinker. Mostly these days beer is the beverage of joy in those parts, hauled in from the wet territory to the east and sold at double price. It causes a few fist fights and wife beatings, but not much else. Whisky is for the blow-off, for the real overspew of that breed's boiling violent illogic that builds up pressure underneath the slit-eyed quiet, and has to go somewhere. It comes out wild; it comes out Cooney Mitchell and Bigfoot Wallace and the cowboys in the Kimball Bend, and makes the midnight horrid and the afternoon, too. So that even drinkers sometimes vote dry, hoping that the voters in the next county will be damned fools enough to vote wet and give them and their friends a nearby swilling place out of earshot of their own kids.

The bootleg kind of liquor doesn't locate itself by law, though. In the cedar hills they make it white, running the steam from soured corn meal and sugar out through copper tubing and selling its condensation right away at two dollars a raw oily half-gallon, though cedar clearing and lawmen in airplanes have hurt the profession's privacy. During the brief glory that was Prohibition, Glen Rose became a resort, hub for a wide ring of thirsty country. There were sanitariums run by chiropractors, at least one of whom wrought witnessed, attested miracles. There were mineral springs, and boosters who spoke of almost every attraction except the real one. There were parks, standing weedy now with bandstands of red petrified wood which testify that here the tip of wanton prosperity's wing once brushed the ground.

In 1932 that boom naturally broke. Now most of the

homemade soul balm is drunk up locally, with a little going to outsiders who for one reason or another like it. West
Texas, too, dry and wide, offers a field for enterprise. One
part-time maker told me that starting from scratch, keeping
no still around between times to be found and blamed on
him, he could stew up a truckload batch of white whisky
for $800 which, after an evening haul to Lubbock, he could
sell for $6,000. He said it was fairly safe if you didn't do it
at regular intervals; if you were regular they'd lay for you.

One short tale? There's an old moonshiner around—call
him Else. He is a man of dignity and of harsh ethics, few
of which fit the interstices of the law or the philosophy of
patio living. A long time back he got caught at his chosen
trade, though to toll him out of the brush they had to break
the law themselves and hold his family hostage. He was
tried and given a year or so in jail but, somehow, was allowed a little time out on bond before he had to turn himself in. On the night before his freedom expired, his friends
gathered to give him a party. Everybody felt bad. There was
whisky, some of it even wood-aged for a month or so. . . .
They gloomed.

"Hod damn it," one said. "This ain't it. We don't want
old Else to recollect us this-a-way, all that time. Like a funeral."

Another said: "What you gonna do, sang songs?"

He said: "Le's have a jury trial."

"Who you want to try?"

"Else, that's who," he said. "I'm the judge. . . ."

They held it, drinking hard. At the end they had Else,
swaying with whisky, stand up before the bench and the
judge said: "They done found you guilty of bein' damn fool
enough to git caught. What you got to say?"

"Sommidgin' thang," Else answered. "G'lty."

"All right," the judge said. "I hereby by God sentence you to git beat up. Now."

And they all piled on him, swinging and kicking. After a while they lost track of who it was they were after and just fought, a flailing mound of them, until nobody had any fight left in him. Old Else, who lost four teeth and had a thumb broken, still says it was the nicest party he ever went to.

~~~~~~~~~

ALL TO THE FACTORIES NOW, all to towns . . . Selling whatever they happen to own, they leave the places which their breed wore out and which in reciprocation wore their breed out, too. They go to Fort Worth and Dallas and Los Angeles and Detroit and almost everywhere, and few come back, for there is no reason to. In corporation plants they learn well or badly those technical specialties that hour-pay requites, mingling there and in the beer halls and in the suburbs into a new and future breed with other kinds of people. With migrant hill Southerners, kinsmen in religion and honky-tonkery and fierce schizoid polarity, and probably often in blood too . . . With that drifting, truly rootless worker mass that two or three generations of big production and war have brewed among us, on all levels from corporation president to shop sweeper . . .

A lament? Ill fares the land, to hastening ills a prey? Not necessarily. A good many ills have been hastening around the Brazos country for a good long while. And besides, what is, is.

But what is, too, is of concern to a farewell-sayer like me, and what is, there, is the slow, sometimes reluctant, sometimes glad end of a people. Davis Birdsong's people, the more-so people . . . The breed is changing.

Not my people, not in lifelong neighborness or the real scaffolding of thought . . . South Texas gets into it, and so does the city, and the wandering.

But if one cares about people at all, he has claim to more than just one kind of them. Young, I breathed in these, like pollen, from the air. . . .

CHAPTER EIGHTEEN

BARNARD'S . . . Above a good hard-bottomed ford you scale four levels of shore, all different—first mud over sand with weedy willows' roots bonding them against the river's wash; then a belt of dry sand nourishing ash trees; then a fine shaded flat of alluvial flood dirt with great cottonwoods and Spanish oaks; and finally, after you mount through sloping thickets, an open uprolling prairie of worn-out fields and pastures, red-gullied, scratchy with poor-land brush and weeds, loud with meadowlarks and doves. The tame Indians raced ponies there while Charles Barnard watched and bet with them, and The People came in arrogant with loot to trade for what whisky Charles's unfortunate thirst might be able to spare them. . . . All that's left now is a dim rectangle of stones beside a new windmill, and an archeological layer, excavable by boot toe, of harness buckles, sun-purpled bottle glass, horseshoes, and porcelain doorknobs. And the feel of old Tomasa's scolding . . . From there, back across the river, you can see a roofless ruin in Kristenstad.

Sand . . . In your ears, your eyes, your bed, your food,

your pipe, your shoes . . . You adjust to the fact of it, and move your feet slowly while cooking.

Turkeys, undomestic blue-headed ones, gobbling on a hill. The brush of those counties is good habitat for them, though there aren't many. They lack wile (does any gallinaceous bird have it except in the defensive mythology of hunters?) and besides are savory enough eating and big enough to attract country persecution, in season and out.

Weather of yellow quietness . . . Gossamer shreds floated shining across the clear air and hung waving off the canoe and laid themselves ticklish athwart my face. In the bottom the deciduous trees were leafless now, winter-stripped; on the hills the dark cedars and live oaks still shaded the white ground. The river had been subsiding day by day, scouring itself clear in the sands. Full of driftingness and sloth, I let it carry me along, dallying, stopping for explorations and to lie in the sun, making no speed at all. I had a feeling that I could go on forever, if there were only river enough and time.

But there weren't.

Ducks . . . You can get a little tired of eating them, though in that country they're good, the short-fibered brown meat untainted yet by coastal fishiness, sweet still with the taste of grain and fresh-water green things gathered all the way down from Canada. Roasted, broiled, or stewed as chunks of breast with bacon and onions . . . There were a lot of them in the long slow stretches between the rock-bottomed rapids—widgeons and mallards, teal and blue-bills and pintails. As I paddled down, groups of six or a dozen or more would swim out from the banks, not much afraid, and would keep on ahead of me downstream, accumulating until at times I'd be herding maybe a hundred. Then the paddle's flash or a rapids below or some other small spur would flush them on short, frantic, sure-beating wings to the sky, and maybe a few would cut back to give me a shot, if I wanted it.

Most of the time I didn't. If I felt like eating ducks I'd usually have killed them by noon. Thanksgiving's brief gluttony was past, and I'd come to some sort of terms with sportsmanship, or whatever you want to call it. I made no more pot shots, but the thrill of using up shells and killing things in quantity had no application there, floating, just feeding myself.

An illusion . . . Three green-winged teal from a big flock of them turned and bulleted back past me very high. I led the lowest one by perhaps twelve feet and fired, and he came down in that long graphlike parabola that charts clean death, to splash hard into the water up and across stream from me. The river was shallow and wide and sand-bottomed there, moving fast though smooth on top. As I turned the boat and paddled toward the duck, the passenger on the bow howling blood, I got suddenly dizzy. On the glassy water I had the feeling of making easy progress upstream, but in fact the river was carrying both me and the duck fast downward, and the cedar hills beyond the flat land of the shore were shifting in what seemed to be the wrong direction. Even after I understood, it was still dizzying, and I had to squint my eyes down so as to see only the duck and the water. I found myself tempted to draw, in the manner of Saint Henry, an allegory between the mixup and our world. There seemed to be a connection, but trying to figure out what it was made me dizzy in another part of my interior, and I gave it up.

That afternoon in the Mitchell Bend (now we're there in

place as in backward-looking time, but the story's already told) I dropped around a little turn, and five more teal were sunning themselves, asleep, on the sixty-degree caved-away slope of a sand bank, just above the water. They sat squatted back on their tails, cinnamon heads down against protruding white breasts. I drifted almost on them, then rapped the side of the canoe. One by one they came awake, stiffening their necks and staring in a kind of low-comedy double take, and flushed in confusion. With a twinge, I swung the gun on the last one as he went, to fill out supper, but he was flying faster than I'd thought, or maybe the twinge had thrown me off; I only speckled the river behind him with both barrels.

Le'm be. . . .

A church camp . . . A cleared ten acres or so planted in Bermuda and dotted with live oaks, with green-roofed white buildings set against the dark hills behind . . . People with children—it was Sunday—walked along a path by the river and looked at me. A good place, a pleasant frame for Old Testamentalism, its structures Old Testamentally stark against the country, not blended in . . . Except in those southern and central parts of the state settled by immigrant Germans a century ago, Texans, like most Americans, lack much devotion to the idea of building into the country, or into a river's shore. But there was no point in wishing, on the Brazos, for the kind of organic houses and inns and cafés which Europeans build overhanging water that's practically tailored into beauty. You can't tailor a river whose yearly custom is to undercut, sweep, tree-bash, and dissolve its shores, not without a millennium of accumulated masonry.

Nor would I want to see it tailored. I didn't want to see it dammed, either, but it was going to be.

All to go, like the breed of people, like the wild things along the shores, like autumn . . . What is, is. What was, was. If you're lucky, what was may also be a part of what is. Not that they often let it be so, now . . .

~~~~~~~~~

We did the Channel Waltz for a long long sandy piece, the river still dropping. Zigzagging with the diagonal bars, getting caught occasionally and having to labor across the shaking lips to the green water below, standing up sometimes while poling to see better what you're getting into, you attain a sense of the channel after a while, though you can't trust it.

You attain a sense of a lot of things, mostly unimportant. Days have songs, for instance, like rapids and steaming logs. The songs take the beat of your paddle's dip, and are likely therefore to be old, slow, sentimental, Gothic things. One day sang "Drink to Me Only" all day long. The next insisted on "Flow Gently, Sweet Afton" and those lyrics which, in spots, are so bad that they can only be comical for a time before they start to dig at your nerves:

I charge thee, disturb not my slumbering fair. . . .

You could go on forever. You know it. Your muscles have gone supple-hard and your hands as crusty as dry rawhide, and your head has cleared, and your boat goes precisely, unstrenuously where and how you want it to go, and all your gear falls into its daily use with thoughtless ease. There is merely not enough river, not enough time. . . . You don't miss anyone on God's earth's face. You're no more bored with the sameness of your days and your diet and your tasks than a chickadee is bored, or the passenger on the sunny bow, or a catfish; each day has its fullness, bracketed by sleep. In the evenings by the fire and in the clear mornings are when you have it strongest—the balance, the rightness, the knowledge.

Or when you think you have it . . . And does it especially matter that, like the dead duck and the river and the shifting cedar hills behind, the knowledge may turn out to be illusory? Illusions are worth having.

You were spare, bare, and ascetic. You knew Saint Henry, Yankee moralist though he might be, and knew too all those other old loners who'd ever baked their bread by fires in manless places. You knew the sovereign pulse of being.

Or you thought you did . . .

Two BOYS were machine-gunning chips in the river with automatic twenty-two's at a place I liked for stopping—a humpy pod of gravel and willows and drift strung to shore only by a low spit of mud. It was mid-afternoon, but I was going consciously slow and the spot looked good. As I neared them, the boys stopped firing and we spoke. They were nice-looking kids, gangly and restless.

One said: "How about a ride?"

"One-way boat," I told him. "I can let you out at Sixty-seven tomorrow or the day after."

"Aw! . . ." he said, and waved me on. Below the bar and out of their sight, I turned the canoe up into quiet water and waited, smoking. In a while the sound of their shooting moved back to shore and into the woods; ricochets moaned around and one came over my head. Then I heard the straight-pipe blast of their car, and paddled up alongside the bar to unload. There'd been no good reason for not stopping while they'd still been there, but I didn't want to talk. The river's aloneness was on me and I liked it and was going to hold onto it while it lasted.

That was a good camp, but the weather went very cold in the night, and the feathers in the old sleeping bag had shifted to head and foot so that my middle parts, where I was touching ground through the leaky mattress, felt ninety years old. I knew what it was, but couldn't wake up enough to get out and shake the bag right again. At dawn there was a raw wind and my throat hurt and the sky, what I could see of it, was whitely gray with low fast-moving clouds. Someone across the river was shouting.

All right, I thought. I'd be able to make it on down that day to a pull-out place. I'd been lucky on the weather anyhow, clear and bright most of the time on into December, on into winter. . . .

"Goatie, goatie, goatie!" the voice across the river hollered, in harmony with a banging on tin.

I crawled up on my elbows until my face and shoulders were in the biting air outside the storm flaps, and looked across. A man and a woman were walking through the brush under pecan trees and calling up Angora goats, maybe to get them to shelter before a blow. They carried buckets with a little feed in them which they were beating and rattling. The woman wore denims, a bright blue jacket, a red scarf, and an orange hunting cap, and jiggled as she walked, goatie-goatie-ing with that excessive zest that women bring to men's tasks, making them caricatures. Even without knowing he had an audience, her quiet husband looked a little embarrassed. But the goats were following, a jostling flock of them that sniffed and shoved at the bucket she carried as she led them up to a higher flat where a new car was parked.

When they had left, driving the car slowly and drumming on its sides so that the goats kept tumbling along behind, I crawled out and put on all the clothes I had and built up the fire. My boots were damp; I shuffled them down into the ashes and red-burnt sand that a part of the bigger evening fire's coals had kept warm. The pup came out, more doubtful than I of the day. He saw what I was doing and sat down against my feet in the warm spot, but hit an ember and yipped and fled back to the tent, scattering ashes.

It didn't go on forever, the river. . . .

That day's song was a piece of Reconstruction jaggedness they used to call "The Good Old Rebel." It had a line about catching the rheumatism a-campin' in the snow that went along with the way my back felt in the region of my chilled kidneys, even after I had on all my clothes and was paddling on the river with hot coffee and fruit inside me. It ended:

I hate the Constitution and the uniform of blue;
I hate the Declaration of Independence, too,
And I don't want no pardon for what I was or am,
And I won't be reconstructed and I do not give a damn.

And then the blustering, cutting day started it all over again, to the tune of "Rambling Wreck." That isn't the right tune, but it was the tune the day used. . . .

A blast of a day, yanking the canoe crooked on the water, riffling the surface so that I couldn't read the channel, making me feel even colder and worse than I'd felt when I awoke . . . None of it seemed to matter much, though. December was a right time for bad weather, and I'd gone about as far as I needed to go to tell my stretch of the river goodbye. I'd made the trip and it had been a good one, and now they could flood the whole damned country if they liked, chasing off the animals and the birds and drowning out the cottonwoods and live oaks and sloshing away, like evil from the font, whatever was left there of Mr. Charlie Goodnight and Satanta the White Bear and Cooney Mitchell, and me.

As they would, for praiseworthy purposes . . . We've learned to change unchangingness, and it seems we'll keep the knowledge working. That long and bedrock certainty of thoughtful men that regardless of the race's disasters the natural world would go on and on is no longer a certainty. It's an improbability instead. Saint Henry's bottom comfort has been yanked from under us; old Hardy's sad assuredness in the time of the breaking of nations is no longer sure. Not just in terms of dams on a salty river unloved, unlovable except by a few loners and ranchers and cedar-hill misanthropes . . . Consider the bug that bites a bureaucrat or the bureaucrat's friend's spinach, and calls down not only on itself but on a stretch of country, which thereupon dies for years, the mimeographically prescribed revenge of a planeload of heptachlor or dieldrin. Consider warblers and television towers, and the ceiling lights at airports. Consider radiation and the sea life of the coral islands. . . .

Consider too, though, and again, and germanely, that it had been a good trip.

Two or three miles above where I thought to pull out, I stopped and ate cheese and onions and biscuit bread on a bar. A line of willows with some leaves left on them baffled the wind a little; I sat with the sun shining out from time to time through rifts in the cold clouds, and juggled gravel. It is whiter down there than in the Palo Pinto country where I'd started, with fossils and other bits of limestone thick among the multicolored chert, a pinto-pony kind of gravel, pretty. I stuck a fragmentary trilobite into my pocket and a couple of bits of white-veined red stuff, aware that when I found them there later, I'd throw them away. It didn't matter:

I'm glad we fought agin her and I only wisht we'd won,
And I ain't ast no pardon for anythang I've done. . . .

That was what the day sang, to the wrong tune.

~~~~~~~~~

I GOT TO THE PLACE at about two thirty, fought eddies and
quicksand to get the canoe beached on firm gravel, and wet
to the knees walked up a little road that comes down to
the river past a shack with a MINNOWS sign nailed slantingly
to a big sycamore. I knew the spot from driving around that
country, but had never stopped there. As I climbed the hill
a very ugly bloated old man rose out of a cane chair under
the sycamore, a sunny nook sheltered from the wind.

He said: "What the hell you up to with that thang?"

"Which?" I said, not knowing whether he meant the pup
or the field glass around my neck or what.

He meant the boat, having watched my maneuvers. I told
him, and asked if there was a telephone nearby.

He said: "You know all about Indians, hey, neighbor?"

Not much, I said; I'd just kicked around a few old camp-
sites.

"Naw!" he said, staring into my face with that disquieting
steadiness that some children and drunks have. "Crap, I
don't believe you'd know no Indian place if you was to
find it."

Probably not, I admitted. Was there a—

"Listen, neighbor. Can you read sign?"

The wind swirled his aura at me, and I got the white cedar-
country whisky smell, strong.

Coon and fox tracks, did he mean?

He said: "Crap! I mean *sign*. Indian sign, neighbor,
where they buried gold and such. . . ."

I said no. He got hold of my arm and pulled me down a path to other sycamores whose trunks had been scratched and had grown out wartily around the scars. They looked like lovers' initials to me. He said they were Comanche treasure maps, if he could only read them. I repeated that I was pretty ignorant. Disgustedly, he said he could see that, now. . . .

It was a queer place, with good springs flowing out of the hillside over humps of soft travertine, and volcanic rocks strewn about. He said somebody else had called them volcanic once, a crazy old bird that drifted up and down looking for treasure. He said it was a God-damn lie.

"Why?"

"Because, neighbor," he said with patience, belching, "hit don't say nothin' in Scripture about no volcanoes in the Newnited States, and you know it."

I said I guessed it didn't, and asked again about the telephone.

"Oh, they's one up at the grocery store," he said. But before I got away he showed me other treasure maps on some black-walnut trees, and told me how the proposed Bee Mountain dam just down the river was going to put him in the boat business and make him rich, and gave me an account of how he'd come to quit liquor. It was very interesting, especially in relation to the smell of his breath.

"Used to drank whisky," he said. "Lots of it. I mean lots. But you know what?"

"What?"

"I woke up one mornin' over in a bar ditch on the Tolar road," he said. "Don't know how I come to git there. I was a-sleepin' in the dew, and what do you reckon they was under my right foot?"

I admitted more ignorance.

"A live God-damn possum!" he said. "A-lookin' at me, that son of a bitch. By God, that done it, neighbor. I quit."

In the ser sta gro up the road, a one-pumper, two women were watching television beside a blistering-hot oil burner made out of blued, thin, stovepipe steel. One of them, old, sat in a wheel chair sucking snuff, with a can that had once held Hunt's peaches perched on the foot rest. The other without rising turned down the loud machine to hear me and said yes, it was there on that shelf—and so it was, among boxes of detergent. I put through a call to Davis collect, and the women said no further word, though they kept the set tuned down during the time I was at the telephone, their eyes remaining on the bright screen. A young man's wide-mouthed face filled it. He sang how the cats was a-rockin' and that wasn't all. . . . Then the camera turned onto three young couples on a dance floor in bright high-school clothing, solemn over the African intricacies of their step. On the shelves of the store the stock was of the kind they usually have, dust-fuzzed and fly-specked: canned goods, soap, combs, bologna and margarine and cheese and lard in a refrigerator case, men's handkerchiefs, razor blades, lipstick, a glass case of candy. . . .

Davis said he'd come. I hung up, and immediately the younger woman twirled up the machine's sound. I offered to pay for using the phone.

"No, you don't owe me nothin'," she said without looking at me.

I thanked her. The old woman in the wheel chair, with a dried, resigned, tragically strong face of the kind that Spanish peasant women sometimes have, had not to my knowledge glanced my way once, and as I left she leaned over to spit with amber exactness into her peach can, without removing her eyes for a second from the fascination of that adolescent dance, the fascination of the future. . . .

~~~~~~~~~

DAVIS CAME in a green pickup truck with a flat-topped arch of galvanized pipe on its rear that would support the stern of the canoe. I was tired and shivery despite a heater in the truck, and when after an hour's driving to the northeast we hit wet territory, I bought a pint of good whisky and we drank some of it, sipping salty chaser water from my canteen, and stopped to eat hamburgers at a neon-bright drive-in. The pup was asleep in my lap, a hot lump.

Davis didn't think much of anyone's having spent three weeks and more alone in a boat on the river. Because he liked me and was maybe a little proud that I'd done anything so crazy, he put his disapproval softly, but he said the trip didn't make much sense to him.

"Should of drownded," he said. "You know what that river's like?"

I guessed I did, a little.

"Shoo," Davis said. "I'll take White Bluff Creek, me. They wouldn't of found no more'n that boat, and maybe a big fat catfish somewheres that ate you up when you got good and rotten."

I said: "Davis, you're a worse parochial than I am."

"A who?"

"Maybe not," I said. "You're a good man, anyhow."

"You're all right, too," he said with a little of the abashment that the gentler emotions rouse in him. "Just the same, hit didn't make no sense."

Before he got me home I was dozing in the warm cab's corner, the pup snuffling in his sleep across my legs. . . .

CHAPTER NINETEEN

"ALL BY YOURSELF?" somebody's wife asked at a party in town. "You didn't get lonesome?"

I liked her and had known her all my younger life, as I had most of the other people in the room. But it was a good place to be, and the thermostat on the wall was set at seventy-five degrees, and outside the windows the cold sleet mixed with rain was driving down at a hard slant, and far far up above all of it in the unalive silent cold of space some new chunk of metal with a name, man-shaped, was spinning in symbolism, they said, of ultimate change. In that place the stark pleasures of aloneness and unchangingness and what a river meant did not somehow seem to be very explicable.

Somebody's wife was waiting for an answer.

"Not exactly," I said. "I had a dog."

AS FOR BIBLIOGRAPHY . . .

Goodbye to a River doesn't lay claim to solid scholarliness, but a good many of the things in it came to me from other people's writings. Some of those writings I read so long ago that I no longer remember what they were, even if their content grains the tissue of my thinking. Others I have consulted and reconsulted, so that to mention them is only honorable. Footnotes seemed not to go with the tone of the book, though where a debt is heavy I've sometimes mentioned a source in the text itself. A few of the books provided mainly peripheral background, among them some with merited fame and currency. The rest are of differing kinds and worth, the ragged records of a region. All helped.

My debts directly to persons rather than to books are so numerous and go back over such a stretch of years that there isn't much point in trying to make a list. I would like specifically to mention Fred Cotten, historian and antiquary, who was generous with his knowledge of the facts and ways of the Brazos country.

Belding, Henry: "Memoirs of Henry Belding." *West Texas Historical Association Year Book*, Vol. XXIX (October 1953).

Catlin, George: *North American Indians.* Philadelphia: Hubbard Brothers; 1891.

Clark, Randolph: *Reminiscences, Biographical and Historical.* Wichita Falls, Texas: Lee Clark, Publisher; 1919.

Clarke, Mary Whatley: *The Palo Pinto Story.* Fort Worth, Texas: The Manney Co.; 1956.

Cotten, Fred R.: "Log Cabins of the Parker County Region." *West Texas Historical Association Year Book,* Vol. XXIX (October 1953).

Dobie, J. Frank: *The Longhorns.* Boston: Little, Brown & Co.; 1941.

————: *The Mustangs.* Boston: Little, Brown & Co.; 1952.

Douglas, C. L.: *Cattle Kings of Texas.* Dallas, Texas: Cecil Baugh; 1939.

Duval, John C.: *Adventures of Bigfoot Wallace,* edited by Mabel Major and Rebecca W. Smith. Dallas, Texas: Tardy Publishing Company; 1936.

An Economic Survey of Parker County, Texas. Austin: University of Texas; 1948.

Erath, George B.: *The Memoirs of Major George B. Erath,* as dictated to Lucy A. Erath. Austin: Texas State Historical Association; 1923.

Ewell, Thomas T.: *History of Hood County.* Granbury, Texas: Frank Gaston, Publisher; 1895.

Fuller, Henry Clay: *A Texas Sheriff: A. J. Spradley, Sheriff of Nacogdoches County for Thirty Years.* Nacogdoches, Texas: Baker Printing Co.; 1931.

Greer, James K.: *Grand Prairie.* Dallas, Texas: Tardy Publishing Company; 1935.

Haley, J. Evetts: *Charles Goodnight, Cowman & Plainsman.* Norman: University of Oklahoma Press; 1949.

The Handbook of Texas (2 vols.), edited by Walter P. Webb and H. Bailey Carroll. Austin: The Texas State Historical Association; 1952.

Hendricks, Leo: *Geology of Parker County, Texas.* Austin:

The University of Texas; 1957.

Hill, Robert T.: *Geography and Geology of the Black and Grand Prairies, Texas.* Washington: Government Printing Office; 1901.

Holland, G. A.: *History of Parker County and the Double Log Cabin.* Weatherford, Texas: The Herald Publishing Company; 1937.

Huckaby, Ida Lasater: *Ninety-four Years in Jack County 1854–1948.* Austin, Texas: The Steck Company; 1949.

Kephart, Horace: *Camping and Woodcraft* (2 vols. in 1). New York: The Macmillan Co.; 1957.

King, Dick: *Ghost Towns of Texas.* San Antonio, Texas: Naylor Co.; 1953.

Lee, Nelson: *Three Years Among the Comanches.* Norman: University of Oklahoma Press; 1957.

Lehmann, Herman: *Nine Years Among the Indians 1870–1879,* edited by J. Marvin Hunter. Austin, Texas: Von Boeckmann-Jones Co., Printers; 1927.

Marcy, Colonel R. B.: *Thirty Years of Army Life on the Border.* New York: Harper & Brothers; 1866.

McConnell, Joseph Carroll: *The West Texas Frontier* (2 vols.). Palo Pinto, Texas: Texas Legal Bank & Book Co.; 1939.

Neighbors, Kenneth F.: "Robert S. Neighbors and the Founding of Texas Indian Reservations." *West Texas Historical Association Year Book,* Vol. XXXI (October 1955).

———: "The Assassination of Robert S. Neighbors." *West Texas Historical Association Year Book,* Vol. XXXIV (October 1958).

Pioneer Days in the Southwest from 1850 to 1879, contributions by Charles Goodnight, Emmanuel Dubbs, John A. Hart, and others. Guthrie, Oklahoma: The State Capital Company; 1909.

Richardson, Rupert Norval: *The Comanche Barrier to*

South Plains Settlement. Glendale, California: The Arthur H. Clark Company; 1933.

Sonnichsen, C. L.: *Ten Texas Feuds*. Albuquerque: University of New Mexico Press; 1957.

Smith, Clinton L. and Jeff D.: *The Boy Captives*, as told to J. Marvin Hunter. Bandera, Texas: Frontier Times; 1927.

Smythe, D. Port: "A Journal of the Travels of D. Port Smythe, M. D., of Centerville, Texas, from That Place to the Mouth of the Palo Pinto, on the Upper Brazos," edited by Donald Day and Samuel Wood Geiser. *Texas Geographic Magazine*, Vol. VI, No. 2 (Fall 1942).

Smythe, H.: *Historical Sketch of Parker County and Weatherford, Texas*. St. Louis: Louis C. Lavat; 1877.

Texas Almanac 1958–1959. Dallas: The Dallas *Morning News*; 1957.

Thoreau, Henry David: *Walden*. Everyman's edition. New York: E. P. Dutton & Co. Inc.; 1943.

————: *A Week on the Concord and Merrimack Rivers*. Concord edition (with *Walden*). Boston and New York: Houghton Mifflin Co.; 1929.

Tilghman, Zoe A.: *Quanah, the Eagle of the Comanches*. Oklahoma City, Oklahoma: Harlow Publishing Corporation; 1938.

The Trail Drivers of Texas, compiled and edited by J. Marvin Hunter. Second Edition Revised. Nashville, Tennessee: Cokesbury Press; 1925.

Turner, Frederick Jackson: *The Frontier in American History*. New York: Henry Holt & Co., Inc.; 1920.

Wallace, Ernest, and Hoebel, E. Adamson: *The Comanches, Lords of the South Plains*. Norman: University of Oklahoma Press; 1952.

Webb, Walter Prescott: *The Great Plains*. Boston & New York: Houghton Mifflin Co.; 1936.